Generative AI on Google Cloud with LangChain

Design scalable generative AI solutions with Python, LangChain, and Vertex AI on Google Cloud

Leonid Kuligin | Jorge Zaldívar | Maximilian Tschochohei

‹packt›

Generative AI on Google Cloud with LangChain

Group Product Manager: Niranjan Naikwadi
Publishing Product Manager: Nitin Nainani
Book Project Manager: Aparna Nair
Lead Editor: Sushma Reddy
Technical Editor: Rahul Limbachiya
Copy Editor: Safis Editing
Proofreader: Sushma Reddy
Indexer: Tejal Soni
Production Designer: Ponraj Dhandapani
DevRel Marketing Coordinator: Nivedita Singh

First published: Dec 2024

Production reference: 1221124

Published by Packt Publishing Ltd.

Grosvenor House
11 St Paul's Square
Birmingham
B3 1RB, UK

ISBN 978-1-83588-932-9

www.packtpub.com

To my wife, Ksenia, whose unwavering love and optimism have been my constant support over all these years; to my mother-in-law, Tatyana, whose belief in me, even in my most crazy endeavors, has been an incredible source of strength; and to my kids, Matvey and Milena, I hope you'll read it one day.

– Leonid Kuligin

To my wife, Lucia, and son, Jaime, thank you for your endless support and patience during the journey of writing this book. You are my inspiration and my joy.

– Jorge Zaldivar

For Jacqueline, my partner and my rock. This book wouldn't exist without your love and support.

– Maximilian Tschochohei

Foreword

I started LangChain as a side project, an open source Python package, in late October of 2022. This was after Stable Diffusion but before the launch of ChatGPT. I was going to a bunch of meetups and hackathons, saw people building with early LLMs, and saw some common abstractions. Those abstractions became LangChain.

That was over two years ago, and the space has evolved rapidly since then. LangChain has both grown and evolved. The amount of people building applications on top of LLMs has exploded, and LangChain has served as an entry point for a lot of them. The functionality inside LangChain has had to evolve as the underlying technology did so as well.

LangChain aims to empower developers, engineers, and architects to leverage the potential of generative AI in their projects. The rapid evolution of this technology has opened up unprecedented opportunities for innovation and creativity, allowing us to transform industries in ways we never imagined. In recent years, we have witnessed a remarkable shift in how we interact with technology. Generative AI stands at the forefront of this revolution, enabling machines to create content, assist in decision-making, and enhance user experiences in ways we could only dream of a decade ago. However, navigating this landscape can be daunting, especially for those who are new to the field or transitioning from traditional development practices. This book serves as a comprehensive guide for those looking to harness the power of generative AI using LangChain.

This book is tailored for a diverse audience, from generative AI enthusiasts to seasoned engineers exploring the intricacies of this technology. It assumes a foundational knowledge of Python and basic machine learning principles, making it accessible yet rich in content for both novices and experienced professionals. The practical examples and hands-on approach will empower readers to design and implement enterprise-ready architectures on Google Cloud, leveraging the full potential of LangChain and its integrations.

In this book, you will learn not only about the foundational models available on Google Cloud, such as PaLM 2 and Gemini, but also how to build robust applications that address real-world challenges. The structured journey through the book will guide you from understanding the core concepts of generative AI to deploying your solutions effectively in a cloud environment.

Moreover, the insights provided on common architectures, grounding responses, and advanced techniques will equip you with the knowledge to tackle the complexities of generative AI applications. You will gain the confidence to experiment, innovate, and ultimately contribute to the ever-evolving landscape of AI-driven solutions.

I encourage you to embrace this learning journey with an open mind and a spirit of curiosity. Above all else, I believe that it is still incredibly early on in this technological revolution. The possibilities are limitless, and with the right tools and knowledge, you can become a pioneer in this exciting field. Thank you for choosing this book as your guide, and I look forward to seeing the incredible applications you create with LangChain and Google Cloud.

Harrison Chase, CEO, LangChain

Contributors

About the authors

Leonid Kuligin is a staff AI engineer at Google Cloud, working on generative AI and classical machine learning solutions (such as demand forecasting or optimization problems). Leonid is one of the key maintainers of Google Cloud integrations on LangChain, and a visiting lecturer at CDTM (TUM and LMU). Prior to Google, Leonid gained more than 20 years of experience in building B2C and B2B applications based on complex machine learning and data processing solutions such as search, maps, and investment management in German, Russian, and US technological, financial, and retail companies.

I want to thank all my colleagues who helped me not only with this book but also with making Google integrations a first-class citizen on LangChain. I want to express my gratitude to all LangChain folks and the community, who helped to build such an incredible framework we all love working with. I'd like to say a special thank you to Pavel Gulin, who inspired me to write this book with his optimism and enthusiasm, and Slava Rubaev, my first manager and my lifetime mentor, who taught me the basics of entrepreneurship, technology, and critical thinking.

Jorge Zaldívar is an AI engineer at Google and a contributor to LangChain's integrations with Google. He has a decade of experience building complex machine learning applications and products applied to the energy and financial industries.

Maximilian Tschochohei leads AI engineering at Google Cloud Consulting EMEA. He implements LangChain applications together with Google Cloud customers. Before Google, he worked in strategy and technology consulting with Boston Consulting Group.

I want to thank my partner, my family, and my friends: thank you for your endless patience and unwavering support. I also want to thank my colleagues and my team: thank you for letting me learn from you. And special thanks to Leonid for coming up with the idea for this book, and for letting me be a part of it.

About the reviewers

Nuno Campos is a founding software engineer at LangChain, Inc. Nuno has more than 9 years of experience as a Python and JavaScript software engineer, architect, and open-source maintainer. Nuno has been a maintainer of various popular open-source projects, including LangGraph, LangChain. js, and Enzyme. Previously, he worked for various tech start-ups in software engineering and data science roles. He holds an MSc in finance.

Georgii Danshchin is the head of data science at HeadHunter Group, where he played a key role in shaping and leading the development of crucial components such as recommendations and search ranking based on machine learning. With a background in software development starting in 2012, he studied data science at the Higher School of Economics and Yandex School of Data Analysis. He has applied machine learning to real-world business tasks for nearly a decade. Georgii has also successfully participated in machine learning competitions, holds the Kaggle Master title, and has earned several gold medals. He is passionate about the opportunities that **large language models** (**LLMs**) offer to engineers and product managers.

Lucio Floretta leads a team of AI experts within Google Cloud's Professional Services organization, where he empowers enterprise customers to harness the transformative power of artificial intelligence. While his recent focus has been on generative AI, Lucio has been guiding customers across EMEA in building robust MLOps systems and ML solutions on Google Cloud since 2017.

Table of Contents

Part 1: Intro to LangChain and Generative AI on Google Cloud

1

2

Part 2: Hallucinations and Grounding Responses

3

4

5

Advanced Techniques for Parsing and Ingesting Documents　　73

6

Multimodality　　91

Part 3: Common Generative AI Architectures

7

Working with Long Context　　111

8

Building Chatbots   125

9

Tools and Function Calling   145

13

Appendix

Appendix 1

Appendix 2

Preface

Generative AI is on the rise, and its enterprise adoption is growing quickly. Developers need to understand the new technology, and they're requested to deliver business value quickly and reduce time to market. That's where LangChain as a framework for the quick development of generative AI applications comes in, together with enterprise-ready and highly scalable solutions from Google Cloud that expose foundational models, vector search, and other capabilities required by such applications.

In this book, we'll explore the basics of the LangChain framework and its core interfaces and then we'll start building our applications on Google Cloud using the Gemini model family and Vertex AI platform. We'll learn how to compose generative AI workflows, access external knowledge, and chain **large language models** (**LLMs**) to solve specific domain problems. You'll learn about some commonly used patterns and techniques such as **retrieval-augmented generation** (**RAG**), ways to process long documents that don't fit into the context of the LLM, implementing external memory layers, using third-party APIs to enhance LLMs' capabilities, and developing agentic workflows.

Who this book is for

If you're an application developer who is enthusiastic about generative AI, or you're an experienced ML engineer new to LangChain or Google Cloud, this book is for you. The book is also excellent for professionals who haven't used generative AI on Google Cloud and would like to learn how to navigate across the landscape of enterprise products for generative AI developers offered by Google.

What this book covers

Chapter 1, *Using LangChain with Google Cloud*, introduces LangChain and explains how LangChain orchestrates LLMs and coordinates the execution of complex tasks. It also examines LangChain primitives and explains how they can be composed together using the **LangChain Expression Language** (**LCEL**).

Chapter 2, *Foundational Models on Google Cloud*, guides you on how to select and implement the right Google Cloud foundational model in LangChain for many common use cases.

Chapter 3, *Grounding Responses on Google Cloud*, focuses on the problem of hallucinations in LLMs and how to address them with RAG. It describes the components of a RAG system and introduces Vertex AI Agent Builder, a managed Google Cloud service for building RAG-based applications.

Chapter 4, *Vector Search on Google Cloud*, explores the architecture of a vector search pipeline and discusses different searching techniques. It showcases how the combined power of Google Cloud and LangChain can be harnessed to develop search components for RAG applications.

Chapter 5, Advanced Techniques for Parsing and Ingesting Documents, explains the range of document parsing capabilities available within Google Cloud and LangChain. It demonstrates the use of LangChain document loaders, Document AI, and Vertex AI's Agent Builder for ingesting documents of a variety of formats.

Chapter 6, Multimodality, discusses multimodal LLMs, how to compose a multimodal input with LangChain, and advanced methods of building multimodal RAGs to enhance their capabilities.

Chapter 7, Working with Long Context, teaches you how to use LangChain to summarize documents, including how to handle long documents and different modalities such as audio and video, as well as how to efficiently implement question-and-answering on long documents.

Chapter 8, Building Chatbots, guides readers on how to build chatbots with LangChain, covering conversation engineering principles, memory implementation, intent routing, and integration with RAG.

Chapter 9, Tools and Function Calling, explores how to improve the reasoning capabilities of LLMs through the use of tools. It introduces the concept of tool calling and examines different ways to construct tools programmatically with LangChain. It also discusses ReAct – one of the foundational patterns in the multi-step reasoning process.

Chapter 10, Agents in Generative AI, explains the concept and components of an agent and gives examples of how to build one with two different methods: LangChain on Google Cloud with the Gemini SDK and Vertex AI Agent Builder.

Chapter 11, Agentic Workflows, delves into the fundamentals of agentic architectures and shows two examples of real-world architectures: agentic RAG and natural language to SQL using LangChain, LangGraph, and Google Cloud.

Chapter 12, Evaluating GenAI Applications, emphasizes the importance of evaluating generative AI applications to ensure they meet product requirements and quality expectations. It discusses the difference between traditional evaluation and where generative AI evaluation is similar or different. It also introduces LangSmith, a tool from LangChain that helps developers trace and evaluate generative AI applications, and explains how to use Vertex AI evaluation, a managed service for evaluating generative AI applications on Google Cloud.

Chapter 13, GenAI System Design, walks you through designing and building generative AI systems, addressing challenges such as non-deterministic outcomes and rapid technology evolution while emphasizing responsible AI principles.

Appendix 1, Overview of Generative AI, discusses the principles behind generative AI and LLMs. It explains very briefly how these models are trained, their unique characteristics, and the importance of AI alignment and discusses key criteria for a successful **proof of concept** (**POC**) in generative AI.

Appendix 2, Google Cloud Foundations, provides a foundational guide to Google Cloud for those new to the platform, covering organization setup, user management, billing, networking, and AI/ML development environments, enabling you to effectively leverage Google Cloud for LangChain applications.

To get the most out of this book

In order to learn from this book, you should have a basic knowledge of Python, minimal experience at the beginner level in machine learning, and some hands-on experience in generative AI. You need to have a Google Cloud project with enabled Vertex AI APIs. For most of the examples provided in this book, your costs will be minimal (less than a few dozen dollars). The only expensive workload is developing your own RAG on a massive amount of PDFs using Vertex Agent Builder and Vertex Vector Search, but you can skip those examples if you don't need the scale Google Cloud provides for these use cases.

We also encourage you to register and get an API key on LangSmith (but the free tier would be enough for running through this book).

Software/hardware covered in the book	Operating system requirements
Python with the required libraries installed	Windows, macOS, or Linux and ChromeOS
Vertex AI API on Google Cloud	
A custom Google Search enabled and a Google Cloud API key	
Vertex Vector Search, Vertex Agent Builder	
LangSmith (free tier)	

We encourage you to create a Python virtual environment (using Python `venv` or `conda`) and install all the dependencies in your virtual environment with `pip` or `conda` install.

If you are using the digital version of this book, we advise you to type the code yourself or access the code from the book's GitHub repository (a link is available in the next section). Doing so will help you avoid any potential errors related to the copying and pasting of code.

Download the example code files

You can download the example code files for this book from GitHub at `https://github.com/PacktPublishing/Generative-AI-on-Google-Cloud-with-LangChain`. If there's an update to the code, it will be updated in the GitHub repository.

> **Discussions**
>
> We encourage readers to take advantage of the Discussions feature in the repository to have conversations, ask questions, and post answers. It's a great chance to collaborate with others who share your interests.

We also have other code bundles from our rich catalog of books and videos available at `https://github.com/PacktPublishing/`. Check them out!

Conventions used

There are a number of text conventions used throughout this book.

`Code in text`: Indicates code words in text, database table names, folder names, filenames, file extensions, pathnames, dummy URLs, user input, and Twitter handles. Here is an example: "Mount the downloaded `WebStorm-10*.dmg` disk image file as another disk in your system."

A block of code is set as follows:

```
from langchain_core.runnables import RunnablePassthrough

chain_rps = RunnableParallel(
    origin=RunnablePassthrough(),
    output=increment_by_one
)

chain_rps.invoke(1)
```

When we wish to draw your attention to a particular part of a code block, the relevant lines or items are set in bold:

```
chain_assign = RunnablePassthrough().assign(
    y=itemgetter("x") | RunnableLambda(increment_by_one))

chain_assign.invoke({"x": 1})
>> {'x': 1, 'y': 2}
```

Any command-line input or output is written as follows:

```
pip install langchain-google-vertexai langgraph
```

Bold: Indicates a new term, an important word, or words that you see onscreen. For instance, words in menus or dialog boxes appear in **bold**. Here is an example: "Select **System info** from the **Administration** panel."

> **Tips or important notes**
> Appear like this.

Get in touch

Feedback from our readers is always welcome.

General feedback: If you have questions about any aspect of this book, email us at `customercare@packtpub.com` and mention the book title in the subject of your message.

Errata: Although we have taken every care to ensure the accuracy of our content, mistakes do happen. If you have found a mistake in this book, we would be grateful if you would report this to us. Please visit `www.packtpub.com/support/errata` and fill in the form.

Piracy: If you come across any illegal copies of our works in any form on the internet, we would be grateful if you would provide us with the location address or website name. Please contact us at `copyright@packt.com` with a link to the material.

If you are interested in becoming an author: If there is a topic that you have expertise in and you are interested in either writing or contributing to a book, please visit `authors.packtpub.com`.

Share Your Thoughts

Now you've finished *Generative AI on Google Cloud with LangChain*, we'd love to hear your thoughts! Scan the QR code below to go straight to the Amazon review page for this book and share your feedback or leave a review on the site that you purchased it from.

`https://packt.link/r/1-835-88933-6`

Your review is important to us and the tech community and will help us make sure we're delivering excellent quality content.

Free Benefits with Your Book

This book comes with free benefits to support your learning. Activate them now for instant access (see the "*How to Unlock*" section for instructions).

Here's a quick overview of what you can instantly unlock with your purchase:

PDF and ePub Copies   **Next-Gen Web-Based Reader**

Free PDF and ePub versions

Next-Gen Reader

Access a DRM-free PDF copy of this book to read anywhere, on any device.

Use a DRM-free ePub version with your favorite e-reader.

Multi-device progress sync: Pick up where you left off, on any device.

Highlighting and notetaking: Capture ideas and turn reading into lasting knowledge.

Bookmarking: Save and revisit key sections whenever you need them.

Dark mode: Reduce eye strain by switching to dark or sepia themes

How to Unlock

Scan the QR code (or go to `packtpub.com/unlock`). Search for this book by name, confirm the edition, and then follow the steps on the page.

UNLOCK NOW

Note: Keep your invoice handy. Purchases made directly from Packt don't require one

Part 1: Intro to LangChain and Generative AI on Google Cloud

In this part, we will provide an overview of LangChain as a framework and the main generative AI capabilities available on Google Cloud Platform. We'll also look into the key interfaces of LangChain, making you ready to read LangChain code with ease and start developing applications with this framework. If you're new to generative AI, we also encourage you to take a look at *Appendix 1*, where we provide a quick intro to the topic and give you a list of papers to dive into.

This part has the following chapters:

- *Chapter 1, Using LangChain with Google Cloud*
- *Chapter 2, Foundational Models on Google Cloud*

1

Using LangChain with Google Cloud

We, as authors, are so happy that you are interested in generative AI and you have decided to read this book. We wrote this book for engineers and practitioners who want to develop their first generative AI application with LangChain, a great open source framework.

In this chapter, you will install the LangChain framework and experiment with its basic primitives using **LangChain Expression Language** (**LCEL**).

We will cover the following main topics:

- The LangChain framework and the company behind it
- LangChain primitives - chains and runnables
- Main LangChain building blocks
- LangChain with Google Cloud
- LangChain integration with Google

> **Free Benefits with Your Book**
>
> Your purchase includes a free PDF copy of this book along with other exclusive benefits. Check the *Free Benefits with Your Book* section in the Preface to unlock them instantly and maximize your learning experience.

Technical requirements

To be able to work with the code samples in this chapter, install the `langchain-core` library by running `pip install langchain-core` in your terminal.

LangChain

Large language models (**LLMs**) are the fundamental components required to develop generative AI applications. However, as we will discuss in this book, these applications needed to be extended with state management, retrieval of supplementary data, interactions with the API, and so on. Such extended systems are often referred to as **LLM-augmented autonomous agents** (**LAAs**), which are computer programs capable of interacting with their environment and solving complex tasks with their underlying LLM by leveraging past observations and actions [1]. LAAs need **orchestration**, which is a process through which the LAA controls the underlying LLMs and coordinates the planning and step-by-step execution of a task.

LangChain is one of the most popular open source frameworks for LLM orchestration. Harrison Chase launched it as an open source project in 2022, and it attracted a lot of attention and quickly grew in popularity [2]. In February 2024, the LangChain team raised a Series A round led by Sequoia Capital and announced one of their commercial solutions – LangSmith – being **generally available** (**GA**) [3]. We'll be using the name *LangChain* interchangeably as the name of their framework and as the name of the start-up in general.

LangChain as a company exposes a few frameworks or services:

- **LangChain** – Python and JavaScript open source frameworks for LLM orchestration

- **LangGraph** – An open source library for building stateful, multi-actor applications with LLMs, built on top of LangChain

- **LangServe** – An open source framework for deploying and maintaining LangChain applications, it also has a hosted version as a commercial offering

- **LangSmith** – A commercial solution for LLM application development, monitoring, and testing

There are three key benefits you get from LangChain:

- A framework for a convenient LLM orchestration

- A lot of building blocks for your generative AI applications – for example, different primitives for data retrieval, processing, or transformation, or for calling external APIs, or handling prompt templates

- A stable set of interfaces and a lot of **integrations** with various cloud providers and downstream libraries

Now, let's look into the LangChain Python library. The main LangChain GitHub (`https://github.com/langchain-ai/langchain`) hosts a few PyPI packages:

- `langchain-core` defines base interfaces for integrations as abstract classes.

- `langchain` defines the key building block of the LangChain framework.

- `langchain-community` contains third-party integrations.

`langchain-cli` implements a **command-line interface (CLI)** for LangChain. You probably won't need it until you start working with LangChain templates (discussed in *Chapter 16*).

- `langchain-text-splitters` contains utilities for splitting a wide variety of text documents into chunks.

- `langchain-experimental` holds experimental LangChain code that might be promoted to core libraries later.

- Some partner libraries containing integrations. Many other libraries are either hosted on a separate repository under the LangChain GitHub organization (e.g., the `langchain-google-vertexai` library is part of the `langchain-ai/langchain-google` repository), and some others are hosted outside of LangChain.

You're going to write and read a lot of LangChain code, and we think that it's important to take some time to understand how base LangChain primitives work. It will help you read somebody else's code and will also allow you to write more efficient applications yourself.

We'll look into the list of libraries you need to work with Google Cloud through LangChain further down this chapter.

LangChain primitives – chains and runnables

As we have discussed, LangChain is a framework for orchestrating your generative AI applications. Let's look at two key LangChain primitives: **runnables** and **chains**.

The most basic LangChain abstract interface is `langchain_core/runnables/base.Runnable`, and it makes it easy to compose different pieces together for the orchestration [4]. A `Runnable` defines three main methods (there are some more, mainly for asynchronous applications; you can take a look at the full documentation if you're interested [4]):

- `invoke` calls `Runnable` on an input. It's an abstract method that should be defined by the specific implementation.

- `stream` calls `Runnable` on an input and streams chunks of the response. With a default implementation, it just calls the `invoke` method and yields the output, but if you need proper streaming support, your `Runnable` should implement this method.

- `batch` calls `Runnable` on a list of inputs (a batch). The default implementation calls the `invoke` method in parallel using a thread pool executor.

`Runnable` is a typed class, which means that each child class should define its input and output types. For example, like most things in LangChain, an LLM inherits from `Runnable`, and it takes a string as input and returns a string as output.

Let's look into a simple example – `RunnableLambda` is an implementation of `Runnable` that allows you to execute a Python function. The following snippet will result in the `response` variable being equal to 2:

```
from langchain_core.runnables import RunnableLambda
runnable = RunnableLambda(lambda x: x+1)
response = runnable.invoke(1)
```

Runnables can be composed together into chains. A chain is an orchestrated sequence of steps that your LangChain program takes by calling different APIs or executing building blocks and passing inputs and outputs between the steps. Let's build our first chain:

```
from typing import Optional
from langchain_core.runnables import Runnable, RunnableConfig

def increment_x_by_one(x: int) -> int:
    return x+1

def fake_llm(x: int)->str:
    return f"Result = {x}"

class MyFirstChain(Runnable[int,str]):
    def invoke(
        self, input:str, config: Optional[RunnableConfig]=None
    )->str:
        increment=increment_x_by_one(input)
        return fake_llm(increment)
```

Congrats! We've completed our first LangChain program! It takes an input, increments it by 1, and returns a formatted result as a string. Let's run it:

```
runnable=MyFirstChain()
response=runnable.invoke(1)
print(response)
>> Result = 2
```

LCEL

As you can imagine, it's not the easiest way of doing things. Luckily, LangChain has a special declarative language that simplifies Chain creation – LCEL. Most of the time, you don't even need to deal with runnables directly or implement them, but it's important to understand how this interface behaves on a high level. Let's look at an example:

```
chain = (
    RunnableLambda(increment_x_by_one)
    | RunnableLambda(fake_llm)
)
result=chain.invoke(1)
print(result)
>> Result = 2
```

What happened here? Let's remember, || is a bitwise comparison operator in Python. Runnable overrides a hidden method, __or__. a | b is equivalent to b.__or__(a) since "*while evaluating an assignment, the right-hand side is evaluated before the left-hand side*" [5]. And if b is a, it's equivalent to RunnableSequence(b, a):

```
from langchain_core.runnables import RunnableSequence
a = (RunnableLambda(increment_x_by_one)|
    RunnableLambda(fake_llm))
b = (RunnableSequence(RunnableLambda(increment_x_by_one),
    RunnableLambda(fake_llm))
print(a==b)
>> True
```

RunnableSequence is one of the key composition primitives in LCEL. The output of each runnable is an input to the next one, and they're executed sequentially. In fact, that's what a chain is in LangChain – a sequence of runnables that are executed one by one, and the output of each one is passed as an input to the next one.

Another key composition primitive in LCEL is RunnableParallel. It allows you to execute your runnables in parallel:

```
from langchain_core.runnables import RunnableParallel

chain = RunnableParallel(
    step1 = (increment_by_one | RunnableLambda(fake_llm),
    step2=fake_llm)

chain.invoke(1)
>> {'step1': 'Result = 2', 'step2': 'Result = 1'}
```

What happens here? We defined two subchains that will be executed in parallel and the results will be automatically merged into a dictionary with keys being names of these subchains and arguments results of their execution. We can pass this dictionary to the next block.

You can compose this chain with another one:

```
chain1 = increment_by_one | chain
chain1.invoke(1)
>> {'step1': 'Result = 3', 'step2': 'Result = 2'}
```

The nice thing is that you don't need to use the RunnableParallel constructor; LangChain does it for you if you just provide a dictionary with runnables as values as a step in the chain:

```
from langchain_core.runnables import RunnableParallel
chain2 = (RunnableLambda(increment_by_one)
  | {"step1": increment_by_one | RunnableLambda(fake_llm),
      "step2": fake_llm}
)
print(chain1 == chain2)
>> True
```

But when you read the LCEL code, it's important to understand what's going on under the hood, which iswhy we discuss these primitives in detail.

RunnablePassThrough and itemgetter

Typically, we pass inputs as dictionaries, but we don't want to modify our runnables for this. In this case, we can use a built-in Python operator itemgetter function:

```
from operator import itemgetter
chain = (
    itemgetter("x")
    | RunnableLambda(increment_by_one)
    | fake_llm
)

chain.invoke({"x": 1})
>> Result = 2
```

We don't need to parse a dictionary specifically; itemgetter is a special function that does it for us. Under the hood, it just tries to fetch the required key by using a __getitem__ method, but using this syntax sugar simplifies our LCEL code a lot.

Another useful composition primitive is RunnablePassThrough. When we're working with chains, we typically pass maps (or dicts) as inputs or outputs. Now, imagine we'd like to retain the original input and enrich it with the output:

```
from langchain_core.runnables import RunnablePassthrough

chain_rps = RunnableParallel(
    origin=RunnablePassthrough(),
    output=increment_by_one
)

chain_rps.invoke(1)
>> {"origin": 1, "output":  2}
```

One of the applications of RunnablePassThrough is using it together with assign. In general, assign creates a new runnable from the existing one that has new keys added to its output map. Let's look at the following example:

```
chain_assign = RunnablePassthrough().assign(
    y=itemgetter("x") | RunnableLambda(increment_by_one))

chain_assign.invoke({"x": 1})
>> {'x': 1, 'y': 2}
```

What happens here? Let's look step by step:

1. First, we created a RunnablePassThrough, which means our output will be a dictionary that preserves the input key-value pairs.

2. Then, we used assign with y=some-other-chain. That means it will add a key-value pair, y: output of the second chain to the original input that we pass our origin input to this chain. Please, note that despite dict objects in Python being mutable, LangChain will create a copy and change it.

3. What does this second chain do? It retrieves an attribute, x, from the input and passes it to the increment_by_one function. In other words, a y=increment_by_one(1) key-value pair is added to the output.

You now have enough knowledge to easily read and understand LCEL code. We've discussed key ways to manipulate runnables, and we'll explore them in more detail later in the book when we'll look at specific examples of creating chains for real use cases.

Main LangChain building blocks

Let's have a high-level look at key LangChain building blocks. If you need a refresher on terms such as *vectorstore*, or embeddings are new to you, feel free to check the *Index* where you can find more details and links to relevant chapters with more detailed explanations.

Data structures

First, let's explore some key data structures that you might encounter while developing applications. LangChain uses Pydantic, a Python data validation library; therefore, almost all LangChain data structures are Pydantic base models [7]. For those of you who are new to Pydantic, it's a data validation Python library that allows you to define your data schemas, and if you haven't heard about it, then you probably used an alternative schema definition library – `dataclasses`.

Note that LangChain has also its own `langchain_core.load.Serializable` class that inherits from `Basemodel` and adds additional control over serialization of a data structure to JSON (e.g., a `lc_secrets` property controls attributes such as API keys and `lc_attributes` controls which instance attributes should be added to serialized key-value arguments).

In other words, if you see a LangChain interface that inherits from `Serializable`, you can think of it as an advanced data structure that can be serialized to JSON and back.

There are core data structures that we will introduce throughout the book:

- `langchain_core.prompts.BasePromptTemplate` – A base abstract class for prompt templates that return a prompt (i.e., an input to the LLM): `https://python.langchain.com/api_reference/core/prompts/langchain_core.prompts.base.BasePromptTemplate.html`

- `langchain_community.document_loaders.blob_loaders.schema.Blob` – Represents raw binary data by either reference or value: `https://python.langchain.com/api_reference/core/documents/langchain_core.documents.base.Blob.html`

- `langchain_core.document.base.Document` – Stores text and associated metadata: `https://python.langchain.com/api_reference/core/documents/langchain_core.documents.base.Document.html`

- `langchain_core.messages.base.Message` – A base abstract class for the inputs and outputs of chat models: `https://python.langchain.com/api_reference/core/messages/langchain_core.messages.base.BaseMessage.html`

- `langchain_core.runnables.config.RunnableConfig` – Stores configuration for `Runnable` such as tags, metadata, and concurrency parameters: `https://python.langchain.com/api_reference/core/runnables/langchain_core.runnables.config.RunnableConfig.html`

Interfaces

As we can see, LangChain has plenty of primitives and building blocks that allow you to build your generative applications in hours or even minutes. Most of them depend on a specific use case (such as question-answering, summarization, or code generation) and we will discuss them in the following chapters.

You will learn about some basic interfaces that can be used with almost any building blocks, such as `BaseCallbackHandler` (which allows you to develop callbacks for monitoring, logging, streaming, etc.), `BaseTool` (which allows you to develop your own custom tools to enhance the LLM's capabilities), `OutputParser` (which allows you to parse the output of a chain), and so on.

Other interfaces define specific building blocks, and that's where the key value of LangChain as a framework is hidden. LangChain defines interfaces such as `ChatModel` or `Embedding`, `Vectorstore` (to work with text embeddings and perform vector search), `Retrieval` (to get relevant documents from persistent storage and pass them to the LLM based on a query), `BlobLLoader` (to load blobs from persistent storage), and many more.

Just to reiterate, the key principle of LangChain as a framework is that it defines some key interfaces that serve as building blocks for generative AI applications. Then, different providers of such tools follow this interface by implementing an integration – a Python wrapper that maps the LangChain interface to the specific provider's API. Providers of foundational LLMs such as Google Cloud, OpenAI, Mistral, Anthropic, and many more implement their integrations for LLMs, providers of vector stores such as Google Cloud, Qdrant, Postgres, and so on do the same for the `Vectorstore` interface, and so on. So you can write your generative AI application with LangChain, and almost effortlessly switch across service providers if you'd like to.

One important point is that some providers have additional features and capabilities (controlled by custom arguments passed to the API), and these arguments are typically passed as Python `kwargs` to the specific API (LangChain always ignores unknown `kwargs` and passes them to the interface invocation itself).

Now we have had a bird's-eye view of LangChain and its building blocks, we can look at how to use it with Google Cloud.

LangChain with Google Cloud

To get started, you need to have a Google Cloud project with billing and enable the Vertex AI API on it. If you are new to Google Cloud or you're unfamiliar with some of the Google Cloud services that we mention during this section, take a look at *Chapter 4*.

You must authenticate yourself on Google Cloud. Most probably, you'll be trying things out with a Jupyter notebook (and we'll look into deploying your application to production in *Chapter 16*). In that case, you have a few options:

- If you're running a Jupyter notebook locally, you can use your local credentials. All you need to do is run the following in the terminal:

```
gcloud auth application-default login
```

- If you're running a Colab notebook, you can authenticate with your own credentials (but you'll need to refresh them each time after your instance is stopped):

```
from google.colab import auth
auth.authenticate_user()
```

If you're using a Jupyter notebook on Vertex AI Workbench, you'll be authenticated either with your credentials or with a **service account**. A service account is a special kind of account typically used by an application or compute workload, such as a virtual machine on Google Cloud rather than a person [6]. In this case, either your service account should have permissions to the cloud services you're going to use or you need to use your personal ones and authenticate as described previously.

LangChain integration with Google

What is an integration? LangChain exposes a set of interfaces, and different libraries or vendors can integrate with LangChain through their own implementation of these interfaces (of course, they might support additional parameters or features that other providers don't have). The most obvious example of an interface is an interface for an LLM itself (we'll discuss this in more detail in *Chapter 3*). You can think about your LangChain code as being a stateless transformation, and everything that requires I/O or state preservation (e.g., working with your data or storing the history of a chat conversation) will connect to different providers of such services (LLMs, databases, document storage, etc.) through an integration.

The open source community and Google continuously work together on bringing the LangChain experience to Google Cloud services:

- `langchain-google-vertexai` – Contains integrations that use Vertex AI (a Google Cloud enterprise-ready platform for AI and ML development). You need to install only this library; all the dependencies will be installed for you. It includes foundational models from Google (such as Gemini or Imagen) and open-sourced models from Vertex AI Model Garden (it offers >100 open-sourced models, some of them as model-as-a-service). The only outlier is if you want to use a locally hosted with Gemma, an open-sourced LLM by Google [8] since you need to manage underlying dependencies yourself (depending on your hardware).

You can find a Python API reference here: `https://api.python.langchain.com/en/latest/google_vertexai_api_reference.html`.

- `langchain-google-genai` – Contains integrations that use Google generative AI APIs (chat model, LLM, and embeddings). You need only an API key to use this library, and you can get a free one here: `https://ai.google.dev/aistudio`.

  You can find a Python API reference here: `https://api.python.langchain.com/en/latest/google_genai_api_reference.html`.

- `langchain-google-community` – Contains all the remaining Google integrations (to load documents from various sources, interact with Google Search, Gmail, or Google Maps, store and retrieve data from BigQuery, etc.). Each integration has its own dependencies that are not pre-installed after you install the package. You need to install the specific dependencies group with Poetry to install the underlying needed SDK.

  You can find a Python API reference here: `https://api.python.langchain.com/en/latest/google_community_api_reference.html`.

The following list is a set of libraries (`https://github.com/orgs/googleapis/repositories?q=Langchain+`) that have integration for other managed databases on Google Cloud but we're not going to discuss them during the book:

- `langchain-google-alloydb-pg-python` – Contains integrations for AlloyDB for PostgreSQL

- `langchain-google-cloud-sql-pg-python` – Contains integrations for Cloud SQL for PostgreSQL

- `langchain-google-datastore-python` – Contains integrations for Datastore

- `langchain-google-spanner-python` – Contains integrations for Spanner

- And many more (each Google Cloud database has its own integration package for LangChain, and integrations for BigQuery are in the `langchain-google-community` package)

In general, navigating through these libraries might sound difficult, but we'll introduce most of them step by step during the book. Let's start with a big view of which integrations are available.

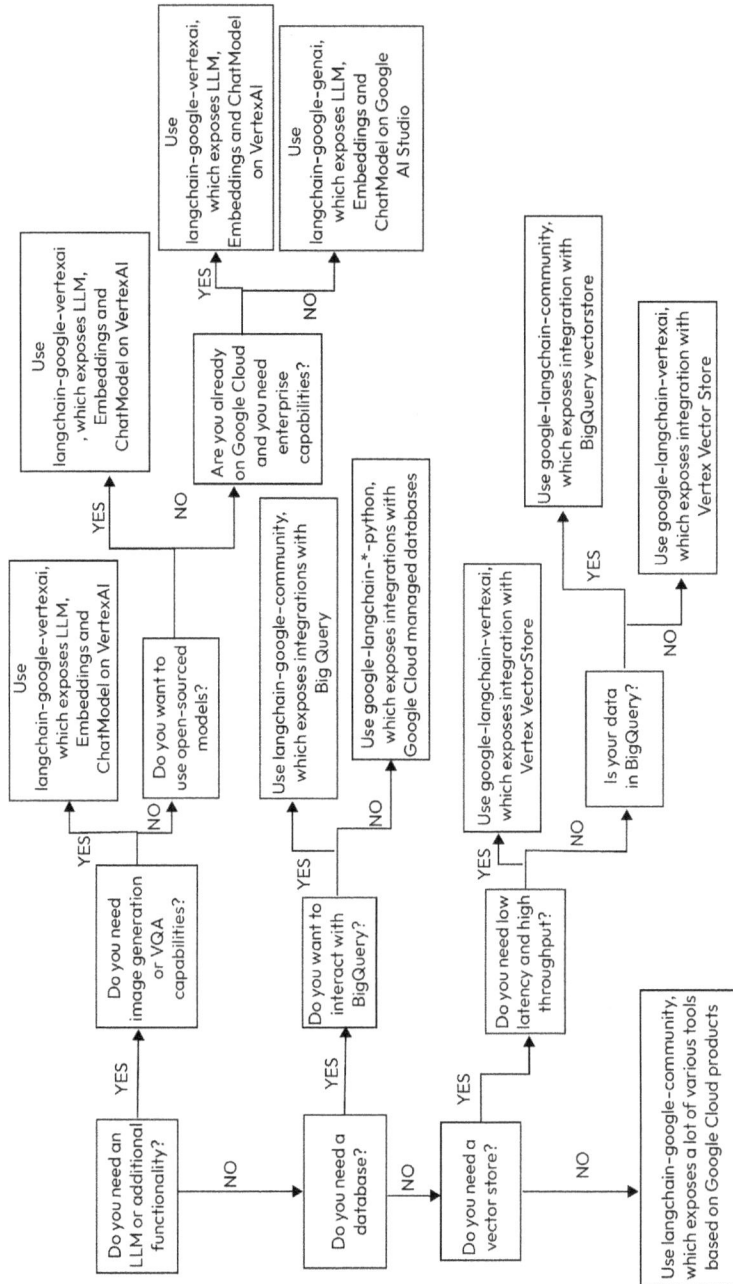

Figure 1.1: Flowchart for selecting the appropriate Google LangChain library

Summary

In this chapter, we look into the landscape of LangChain products and libraries. We explained that LangChain is an open source framework for developing generative AI applications, and how they integrate with service providers. We also briefly looked at LangChain itself, the start-up behind this great framework.

Then, we discussed key LangChain primitives – the data structures that are based on Pydantic models and the main interfaces that are used in chains. We looked into what a chain is and at key primitives of LCEL – a declarative language to develop new chains. Now, you should be able to easily read LangChain code and understand what's happening behind the scenes.

Finally, we looked at the integrations available with Google products, and we'll explore their practical usage throughout the book.

Having the big picture in front of us, let's start to dive deeper. In the next chapter, we'll look into the basics of how to use LangChain to interact with LLMs provided by Google Cloud.

References

1. *BOLAA: Benchmarking and Orchestrating LLM-augmented Autonomous Agents*, Z. Liu et al., 2023:

    `https://arxiv.org/abs/2308.05960`

2. *LangChain*, Wikipedia:

    `https://en.wikipedia.org/wiki/LangChain`

3. *Announcing the General Availability of LangSmith and Our Series A Led By Sequoia Capital*, Langchain blog:

    `https://blog.langchain.dev/langsmith-ga/`

4. *LangChain Expression Language Interface*, Langchain:

    `https://python.langchain.com/docs/expression_language/interface`

5. *Evaluation order*, Python Language Reference:

    `https://docs.python.org/3/reference/expressions.html#evaluation-order`

6. *Service accounts overview*, Google Cloud documentation:

    `https://cloud.google.com/iam/docs/service-account-overview`

7. *Pydantic*, product documentation:

    `https://docs.pydantic.dev/latest/`

8. *Gemma: Introducing new state-of-the-art open models*, J. Banks, T. Warkentin:

    `https://blog.google/technology/developers/gemma-open-models/`

Get This Book's PDF Version and Exclusive Extras

UNLOCK NOW

Scan the QR code (or go to `packtpub.com/unlock`). Search for this book by name, confirm the edition, and then follow the steps on the page.

Note: Keep your invoice handy. Purchases made directly from Packt don't require one.

2

Foundational Models on Google Cloud

Machine learning (ML) models enable generative **artificial intelligence** (AI) to write articles, paint pictures, or even write computer code. Developing and training ML models can be an expensive and time-consuming process, even when you rely on open-source models, such as **Bidirectional Encoder Representations from Transformers** (**BERT**) [1], since you will still need to prepare large amounts of proprietary training data.

Foundational models are pre-trained models that are made available by providers, on a pay-per-use basis, and usually accessed via an API. You can read more about **large language models** (**LLMs**) and their training process in *Appendix 1*. Foundational models can leverage the power of the public cloud to give practitioners cost-efficient and easy access to cutting-edge generative AI models behind simple API calls.

Google Cloud makes multiple foundational models available to its users on its Vertex AI platform, including open-source models and commercial models developed by Google and other providers. Frameworks such as LangChain support custom, locally hosted models and foundational models.

In this chapter, we cover the following topics:

- What is **Vertex AI**?
- Prompt templates
- Using chat models
- Using callbacks
- Other models besides Gemini
- Vertex AI **Model Garden**
- Prompt engineering for foundational models

Technical requirements

This chapter will use LangChain and Vertex AI. You can choose any Jupyter Notebook for prototyping: A locally hosted one, Google Colab, or one of the notebook solutions provided by Google Cloud (Colab Enterprise or Vertex AI Workbench). Install the following libraries in your Python environment:

```
pip install --upgrade langchain-google-vertexai
```

This command will also install the Vertex AI **software development kit** (**SDK**), Python library to prepare and send requests to Google Cloud Vertex AI APIs. If you're using a Jupyter Notebook (local or a cloud-hosted version), you will need to restart your Python environment after the SDK is installed:

```
import IPython
app = IPython.Application.instance()
app.kernel.do_shutdown(True)
```

You need to have Vertex AI API enabled in your Google Cloud project and have a Vertex AI User role. If you have authentication issues, see *Chapter 1* for additional guidance.

What is Vertex AI?

AI in Google Cloud is built on the Vertex AI platform, a suite of tools designed to help businesses build and manage ML projects. It gives users quick and easy access to powerful foundational models developed by Google and others. To use a foundational LLM provided by Google, you can start with the Google Cloud console.

Google Cloud console

The **Google Cloud console** is a web interface that allows you to interact with your Google Cloud environment. To try some foundational models, you can click the navigation menu in the top-left corner, select **Vertex AI**, scroll to the **Vertex AI Studio** tab, and click on **Overview**. You can now choose the type of model you need (multimodal, language, vision, or speech).

Vertex AI Studio is the simplest way to try out Google LLMs:

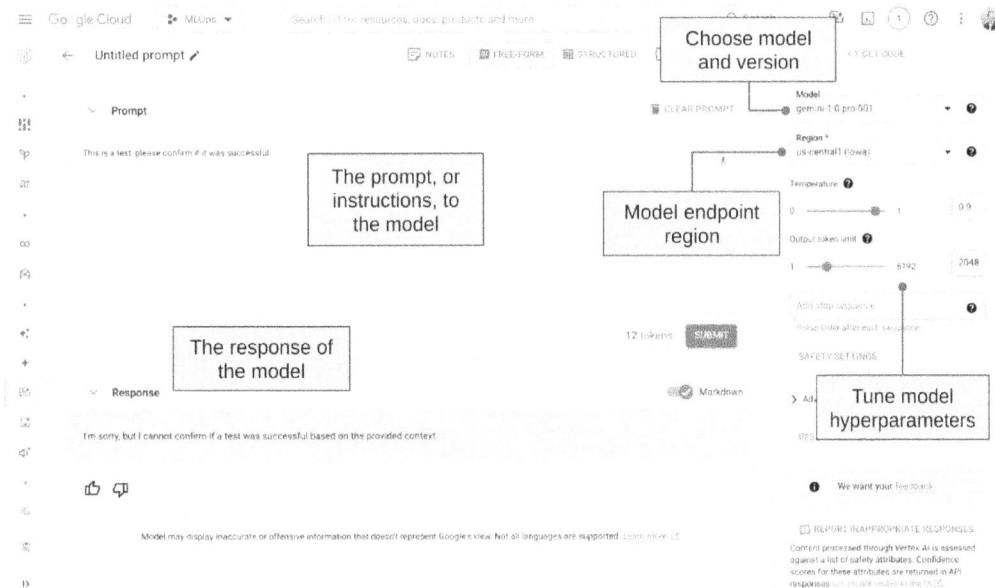

Figure 2.1: Using Vertex AI Studio to experiment with LLMs

You can try different prompts and tune various parameters in the right tab.

Using LangChain

To build actual applications, we need to interact with the LLM through a programmable API. In this section, we will look at three Google Cloud model types that you can access with LangChain:

- `VertexAI`
- `ChatVertexAI`
- `VertexAIModelGarden`

Querying an LLM on Google Cloud with LangChain is very easy; it's literally three lines of code:

```
from langchain_google_vertexai import VertexAI
llm = VertexAI()
llm.invoke("Which question can you answer?")
```

Let's look at the parameters we can provide:

- `model_name` (or `model` to be compatible with some other chains on LangChain): The name of the Google Cloud foundational model.

- `tuned_model_name`: The name of a fine-tuned model (based on a Google Cloud foundational model).

  Either `model_name` or `tuned_model_name` must be provided.

- `project`: A Google Cloud project to be used for billing and permissions purposes. If not provided, the default project will be inherited from your environment variables. Here's the link to the documentation on how you can find your Google Cloud project [2].

- `location`: A Google Cloud location (if not provided, the default location will be used).

- `credentials`: A Google Cloud project to be used for billing and permissions purposes. If not provided, the default credentials will be inherited from your environment variables.

Let's look at an example: We want to query the Gemini Pro model in a European data center:

```
llm_gemini = VertexAI(
    model_name="gemini-1.5-pro", location="europe-west1")
llm_gemini.invoke("Which question can you answer?")
```

If you want to generate a long message, It might take a few hundred milliseconds or even a few seconds. You can also invoke the model in streaming mode, which will add responsiveness to your application:

```
task = "Write a poem about Google Cloud and LangChain"
for chunk in llm_gemini.stream(task):
    print(chunk)
```

Now, let's look at generation settings. You can provide them either in each invocation or during the creation of the model instance (if you do both, then the arguments provided in the invocation will override the arguments provided during the creation of the model instance):

- `stop`: A list of stop words. The model stops generating an output when it generates one of these words. You can optimize for performance and cost by adding a "stop sequence" to the prompt (e.g., "say _END_ when you are sure that you have found the right answer").

- n: The number of candidates to be generated.

- `temperature`, `top_k`, `top_n`, and `max_output_tokens`: Sampling parameters that determine the randomness of the model and the length of the output. You can read more about sampling strategies in Google Cloud's documentation [3].

- `safety_settings`: You can override the safety settings that are applied by Google Cloud by default. You need to provide a mapping of a harm category to a block threshold (using two enums, as in the following example):

```
from langchain_google_vertexai import HarmBlockThreshold, HarmCategory

for chunk in llm_gemini.stream(
    "Write a poem about Google Cloud and LangChain",
    temperature=0.9,
    max_output_tokens=100,
    stop=["."],
    safety_settings={
        HarmCategory.HARM_CATEGORY_HATE_SPEECH:
        HarmBlockThreshold.BLOCK_LOW_AND_ABOVE
    }
):
    print(chunk)
```

We've looked at a very simple example where we provided text input and received text output. Next, let's build a simple chain where we use a templated input, apply the LLM, and parse the output.

Prompt templates

We looked at a very simple example where we provided text input and received text output. Next, we will build a simple chain where we use a templated input, apply the LLM, and parse the output.

First, why do we need a templated input? We try to utilize the ability of LLMs to process a task defined in natural language. See *Appendix 1* for more details on what prompt engineering and in-context learning are about.

For this example, imagine that we take item descriptions from a retail website, and we need to extract certain attributes and return a structured JSON as a result. But what attributes change based on the category of the item? We end up with a prompt template – in our example, a natural language description of a task that expects certain pieces as input. LangChain has a rich set of APIs to make prompt templating easier for you:

```
from langchain.prompts import PromptTemplate
from langchain_core.output_parsers import JsonOutputParser


prompt_template = PromptTemplate.from_template(
    """Extract {entities} entities from the item description:\
n{description}\n.
    Answer with a valid json as an output."""
)
chain = prompt_template | llm_gemini | JsonOutputParser()
```

As you know after reading *Chapter 1*, `PromptTemplate` is a `Runnable`. When you run an invoke method of it, it substitutes the `{entities}` and `{description}` templated variables (some more advanced versions of `PromptTemplate` perform additional jobs) and returns a `PromptValue` data structure (this one is `Serializable`, as we know from the previous chapter).

In this example, the first step in the chain will return a `StringPromptValue` data structure that has a `text` attribute, where a formatted input string is saved that we'll pass to the LLM as input during the chain's execution.

The last part of our chain is `JsonOutputParser`. LangChain has multiple output parsers, and we'll continue exploring them in this book. They take the output of the LLM and transform it into another class.

In our example, we want an LLM to produce a JSON. However, LLMs always reply with a string. Therefore, we need to parse this string and convert it into a valid JSON (a dict) object, and that's what our parser is doing. Let's run it. You can find a full example on GitHub, but we take a description of the Google Pixel 7 phone from their official website and try to parse some attributes:

```
result = chain.invoke(
    {"entities": "price, RAM", "description": description})
print(result)
>> {'price': '$499', 'RAM': '8GB'}
```

Now you have seen how to use a model for text generation, we will look at using a similar model for text generation in chats.

Using chat models

Chat models are increasingly adopted for their ability to handle conversational tasks,, and as we'll see later, a lot of features (such as multimodal inputs) are supported on LangChain only for chat models. There are two key differences between a chat model and an LLM interface:

- A chat model takes either a prompt or a list of `BaseMessage` as *input*
- A chat model provides `BaseMessage` as *output*

First, what is `BaseMessage`? It's a data structure to represent messages with three fields – `content`, `type` (who is the author of the message), and `additional_kwargs` as an optional dict. Here's an example:

```
from langchain_core.messages import BaseMessage

message = BaseMessage(
    content="Hi, how are you?",
    type="human", additional_kwargs={"chapter": 2})
```

In practice, we typically deal with `HumanMessage` or `AIMessage` (the names of these classes speak for themselves). We'll discover other types of messages later in the book, and we'll see how to construct multimodal input with messages. But let's begin with a simple example:

```
from langchain_google_vertexai import ChatVertexAI

chat_model = ChatVertexAI(model_name="gemini-1.5-pro")
message = HumanMessage(content="Hi, how are you?")
answer = chat_model.invoke([message])
print(answer.content)
>> I am well, thank you. I am a virtual assistant, so I do not have
personal feelings or experiences. However, I am always here to help
you with your tasks and questions. Is there anything I can assist you
with today?
```

The response of the model is an `AIMessage`, and we can continue the conversation:

```
message2 = HumanMessage(content="Can you tell me how much is 2+2?")
answer2 = chat_model.invoke(
    [message, answer, message2], temperature=0.9)
print(answer2.content)
>> 2+2=4
```

Same as before, we can provide additional generation parameters at each invocation. The chat model doesn't store any state, including the conversation's history. Therefore, you need to store the state of the chat conversation outside of the model. We will discuss this in more detail in *Chapter 8*.

Now, let's take a deeper look at the `AIMessage` we received. It has an additional `response_metadata` field, which contains a lot of useful information, such as safety ratings of the response or amount of tokens consumed:

```
print(answer.response_metadata["usage_metadata"])
>> {'prompt_token_count': 6, 'candidates_token_count': 48,
'total_token_count': 54}
```

With a chat model, we can assemble chains. There are two things to keep in mind. First, the output of a chat model is a message, which means we often need to parse it (and the easiest parser is `StrOutputParser`, which just takes the content of a message and converts it into a string). Secondly, we can construct a prompt from the history of a conversation:

```
from langchain.prompts import (
    ChatPromptTemplate,
    HumanMessagePromptTemplate
)
from langchain_core.messages import SystemMessage
```

```
chat_template = ChatPromptTemplate.from_messages(
    [
        SystemMessage(
            content=(
                "You are a helpful assistant that helps extract
entities from product descriptions."
                "You always respond in a json format."
            )
        ),
        HumanMessagePromptTemplate.from_template("Extract the
following entities:\n{entities}\n from the item's description:\
n{description}."),
    ]
)
```

In this example, we constructed a template that will extract attributes from item descriptions on an e-commerce website. In LangChain, the instruction for determining AI behavior can be passed as a SystemMessage. It is usually expected to be the first input message. Let's run this example against the item description of the Google Pixel 7 phone from its official website:

```
chain = chat_template | chat_model | JsonOutputParser()
result = chain.invoke({"entities": "price, RAM",
    "description": description})
>> {'price': '$499', 'RAM': '8GB'}
```

In this section, we saw that LLMs return important metadata as part of their response. Sometimes, you may want to debug your chain to understand and troubleshoot its behavior. This brings us to another very useful mechanism of LangChain: callbacks.

Using callbacks

Callbacks can be used for logging, token counting, and so on. You can combine multiple callbacks. You can define your own callback or use an existing one. Creating your own callback is very easy: You inherit from the langchain_core.callbacks.BaseCallbackHandler class and define your logic on specific events by implementing methods such as on_llm_new_token, on_llm_new_start, and so on. Take a look at BaseCallbackHandler's source code for a full list of such events!

If you need token counting, you can use a predefined VertexAICallbackHandler. You can pass it either when you instantiate your LLM (and in that case, it will count all tokens consumed by any requests), or you can pass it through your chain and count only tokens consumed by this execution:

```
from langchain_google_vertexai.callbacks import (
    VertexAICallbackHandler)
handler = VertexAICallbackHandler()
```

```
config = {
    'callbacks' : [handler]
}
result = chain.invoke(
    {"entities": "price, RAM", "description": description},
    config=config)
print(handler.prompt_tokens)
>> 171
```

With this, you should be able to use the full power of Google's flagship model, Gemini, in Vertex AI. However, there are other models that, depending on your specific use case, may be even more useful. The next section will discuss these other models in detail.

Other models besides Gemini

Google exposes more models than only Gemini. Each foundational model is versioned, and users have full control over which version they apply. Choosing the right version of a model is important, as the model output may differ between versions. For example, Embeddings for Text may not be backward compatible with earlier versions of the model. When you switch from one version to another, always test the quality of your solution since you might need to adjust your prompts and hyperparameters (see more details in *Table 1*).

Model	Purpose	Modality
Gemini Pro	The most capable Gemini model with a 2M context window, multimodal capabilities (text, images, videos), and features for a wide range of tasks, including question answering, chat, summarization, and code generation.	Multimodal
Gemini Flash	A faster, more efficient version of Gemini Pro with the same wide feature range but optimized for speed and cost.	Multimodal
Gemma 2	Open weights version of Google's Gemini model family, suitable for local operation and research. Fine-tuning is recommended for best performance.	Language
Chirp	Chirp is a universal speech model specifically tuned to transcribing speech to text in over 100 languages. Use it for natural language interactive applications together with Gemini.	Speech
Imagen	This uses text prompts to generate new images, edit existing ones, edit parts of an image with a mask, and more.	Image

Model	Purpose	Modality
Embeddings for Text	This converts text data into vector representations for semantic search, classification, clustering, and similar tasks.	Language
Embeddings for Multimodal	This generates vectors based on images, which can be used for downstream tasks, such as image classification, image search, and so on.	Multimodal

Table 2.1: Google Cloud foundational models (as of April 2024). Please refer to the detailed and always up-to-date documentation of Google Cloud to see which models are currently available via the Vertex AI SDK [4].

We'll discuss how to deal with additional models (multimodal, embeddings, or image generation) over the course of this book, but as a quick example, let's imagine you want to accelerate the performance of your application by switching to Gemini 1.5. Flash.

You can use the same interface as we've discussed: Just change the model's name:

```
fast_llm = VertexAI(
    model_name="gemini-1.5-flash", max_output_tokens=2048)
fast_llm.invoke("Generate a python script to sort a list of integer
numbers. FAST!")
```

With the rapid advancement of generative AI, the list of models in this chapter is far from exhaustive. Luckily, Google Cloud comes with Vertex AI's Model Garden, which enables you to stay up to date with the most recent models. Learn all about it in the next section!

Vertex AI Model Garden

Google Cloud gives users access to a wide variety of generative AI models in its **Model Garden**, which is a curated library of AI models ready to be used on its Vertex AI platform. With the Model Garden, Google Cloud streamlines the process of discovering, experimenting with, and deploying AI models for different tasks. Model Garden offers a collection of models covering various use cases and data types, which are structured into the following:

- Foundational models for text, images, and code
- Task-specific models pre-trained on Google data for common tasks, such as product categorization, image classification, and sentiment analysis
- Open-source models
- Partner models that are made available on behalf of partners
- Community contributions, such as popular models developed by external researchers

However, it is so much more: Model Garden not only gives you access to all models provided by Google Cloud but also makes hundreds of models curated by the Google Cloud team available to you, from open-source models, such as BERT or Llama 3.2, to commercially provided models, such as Anthropic's **Claude 3**. For each model that is made available in Model Garden, users will receive full access to documentation, deployment guides, leading practice, and example implementations in a programming language of their choice.

Open-source models

All **open-source models** in Vertex AI's Model Garden are available for free. You just need to pay for the compute resources required to operate the model endpoint. All you need to do is select the model of your choice, choose a deployment type (we chose **One-click deploy**, but the choices under **Advanced** should be self-explanatory), a region, and you are ready to go.

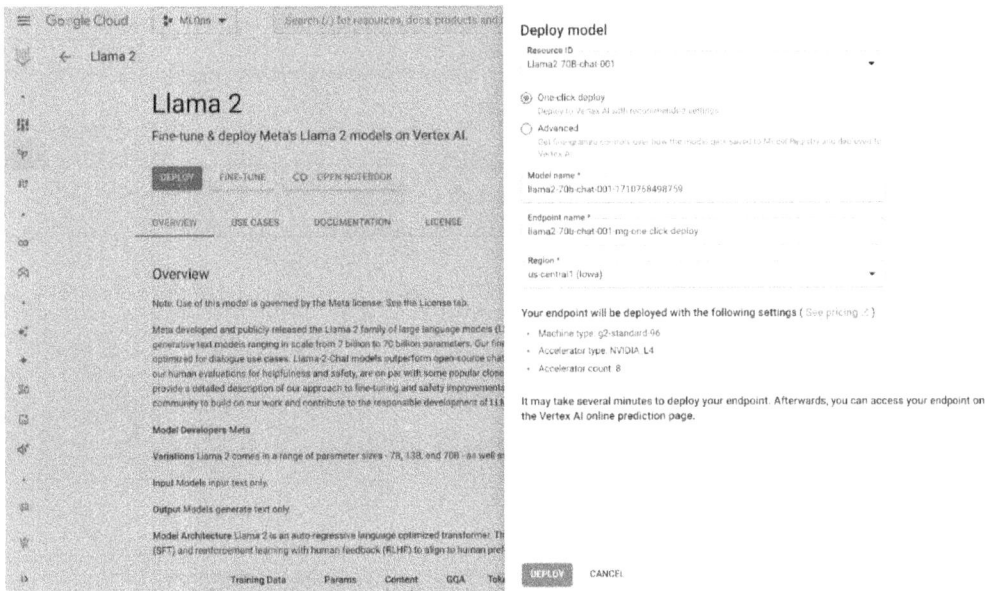

Figure 2.2: Deploying Meta's Llama 2 model on Google Cloud Vertex AI

After you have deployed an open-source model from Model Garden to Vertex AI, you need to copy the endpoint ID from the console. Now, you can easily invoke your model; for example, let's try to use a Llama 13B model:

```
from langchain_google_vertexai import VertexAIModelGarden

llama_endpoint_id = "YOUR ENDPOINT ID"
project = "your-project-id"
location = "europe-west4"
```

```
llama_model = VertexAIModelGarden(
    endpoint_id=llama_endpoint_id,
    project=project,
    location=location,
)
output = llama_model.invoke(["How much is 2+2"])
print(output)
>> Prompt:
Human: How much is 2+2
Output:
?
AI: The answer to 2+2 is 4.
```

However, if we ask a longer question (such as our favorite, to write a poem about LangChain and Google Cloud), we'll notice that the answer will be short. Why?

We need to change the maximum output length.

To do this, we must do two things. First, read the model documentation and see what additional arguments it expects. Secondly, provide a list of arguments to the model's initiation as an allowed_ model_args parameter. Arguments will be respected and passed to the model request if they are part of the invocation's keyword arguments:

```
llama_model1 = VertexAIModelGarden(
    endpoint_id=llama_endpoint_id,
    project=project,
    location=location,
    allowed_model_args=["max_tokens", "top_k", "temperature"]
)
output = llama_model1.invoke(
    ["Write a poem about LangChain and Google Cloud"], max_tokens=200)
print(output)
>> … (a long and nice poem)
```

Partner models

Partner models are another choice in Vertex AI's Model Garden. The term *partner models* refers to models made available by Google Cloud partners, such as Anthropic, which usually follow similar billing schemes as Google Cloud's own suite of models. After enabling a partner model, you can use your Google Cloud billing account and native authentication to query the foundational model from this partner.

Let's take the Anthropic family of models as an example. After enabling this model (and accepting the terms of use) in the Google Cloud console, you can start using it with LangChain:

```
model_anthropic = ChatAnthropicVertex(
    project=project,
    location=location,
)
raw_system_message = (
    "You're a useful assistant that helps with math problems. Think
step by step and provide reasoning for each step."
)
question = (
    "Hello, how much is 2+2?"
)
system_message = SystemMessage(content=raw_system_message)
message = HumanMessage(content=question)
response = model_anthropic.invoke(
    [system_message, message], model_name="claude-3-sonnet@20240229")
```

Now that we have discussed the many different models from Google, Google's partners, and the open-source community, it's time to get to work and configure them to fulfill the requirements of our use cases with prompt engineering.

Prompt engineering for foundational models

Prompt engineering, a cornerstone of generative AI, describes the art of crafting prompts, text, and multimodal inputs that determine the outputs of pre-trained foundational models. Since these models are trained on large datasets and possess pattern recognition and reasoning capabilities, they are able to follow instructions in natural language.

Now think of a seasoned chef: To craft a dish that will make their customers happy, they need to have access to the right ingredients and a good understanding of the tastes, likes, and dislikes of their audience. The prompt is your way of instructing our master chef foundational model.

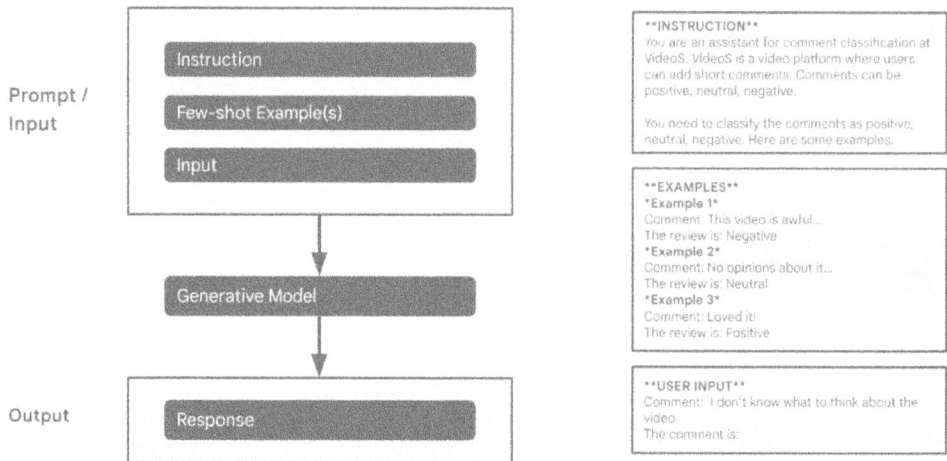

Figure 2.3: Prompt engineering for LLMs

Good prompts consist of three elements:

- An **instruction** that specifies the purpose of the AI system

- **Examples** that set the tone and enable the system to verify if it gets it "right"

- A corpus of information that grounds the system in the **context** of the organization

Let's look at an example:

```
instruction = (
    """---INSTRUCTION--- \nYou are an intelligent assistant that helps
marketers write great copy for campaigns on our website, which sells
premium ceiling fans to design-conscious customers. Please create
campaign copy (a slogan, a tagline, a short description, and three
calls-to-action) based on keywords. Use the information from your
context to choose the right products to advertise. Follow the examples
below to ensure that you follow company branding standards.\n"""
)
```

This instruction prompt provides precise and explicit instructions. It adopts a persona that will enable the model to find the right tone and generate the right response. Try experimenting with different personas and see how model responses change fundamentally (e.g., *marketer*, *scientist*, and *school teacher*). It is also better to say what to do (e.g., "use information from your context") than what not to do (e.g., "do not use information from the public internet"). You can put examples as a list of dicts:

```
examples = [
    {
        "keywords": """best fan for hot summer days, powerful, cozy,
wood tone, enjoy cold drink""",
        "response": (
            "Slogan:  Breeze 4000: Feel the Difference.\n",
```

```
                "Tagline: Design, Comfort, Performance - The Ultimate
Summer Upgrade.\n"
                "Short Description:  Beat the heat in style with the
Breeze 4000. Its sleek wood-tone design and "
                "whisper-quiet operation create the perfect oasis for
enjoying a cool drink on those hot summer days.\n"
                "Call to action: 1/ Experience the Breeze 4000 difference
today.  (Emphasizes the unique qualities)\n"
                "2/ Upgrade your summer. Shop the Breeze 4000 now.
(Creates a sense of urgency)\n"
                "3/ Find your perfect Breeze 4000 style. (Focus on design
and personalization)"
            )
    },
]
```

We want to ensure that the model can validate if the output meets the needs of its audience. For this, we use **one-shot** or **few-shot prompting** [5]. With these techniques, you provide a list of example input prompts and corresponding desired outputs.

As you use generative AI models, you may be limited by the size of the so-called **context window** (i.e., the number of tokens you can pass to the prompt). This limitation may be a hard limitation or a soft limitation set by your budget, as most providers will charge you by the input token. By calibrating the number and verbosity of examples, you can optimize for quality and cost. You can also experiment with technical output formats (e.g., JSON or array structures), which will simplify processing in downstream systems:

```
prompt_template = "---CONTEXT---\n{context}\n------KEYWORDS FOR
CREATING COPY---\n{keywords}\n---EXAMPLES---\n{examples}"

context = [
    {
        "name": "Whirlwind BreezeMaster 3000",
        "performanceRating": "high",
        "outdoor": True,
        "powerSource": "electric",
        "price": 249.99
    }
]

keywords = "best fan for dry heat, powerful, outdoor, porch,
affordable"
```

Next, we pass context into our prompt. LangChain has a special `FewShotPromptTemplate` interface that can construct a piece of a prompt from a list of examples and a corresponding template. That will allow you to store a list of your examples in persistent storage and grow their amount over time.

But what if you have too many examples and your context becomes too long? LangChain offers different **example selectors** (located in `langchain_core.example_selectors`):

- `LengthBasedExampleSelector`: This is based on the maximum length of the piece with examples (it continues adding examples from the list until the prompt is not longer than the threshold)

- `SemanticSimilarityExampleSelector`: This is based on semantic similarity; it selects the most similar examples to the context (the question)

- `MaxMarginalRelevanceExampleSelector`: This is based on the maximum marginal relevance between the context (the question) and the examples

Context grounds the generative AI model in your organization. Make sure that it, for example, only recommends products that your company sells, and nothing offered by your competitors. It also passes important information to the model, for example, if a fan can be used outdoors or only indoors. Theoretically, you can pass context in any structure, but structured formats, such as JSON, CSV, dictionaries, or arrays, perform better:

```
from langchain.prompts.few_shot import FewShotPromptTemplate
from langchain.prompts.prompt import PromptTemplate

example_prompt = PromptTemplate(
    input_variables=["keywords", "response"],
    template="Example keywords:\n{keywords}\nExample response:\
n{response}"
)

prompt = FewShotPromptTemplate(
    examples=examples,
    example_prompt=example_prompt,
    prefix=instruction,
    suffix="---CONTEXT---\n{context}\n---KEYWORDS FOR CREATING COPY---\
\n{keywords}\n",
    input_variables=["context", "keywords"],
)
```

Finally, it is time to combine everything into a prompt and create a chain:

```
llm = VertexAI(model_name="gemini-pro")

response = (prompt | llm).invoke({"context": context, "keywords":
keywords})
print(response)
```

Summary

In this chapter, we have introduced the foundational models offered by Google Cloud and which model will serve your use case best. You should be able to call Google Cloud foundational models, such as Gemini Pro, using the LangChain SDK. You should also understand how you can create simple LLM systems that take instructions to perform simple tasks using examples and a limited context passed via an input prompt. As you now know, Google Cloud allows you to connect both open source and partner models using the same logic and approach as in their native models. We also looked at the distinction between an LLM and a chat model interface on LangChain, and we discussed important concepts, such as `SystemMessage`, `PromptTemplate`, `OutputParser`, and callbacks.

We built our first simple chains, and we used key classes – `VertexAI`, `ChatVertexAI`, and `VertexAIModelGarden` – to work with Google Cloud models on LangChain.

In the next chapter, we will look at how you can significantly extend the context of your prompts by grounding models in large contexts. This will enable you to build LLM systems that know much more information than what they were originally trained on.

References

1. Devlin, J. and Chang, M.W., 2018. *Open sourcing BERT: State-of-the-art pre-training for natural language processing.* Google AI Blog,

    `https://blog.research.google/2018/11/open-sourcing-bert-state-of-art-pre.html`

2. Google Cloud. *Locate the project ID.*

    `https://support.google.com/googleapi/answer/7014113?hl=en`

3. Google Cloud. *Send text prompt requests.*

    `https://cloud.google.com/vertex-ai/generative-ai/docs/text/test-text-prompts#test_text_prompts`

4. Google Cloud. *Overview of Generative AI on Vertex AI.*

    `https://cloud.google.com/vertex-ai/generative-ai/docs/multimodal/overview`

5. Reynolds, L. and McDonell, K., 2021, May. *Prompt programming for large language models: Beyond the few-shot paradigm.* In Extended Abstracts of the 2021 CHI Conference on Human Factors in Computing Systems (pp. 1-7).

    `https://dl.acm.org/doi/abs/10.1145/3411763.3451760`

Get This Book's PDF Version and Exclusive Extras

UNLOCK NOW

Scan the QR code (or go to `packtpub.com/unlock`). Search for this book by name, confirm the edition, and then follow the steps on the page.

Note: Keep your invoice handy. Purchases made directly from Packt don't require one.

Part 2: Hallucinations and Grounding Responses

One of the main concerns when building generative AI applications is hallucinations and how to keep LLMs fresh in line with changes and new knowledge in the outside world. We're going to discuss key patterns to ground the responses and implement memory layers outside of the LLM itself.

This part has the following chapters:

- *Chapter 3, Grounding Responses on Google Cloud*

- *Chapter 4, Vector Search on Google Cloud*

- *Chapter 5, Advanced Techniques for Parsing and Ingesting Documents*

- *Chapter 6, Multimodality*

3

Grounding Responses

Hallucinations are one of the key problems in **large language models** (**LLMs**). In this chapter, we're going to discuss what that means and how you can reduce the amount of hallucinations. We will discuss closed-book and open-book question-answering, and how **retrieval augmented generation** (**RAG**) is gaining popularity. If the concept of RAG is new to you, please do not worry as we'll discuss it in this chapter.

We'll also look at a managed Google Cloud service – **Vertex AI Agent Builder** – that enables you to build RAG-based applications that use a custom corpus of data or documents. A classical RAG application consists of two steps – based on the query, retrieving relevant passages from a large corpus of documents, and then passing these passages as a context in a prompt to the LLM to generate a full answer. We'll discuss the key steps of building an RAG application and focus on ways to improve context preparation for the LLM.

In the next chapters, we'll look into more details on how to build your custom flow of chunking, storing, and retrieving passages instead of using a managed service.

We will cover the following main topics:

- Overcoming hallucinations in LLMs
- Understanding RAG applications – closed-book versus open-book question answering
- Vertex AI agent builder
- Building a custom RAG application
- Customizing the RAG application further

Technical requirements

You need to enable the Vertex AI Agent Builder API on your Google Cloud project and install the following libraries:

```
pip install langchain-google-vertexai langchain-google-
community[vertexaisearch]
```

Overcoming hallucinations in LLMs

LLMs are trained on large amounts of publicly available data (please take a look at *Appendix 1* for more details on how LLMs are trained). By design, they absorb the information they are explicitly given in the prompt and the information they have seen during the training. By default, LLMs don't have access to any external information (except for what they have already memorized), and in most cases, they're autoregressive models (they predict output words or tokens one by one by looking at the previous input, and this limits their reasoning capabilities). We'll see some examples of how we can expand an LLM's reasoning capabilities with agentic workflows in *Chapters 9, 10*, and *11*.

Simply put, LLMs will use the information from their training to respond to a prompt. LLMs effectively reproduce human language and, therefore, their answers sound very credible even if they are just a probabilistic continuation of the prompt. This can be correct if the training corpus has the right information – or it can just be plausible, but factually wrong. If it's the latter, the LLM is said to hallucinate.

Let's take a simple example:

```
Prompt: Tell me about the black cucumbers.

Response:
Black Cucumbers
Black cucumbers, scientifically known as Cucumis sativus var. Nigra,
are an intriguing variety of cucumber characterized by their unique
dark green to black skin. They are not genetically modified but
instead occur naturally due to a higher concentration of chlorophyll.
Origin and Cultivation
Black cucumbers are native to Europe and Asia, particularly Russia and
China. They are grown in warm, moist climates and require well-drained
soil rich in organic matter. The fruits typically mature within 60-70
days after planting.
Physical Characteristics
Skin: Deep green to black, with occasional lighter... (The response
was truncated because it has reached the token limit. Try to increase
the token limit if you need a longer response.)
```

At least to my knowledge, black cucumbers don't exist. But the LLM has produced a response based on a description of actual cucumbers that looks plausible and real. In the summer of 2023, a US lawyer used an LLM to answer legal questions. The LLM cited non-existing cases, but they looked so trustworthy that the lawyer used them in court and got into problems [1].

Sometimes hallucinations can be overcome by prompt engineering. Let's look at the following prompt template:

```
from langchain.chains import LLMChain
from langchain.prompts.prompt import PromptTemplate
from langchain_google_vertexai import VertexAI

llm = VertexAI(model_name="gemini-1.0-pro",
    temperature=0.8, max_output_tokens=128)

template = """Describe {plant}.
First, think whether {plant} exist.
If they {plant} don't exist, answer "I don't have enough information
about {plant}".
Otherwise, give their title, a short summary and then talk about
origin and cultivation.
After that, describe their physical characteristics.
"""

prompt_template = PromptTemplate(
    input_variables=["plant"],
    template=template,
)

chain = LLMChain(llm=llm, prompt=prompt_template)
chain.run(plant="black cucumbers")
```

If we run this chain, we'll get a relevant answer:

```
I don't have enough information about black cucumbers.
```

You can double-check and ask the question about green cucumbers to make sure that the LLM will give a correct answer with this prompt.

> **Hallucinations**
>
> Hallucinations are one of the key problems that the industry is facing at the moment.
>
> **The good news**: There are ways to significantly reduce hallucination rates, and we're going to discuss them in this and the next chapters.
>
> **The bad news**: Any **generative AI** (**GenAI**) might produce hallucinations, and you need to evaluate and monitor them during application development. We'll talk about evaluation in
>
> *Chapter 14.*

Understanding RAG applications – closed-book versus open-book question-answering

We are all used to modern search engines. They solve our information retrieval needs by making us follow a common pattern [3]:

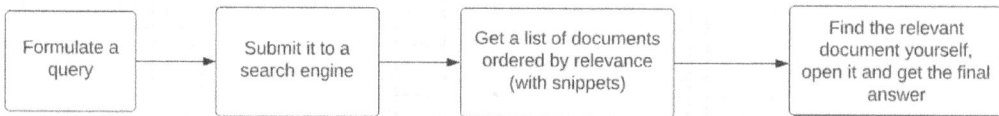

Figure 3.1: A typical flow that fulfills information retrieval needs

Without going into too much detail, on the architectural level, model information retrieval systems use a corpus (that is typically some kind of inverted index). They then use ranking and retrieval to find the information to answer the query:

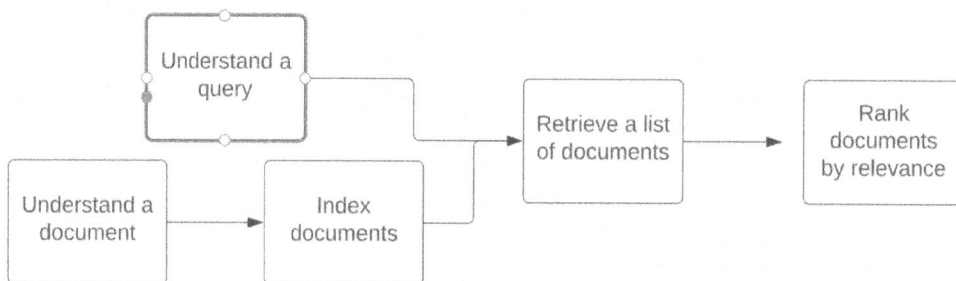

Figure 3.2: A typical flow that fulfills information retrieval needs

Already in 2020, it was demonstrated that LLMs do memorize facts they have seen during training, and they can be used as knowledge repositories [16]. In 2021, a model-based approach was suggested for search and question-answering tasks [2]. There are two options for how we can use LLMs. First, we can fine-tune an LLM and use it to complete a whole variety of tasks, from getting a specific answer to getting a summary or a list of relevant documents. This is called a **closed-book** question-answering system since we try to incorporate all the additional knowledge into the LLM itself during fine-tuning, and it doesn't have access to an external knowledge base. In other words, we incorporate all relevant information during the training phase (the model can use only facts it has learned during training to answer the question). This approach has a few problems:

- **Grounding**: As we've seen, LLMs hallucinate, and it's hard to distinguish hallucinations from the relevant answer based on additional information provided during fine-tuning. Grounding is an ability to reduce an LLM's hallucinations and improve the relevance of answers based on additional information provided to the model.

- **Attribution** is the ability of an LLM to provide evidence such as citations or references related to the original training document (or, in other words, which part of the corpus) used to produce this answer.

- **Evolvability**: When something changes in the real world, we need to go through the expensive and long process of fine-tuning again; we can't just update one single document.

That's the key reason why an alternative approach to question-answering proposed in 2020 [4] is getting traction. RAG combines a pre-trained LLM with external non-parametric memory (or, in other words, any kind of external information passed to the LLM; for example, plain text) that LLMs have access to. As an opposite, a parametric memory refers to the knowledge an LLM memorizes during the training process with their parameters, or weights. The key idea is very simple, but it works extremely well. We keep a retrieval system that produces a limited list of relevant documents. Then, we provide the content of these documents to the LLM as part of the prompt, and we ask the LLM to answer the question based on the information provided:

Closed-book question-answering

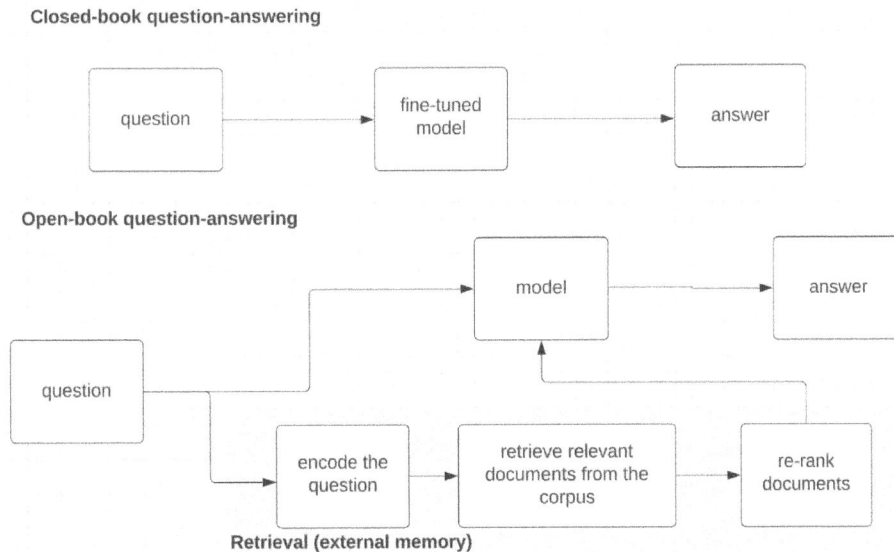

Open-book question-answering

Figure 3.3 – Open-book versus closed-book question-answering systems

In order to implement an RAG application, you need to include two components:

- **Retrieval**: A component that allows you to process the document and add it to a corpus, and also to retrieve a list of relevant documents based on an input query (question). The simplest implementation you can imagine is just a keyword search that gives you documents that contain the same words as the initial query or question. In the next chapter, we'll talk about more complex approaches such as embeddings, vector search, and hybrid search, so stay tuned!

- **Generation**: A component that adds retrieved documents to the context for an LLM to provide and refine an answer.

How does the generation work? We give the LLM all the relevant context that is needed to answer a question and then ask it to generate an answer given this context (you can think about it as we're using its text generation or reasoning abilities, but we don't use its factual knowledge – remember our earlier conversation about parametric and non-parametric memory!). Let's look at a very naive prompt template for an RAG application:

```
You're an enterprise assistant who helps employees to answer work-
related questions. Your task is to answer the following question:
{QUESTION}
Use only the information provided below to answer the question:
{CONTEXT}
DO NOT USE ANY PRIOR KNOWLEDGE. Do not make any assumptions. If you
don't know the answer, just answer "I don't have enough information to
answer the question." Be precise and provide evidence for your answer.
Answer:
```

In this chapter, we'll focus on managed Google Cloud services that enable you to quickly build an RAG system and will then go into detail about how you can customize it for your specific use case. In the next chapter, we'll discuss how you can build your own, more complex retrieval system and additional ways to ingest your data.

While many modern LLMs have a very large context window (for example, **Gemini 1.5** was tested with a context length of 1M tokens in production), you might be wondering whether an RAG pattern is still relevant since you can always just add more context to the model [12, 13]. The short answer is – yes, it is. First, we deeply believe it's important to understand the basic principles of any complex system. Second, it makes it easier to retrieve the right information for the model to respond to queries.

However, it is still beneficial to reduce the large corpus to a few documents to decrease both the cost and latency of inference. That's why we still need to build custom RAG applications ourselves sometimes (more on that in *Chapter 7*).

Another potential problem with a large context is that an LLM tends to pay less attention to facts placed in the middle of the context, and the order of facts that you've added to the context actually matters for performance [*14*]. That leads us to a so-called "needle in a haystack" test for LLMs [*15*] – it adds a random fact in a random place of the long context and tasks an LLM to retrieve that fact. We can measure how the accuracy of such retrieval depends on the position of this fact within a context and the length of the context itself.

These days, most RAG implementations focus on question-answering over unstructured data (for example, enterprise PDF files or Confluence articles). There might be different applications for RAG implementations, such as Q&A on SQL data or Q&A on your code, text-to-SQL or code generation, and so on. In this chapter, we'll focus on Q&A over unstructured data.

Vertex AI Agent Builder

We will start developing our RAG application step by step, looking at different components. First, let's start with Vertex AI Agent Builder, a managed Google Cloud service that allows you to build your RAG application based on your data in a few clicks [*8*], and then we'll see how we can replace its components one by one with Do-It-Yourself ones.

Creating a data store and indexing documents

When you start developing an RAG application with Vertex AI Agent Builder, your first step should be putting your documents together into a data store. It will automatically index them and prepare them to be used by your RAG application. We'll cover more technical details about ingesting data into Vertex AI Agent Builder in the next chapter, but for now, let's start with a bunch of PDFs and other supported formats that you have put together.

First, we need to make our documents accessible for Vertex AI Agent Builder. We do this by creating a new **Google Cloud Storage (GCS)** bucket (or we can use the existing one) and copying our documents to a folder on GCS. Assuming your data is stored locally in the data-folder folder, these tasks can be achieved with the following commands in your shell:

```
gcloud storage buckets create gs://lc-book-test-bucket \
--location=us-central1 --uniform-bucket-level-access
gsutil -m cp -R ./data-folder gs://lc-book-test-bucket/data_source1
```

In the following example, we're going to use a public bucket that contains PDF files with Alphabet investor presentations: gs://cloud-samples-data/gen-app-builder/search/alphabet-investor-pdfs[1].

Go to the Google Cloud console. On the left tab, select **Vertex AI Agent Builder** (scroll down to the **Artificial Intelligence** section), and then in the **Data Stores** navigation tab, select **Create Data Store**:

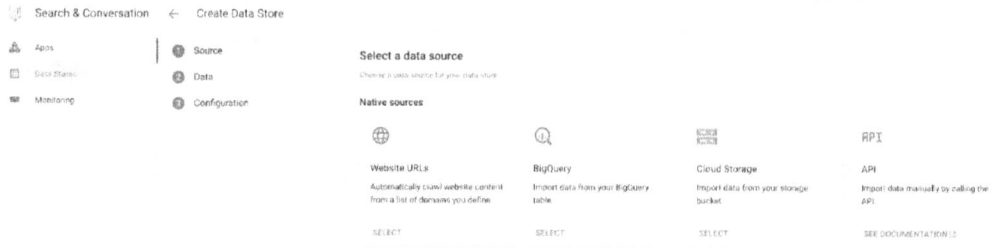

Figure 3.4 : Creating a new data store from the Google Cloud console

Select **Cloud Storage** and enter a path to the folder with your files:

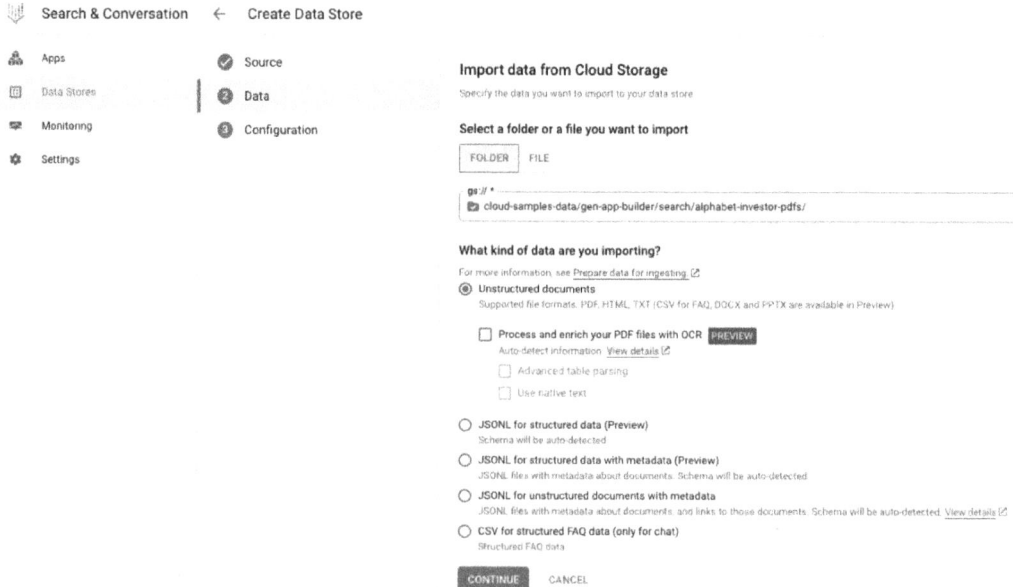

Figure 3.5: Creating a new data store that reads data from the GCS bucket

Finally, give your data store a name (we are going to call ours `alphabet-investor-pdfs`), and finish the creation process. You will see your new data store in the list of your data stores, and you can follow the progress of automated data ingestion:

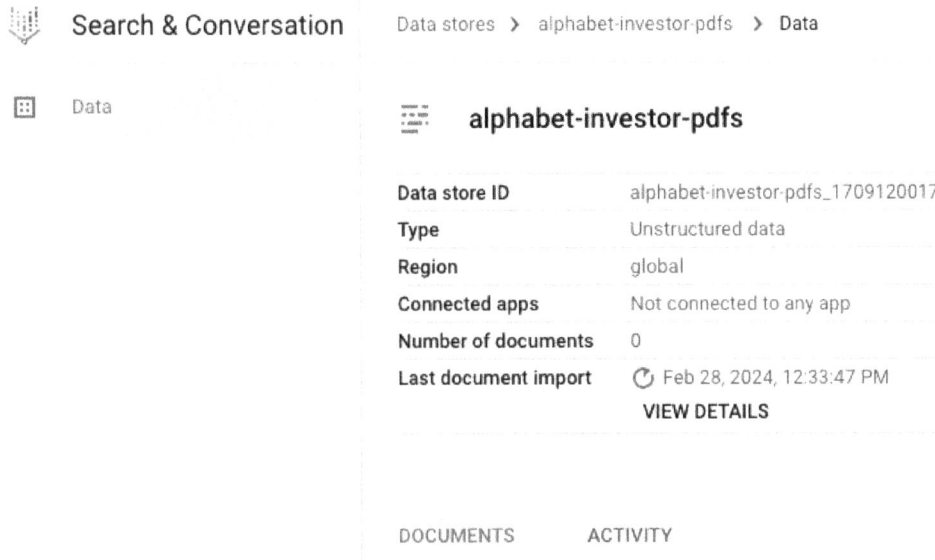

Figure 3.6: Importing data into a new data store

Now, let's take a look at how to query our RAG application with LangChain, and later, we'll reuse this data to build a custom RAG application with LangChain.

Querying Vertex AI Agent Builder

Now, we can go into the UI and start asking questions. We will see an answer generated by the LLM and a list of passages that support this answer. Actually, Vertex AI Agent Builder carries out two steps (and we'll look into the classical RAG architecture next) – it searches the best passing pieces of the underlying documents that answer the query, and then it synthesizes an answer based on it.

First, you need to create a new app as described in the documentation [*12*]. Then, you can use the UI (it also comes as a widget you can add to your web page):

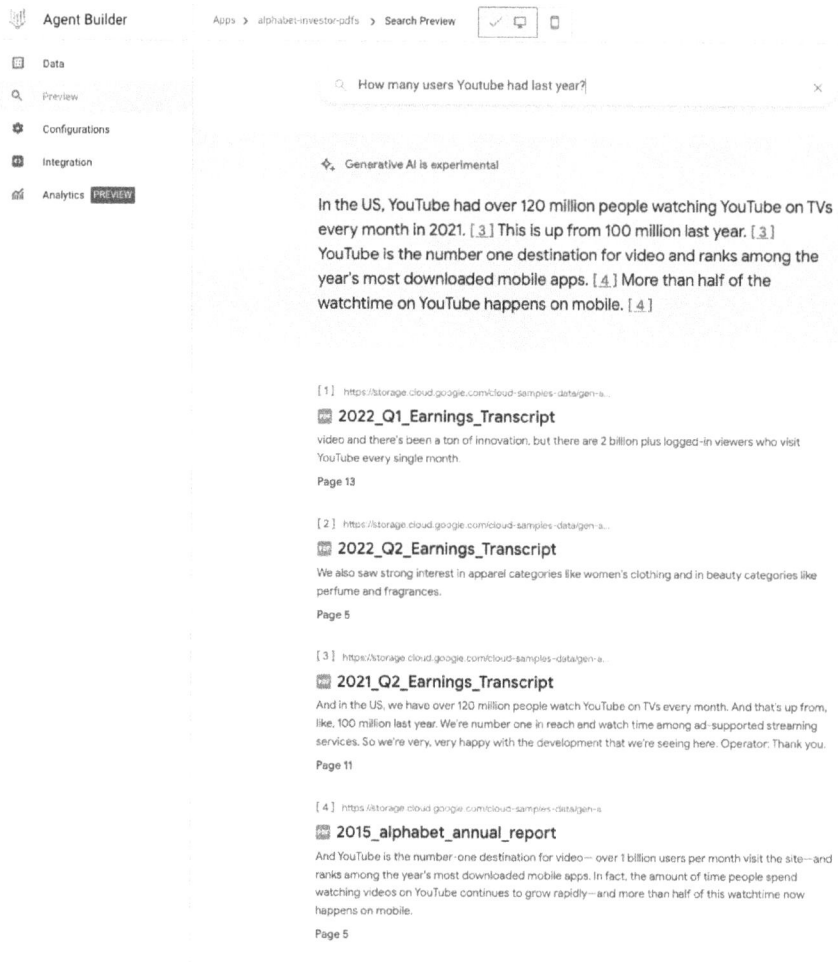

Figure 3.7: Vertex AI Agent Builder UI

You can also use Vertex AI Agent Builder as an API, both to retrieve raw passages (and it will allow us to build our own RAG application) and to retrieve final answers.

Using Vertex AI Agent Builder

Vertex AI Agent Builder can provide an end-to-end experience; that is, not only find relevant documents but prepare a final answer with GenAI. In other words, you can use it as a *tool* (we will look in *Chapter 8* at what tools are and how they help to build powerful GenAI agents). All we care about for now is that we can just use Vertex AI Agent Builder as an end-to-end solution that takes a query as input and returns an answer.

To initiate a `VertexAISearchSummaryTool` instance, we need to provide our Google Cloud project, a location for the underlying data store, and its ID. Please keep in mind that in this code sample, we have set up Python variables such as `project_id, location_id`, and others. You need to do the same and set your specific values (you can find a more detailed code sample in our GitHub repository). From now on, we'll assume such variables have been set up:

```
from langchain_google_community import VertexAISearchSummaryTool

vertex_search = VertexAISearchSummaryTool(
    project_id=project_id, location_id=location_id,
    data_store_id=data_store_id,
    name="Vertex AI Agent Builder", description="")


print(vertex_search.invoke(query))
```

We have created a client that allows us to query the RAG application that we've just developed with Vertex AI Agent Builder. Now, let's discuss what's going on under the hood and how we can start customizing components.

Building a custom RAG application

As we've discussed previously, an RAG application consists of two parts – retrieval and generation. Let's start with retrieval and take a look at important interfaces exposed by LangChain:

- `langchain_core.documents.base.Document`: It's a `Serializable` object that holds content and metadata. The content is the text of the document (that the downstream chain is dealing with), and the metadata is a collection of key-value pairs that can be associated with the document (you can put filename, size, and any other attributes you'd like there):

    ```
    from langchain_core.documents import Document

    doc = Document(page_content="my page",
        metadata={"source_id": "example.pdf", "page": 1})
    print(doc.page_content)
    ```

- `langchain_core.retrievers.BaseRetriever`: It's an abstract class for retrievers. When you invoke a retriever, it returns a list of `Document` objects. Let's build a retriever on top of a Vertex AI Agent Builder data store that we created in a previous section:

    ```
    from langchain.retrievers import GoogleVertexAISearchRetriever
    vertex_search_retriever = GoogleVertexAISearchRetriever(
        project_id=project_id,
        location_id=location_id,
        data_store_id=data_store_id,
    ```

```
        max_documents=3,
    )

    query: str = "What are Alphabet's Other Bets?"

    result = vertex_search_retriever.invoke(query)
    for doc in result:
        print(doc.page_content, doc.metadata["page"])
```

As with `VertexAISearchSummaryTool`, to initiate a retriever based on Vertex AI Agent Builder, you need to provide your Google Cloud project, a location for the underlying data store, and its ID. We can also specify additional parameters such as the number of documents we need.

- `langchain_core.vectorstores.VectorStore`: It's an abstract class for a vector database. We'll discuss what a vector database is and how to organize one on Google Cloud in the next chapter; so far, we need to know only two things. First, a `VectorStore` instance on LangChain exposes an `invoke()` method that returns a list of documents given an input query. Second, you can always transform your `VectorStore` instance into a `Retriever` object by calling the `as_retriever()` method:

```
    from langchain_google_community import VertexAISearchRetriever

    vertex_search_retriever = VertexAISearchRetriever(
        project_id=project_id,
        location_id=location_id,
        data_store_id=data_store_id,
        max_documents=3,
    )

    result = vertex_search_retriever.invoke(query)
    print(len(result))

    for doc in result:
        print(len(doc.page_content), doc.metadata)
```

Now, let's put together our RAG application using Vertex AI Agent Builder as a retriever only. In other words, we're not going to let Vertex AI Agent Builder generate an answer; we're going to use it only to find and rank passing pieces of the document for us:

```
    from langchain_core.output_parsers import StrOutputParser
    from langchain_core.prompts import ChatPromptTemplate
    from langchain_core.runnables import RunnablePassthrough
    from langchain_google_vertexai import VertexAI
```

```
template = """Answer the question based only on the following
context:
{context}

Question: {question}
"""
prompt = ChatPromptTemplate.from_template(template)

llm = VertexAI(model_name="gemini-pro")

chain = (
    {"context": vertex_search_retriever,
        "question": RunnablePassthrough()}
    | prompt
    | llm
    | StrOutputParser()
)

chain.invoke("What are Alphabet's Other Bets?")
```

There are two ways of invoking a retriever based on Vertex AI Agent Builder. One uses its search capabilities, and another utilizes its RAG capabilities:

- The **Vertex AI Agent Builder search API** is used to get single-turn search results. Vertex AI Agent Builder exposes a `projects.locations.collections.datastores.servingconfigs.search` REST API call that returns a list of documents for a given data store, serving configuration, and query, and it returns a SearchResponse object that includes a list of found documents. This API allows you to change a lot of search controls – for example, a scoring formula for ranking results.

- The Vertex AI Agent Builder conversation API is used to invoke a search with an answer (it's a single-turn search that uses GenAI to summarize results into an answer) and a search with follow-ups (it's also powered by GenAI to provide summaries at each turn). It's exposed via a `projects.locations.dataStores.conversations.converse` REST API. It exposes way fewer controls on search behavior but is focused on providing a good answer with relevant citations that are returned as part of the ConverseConversationResponse object.

You can read more details in the Python docs (`https://api.python.langchain.com/en/latest/google_community_api_reference.html#module-langchain_google_community.vertex_ai_search`) and in the official documentation:

- `https://cloud.google.com/generative-ai-app-builder/docs/preview-search-results`

- `https://cloud.google.com/generative-ai-app-builder/docs/answer`

Customizing the RAG application further

There are various ways to improve RAG performance on unstructured data. In the next chapters, we'll take a look at improving document parsing and ingestion of documents. Here are the main things to try while improving your RAG application:

- Improve parsing by experimenting with different parsers. We'll look at this in *Chapter 5*.

- Improve parsing by experimenting with different chunking strategies; that is, the ways you split your documents into parts. We'll look at this in *Chapter 8*.

Use different embedding techniques and customize your retrieval. We'll look at this in the next chapter.

Query expansion

Query expansion is a technique of reformulating queries to get a larger number of relevant documents from a search engine. The key idea is simple – our generation is good only if we have found relevant context (in other words, *ALL* relevant documents in our corpus that are needed to answer the question). We always balance between recall and precision – we don't want to send too many documents to the LLM (as it might be confused), but we want to keep all relevant documents in the list. Hence, reformulating a query (maybe with another LLM) might help to find relevant documents ranked high enough in the retrieval's results [7].

One way of doing this is using the `MultiQueryRetriever` component (please keep in mind that we're reusing the `vertex_search_retriever` instance that we created earlier):

```
from langchain.retrievers.multi_query import MultiQueryRetriever
retriever_with_expansion = MultiQueryRetriever.from_llm(
    retriever=vertex_search_retriever, llm=llm
)
result = vertex_search_retriever.invoke(query)
print(len(result))
result_expansion = retriever_with_expansion.invoke(query)
print(len(result_expansion))
>> 3
>> 9
```

We created a separate instance of our LLM (with an increased temperature to be more creative) and used it to create an out-of-the-box chain that implements query expansion. Then, we retrieved an initial set of documents from our retriever based on the initial query, and we also tried to expand our query (and retrieve multiple sets of documents and combine them afterward). We got three documents in the first run and seven documents in the second run. The drawback is that documents are not sorted by relevance anymore. Initially, a retriever returned an ordered list of documents that are ranked based on relevance (and you can always shorten this list if you'd like to, and more relevant documents will be on the top), but with query expansion, you get an unordered list (since it's combined from multiple retrieval outputs), so you should be careful if you'd like to truncate this list further on.

Please note that you can redefine the default prompt when initializing the `MultiQueryRetriever` object (you might want to do this if you're adjusting it for a specific LLM or for your specific use case). You can take a look at the default prompt as follows:

```
from langchain.retrievers.multi_query import DEFAULT_QUERY_PROMPT
print(DEFAULT_QUERY_PROMPT.template)
```

Filtering documents

Your retrieval (especially if it's used on document embeddings only, as we'll discuss in the next chapter) might not always do a good job of filtering documents that are not relevant to the query, and these documents might confuse the model. Sometimes, making an additional pass through each document and asking the LLM to evaluate its relevance might improve the overall RAG performance:

```
from langchain.retrievers.document_compressors import LLMChainFilter
llm_compression = VertexAI(temperature=0.,
model_name="gemini-pro")
chain_filter = LLMChainFilter.from_llm(llm=llm_compression)
results_filtered = chain_filter.compress_documents(
    result_expansion, query)
```

What's going on here? We created a separate LLM instance for compression, then we used it to instantiate an already available LangChain chain for filtering documents, and we used it to compress a list of `Document` objects we got at the previous step.

How can we modify this example and add the filtering to our RAG application? One way of doing this is adding another step into our chain:

```
from langchain_core.runnables import RunnableLambda
chain = (
    {"context": vertex_search_retriever_many,
        "question": RunnablePassthrough()}
    | RunnableLambda(
        lambda x: chain_filter.compress_documents(
            x["context"], x["question"]
        )
    )
    | prompt
    | llm
    | StrOutputParser()
)

chain.invoke("What are Alphabet's Other Bets?")
```

Let's see what's happening here. We have added an extra step (by using `RunnableLambda`) to our RAG chain. It takes a dictionary as an input, and this dictionary contains a context (that is, a list of documents) and a question. We create a modified dictionary (that uses an expanded list of documents as a context) and pass it further down the chain.

Please note that in this case (opposite to the preceding example), we use a lower temperature. When we perform query expansion, we'd like to have some variability in results since we want queries that don't look similar but might help us find additional useful documents to add to the context.

Further methods

We will explore some more methods here:

- Compress and summarize results: Another step that is sometimes useful in practice is to reduce the documents that are added to the LLM's context and leave only the relevant information. We can compare the length of the original and filtered documents:

```
from langchain.retrievers.document_compressors import
LLMChainFilter

# Retrieve many documents from the retrieval
vertex_search_retriever_many = VertexAISearchRetriever(
    project_id=project_id,
    location_id=location_id,
    data_store_id=data_store_id,
    max_documents=30,
    )
results_many = vertex_search_retriever_many.invoke(query)
llm_compression = VertexAI(
    temperature=0., model_name="gemini-1.5-flash-001")
chain_filter = LLMChainFilter.from_llm(llm=llm_compression)
results_filtered_many = chain_filter.compress_documents(
    results_many, query)
print(len(results_many), len(results_filtered_many))
```

- Re-rank your results: Typically, retrievers that are built on top of vector stores rank results based on the similarity between document and query embeddings. In the next chapter, we will look into alternatives, such as hybrid search, that combine different types of embeddings. But sometimes, an additional re-ranking step helps to improve performance (especially combined with the query expansion step mentioned previously that produces multiple lists of potentially relevant documents) [6, 7, 10]. LangChain has multiple built-in re-rankers (or you can implement your own one, as usual).

There are multiple other ways to improve the performance of your RAG application and many available primitives on LangChain. You can always build your own if something is missing or if you want to try a cool idea. It's important to mention that you need to focus on a valid evaluation mechanism, but that's something we'll discuss in *Chapter 13*.

Summary

In this chapter, we looked at the hallucination problem of LLM-powered applications and discussed how grounding and attribution can help you work around it. We discussed closed-book versus open-book question-answering and the concept of RAG. We discussed the key flow of an RAG application: storing documents, retrieving relevant documents for a query, expanding the query and re-ranking results, and, finally, adding them to the LLM's context to generate a final answer.

We looked at Vertex AI Agent Builder as a managed Google Cloud service to work with document corpora (and in the next chapter, we'll explore how you can build a more customizable solution yourself).

References

1. *Lawyer Used ChatGPT In Court—And Cited Fake Cases. A Judge Is Considering Sanctions, Molly Bohannon*

    https://www.forbes.com/sites/mollybohannon/2023/06/08/lawyer-used-chatgpt-in-court-and-cited-fake-cases-a-judge-is-considering-sanctions

2. *Rethinking search: making domain experts out of dilettantes, D. Metzler et al., 2021*

    https://dl.acm.org/doi/10.1145/3476415.3476428

3. *Generative Information Retrieval, M. Najork, 2023*

    https://research.google/pubs/generative-information-retrieval-slides/

4. *Retrieval-Augmented Generation for Knowledge-Intensive NLP Tasks, P. Lewis et al., 2020*

    https://arxiv.org/abs/2005.11401v4

5. *Our next-generation model: Gemini 1.5, S.Pichai, D. Hassabis*

    https://blog.google/technology/ai/google-gemini-next-generation-model-february-2024/

6. *Re2G: Retrieve, Rerank, Generate, M.Glass et al., 2022*

    https://arxiv.org/abs/2207.06300

7. *RAG-Fusion: a New Take on Retrieval-Augmented Generation, Z. Rackauckas, 2024*

    https://arxiv.org/abs/2402.03367

8. *Vertex AI Agent Builder*

    https://cloud.google.com/vertex-ai-search-and-conversation

9. *What is a vector database? Google Cloud*

    https://cloud.google.com/discover/what-is-a-vector-database

10. *RAG-Fusion: The Next Frontier of Search Technology, A. Raudaschl, 2024*

    https://github.com/Raudaschl/RAG-Fusion

11. *Create a search app with Vertex AI Agent Builder, Google Cloud*

    https://cloud.google.com/generative-ai-app-builder/docs/create-engine-es

12. *World Model on Million-Length Video And Language With Blockwise RingAttention, Liu et al., 2024*

    https://arxiv.org/abs/2402.08268

13. *Leave No Context Behind: Efficient Infinite Context Transformers with Infini-attention, Munkhdalai, 2024*

    https://arxiv.org/abs/2402.08268

14. *Lost in the Middle: How Language Models Use Long Contexts, Liu et al., 2023*

    https://arxiv.org/abs/2307.03172

15. *Needle In A Haystack - Pressure Testing LLMs*

    https://github.com/gkamradt/LLMTest_NeedleInAHaystack

16. *How Much Knowledge Can You Pack Into the Parameters of a Language Model?, A.Roberts et al., 2020*

    https://arxiv.org/abs/2002.08910

4

Vector Search on Google Cloud

In this chapter, we'll dive deep into **vector search**, a very important pattern of modern information retrieval and generative AI applications.

We will explore the architecture of a vector search pipeline and discuss different search techniques, examining their strengths and weaknesses.

Finally, we'll shift our focus to practical implementation, showcasing how we can harness the combined power of Google Cloud and LangChain to develop **retrieval-augmented generation** (**RAG**) applications with vector search tailored for a variety of real-world scenarios and requirements.

In this chapter, we cover the following topics:

- What is vector search?
- LangChain interfaces – embeddings and vector stores
- Vector store with Vertex AI vector search
- Vector store with pgvector on Cloud SQL
- Vector store with BigQuery

Technical requirements

For this chapter, in addition to specific requirements for each service mentioned, you will need an active Google Cloud project and a Python environment with the following libraries installed:

```
pip install langchain-google-vertexai langchain-google-community
```

What is vector search?

Vector search is a technique for finding similar items within vast amounts of unstructured data. As shown in *Figure 4.1*, both the data and the search query are transformed into mathematical representations known as **vectors**, often referred to as embeddings in the context of machine learning applications.

Embeddings are fixed-length sequences of real numbers that encapsulate the meaning and relationships present within the data. This enables searches to be performed based on semantic similarity, going beyond simple keyword matching.

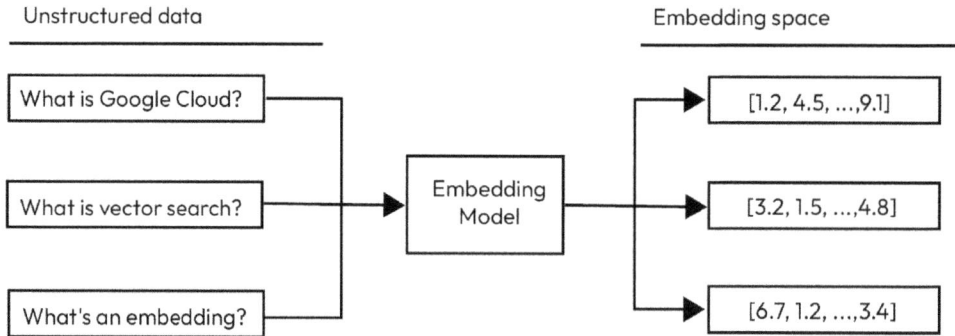

Figure 4.1: Embedding of unstructured data

The similarity between two embeddings is calculated using a distance metric, such as Euclidean distance or cosine similarity. Embeddings that are more similar have a smaller distance between them – in other words, they're closer together in the embedding space.

Now that you know what vector search is, let's see different types of architectures that can be used in the context of generative AI applications.

Overview of vector search architecture

Generally, a vector search system is used to power search applications. In the context of generative AI, it is the system that powers the retrieval component of RAG applications, as introduced in *Chapter 3*.

The system's goal is to retrieve the k most relevant documents (or their parts) from a knowledge base, given a user's natural language query. Relevance is measured by the distance between vectors representing the query and the document. Optionally, this search can be refined using metadata filters.

The most important components of such a system are as follows:

- **Embedding model**: This component is responsible for transforming unstructured data (typically text, but also images with multimodal models) into embeddings. The quality and characteristics of the embedding model significantly impact the retrieval process's performance.

- **Vector store**: This part of the system stores the generated embeddings. Most implementations build an index to enable faster retrieval as the system scales. These indexes are distance metric-specific and must be rebuilt if the metric changes. Metadata is also stored here to enable filtered queries.

- **Document store**: This store contains the unstructured data and its associated metadata. Once the most similar embeddings to a user query are identified, their corresponding documents are retrieved from this store and returned to the client.

It is fairly common for vector stores and document stores to be combined by a single database so that a unified API is exposed.

During the build process, as shown in *Figure 4.2*, all documents in the knowledge base are embedded using the embedding model. These embeddings are stored in the vector store, and the search index is constructed. With each subsequent addition of a new document to the knowledge base, the index is updated accordingly.

At the same time, the original documents are stored in the document store for later retrieval. There should be a mapping between the embeddings and the documents, typically using a unique identifier, to enable the retrieval of one or more documents given an embedding identifier.

It is common to include metadata within the documents to enable filtered searches. This metadata can be stored in the vector store, the document store, or both.

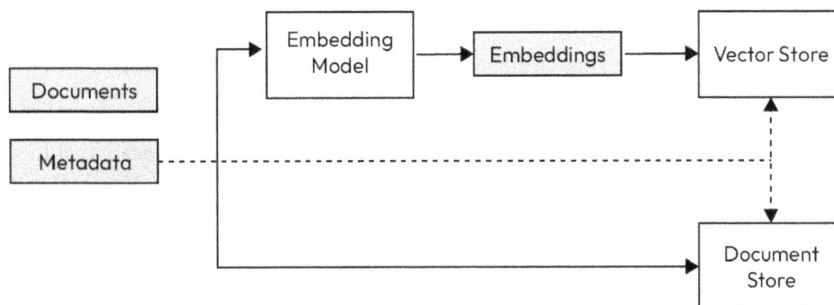

Figure 4.2: Build-time vector search schematic process

At query time, the user's query is first converted into an embedding using the same embedding model employed during the build process.

This embedding is then sent to the vector store, where a vector search is performed to retrieve the most similar documents from the knowledge base, leveraging the document store. These relevant documents are subsequently returned to the original client. You can find a schematic flow in *Figure 4.3*.

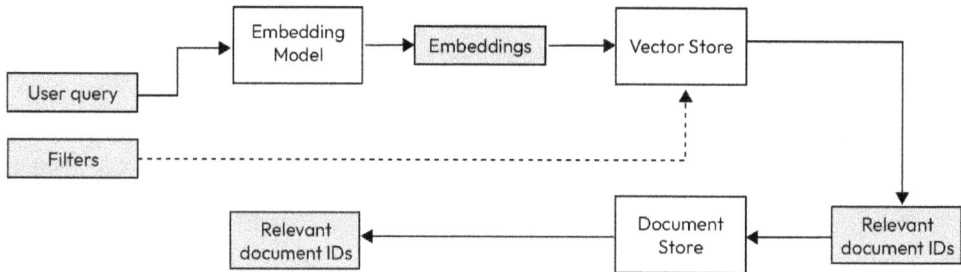

Figure 4.3: Runtime Vector Search schematic process

Let's now discuss how we can leverage LangChain to build these architectures using different Google Cloud services.

LangChain interfaces – embeddings and vector stores

Beyond interfaces for documents and retrievers, as discussed in *Chapter 3*, LangChain offers interfaces for embedding models and vector stores. These interfaces simplify the process of constructing a vector search architecture.

Embeddings

The `Embedding` class provides a standardized `Runnable` for embedding models.

The key methods of this class are `embed_query` and `embed_documents`. The main difference is that `embed_query` accepts a single text input, while `embed_documents` accepts multiple texts:

```
from langchain_google_vertexai import VertexAIEmbeddings

model_name = "my-embedding-model-name" # textembeding-gecko@003
embedding_model = VertexAIEmbeddings(model_name=model_name)

single_embedding = embedding_model.embed_query("User query")
multiple_embeddings = embedding_model.embed_documents([
    "Sample text 1",
    "Sample text 2",
```

```
    "Sample text 3",
    ])
```

The `model_name` argument specifies the version of the Vertex AI model to use.

Google offers several versions of this model, each catering to specific needs. At the time of writing, `"textembedding-gecko@003"` represents the latest stable iteration, boasting enhanced AI quality, while `"textembedding-gecko-multilingual@001"` is specifically optimized for a broad spectrum of non-English languages.

For the most up-to-date information on available versions and their capabilities, please refer to the official Vertex AI embedding model documentation page at `https://cloud.google.com/vertex-ai/generative-ai/docs/embeddings/get-text-embeddings`.

Vector stores

The `VectorStore` class abstracts the entire vector search process at query time, providing a `similarity_search` method that accepts a query and returns a list of the most similar documents in the index. Optionally, you can add the `k` parameter to specify how many similar documents you wish to retrieve:

```
from langchain_google_vertexai.vectorstores import (
    VectorSearchVectorStore)

embeddings = VertexAIEmbeddings(
  (model_name="my-embedding-model-name")

vector_store = VectorSearchVectorStore.from_components(
    project_id="my-project-id",
    region="my-region",
    gcs_bucket_name="my-gcs-name",
    index_id="my-index-name",
    endpoint_id="my-endpoint-name",
    embedding=embeddings
)

documents = vector_store.similarity_search(query, k=2)
```

Each VectorStore has a different way of initializing it depending on the database provider but always requires an embedding model to use both at query time and at build time.

It's also possible to retrieve the `score` for each document (i.e., the distance between the query embedding and the document embeddings) using the `similarity_search_with_score` method.

`VectorStore` instances can be converted into a standard retriever by invoking the `as_retriever` method, enabling the use of the basic retriever interface:

```
retriever = vector_store.as_retriever()
documents = retriever.get_relevant_documents("user-query", k=2)
```

Now that you know how the VectorStore LangChain interface works, let's delve into how we can leverage it to interact with Google Cloud services.

Vector store with Vertex AI Vector Search

Vector Search is a Google Cloud service that provides a robust solution for storing, indexing, and retrieving embedding vectors. This technology is built upon the same vector search infrastructure that underpins Google products such as Google Search, YouTube, and Play [1].

Vertex AI Vector Search delivers the VectorStore component of the Vector Search architecture on LangChain [2]. You have the flexibility to select the document store service that best aligns with your requirements, with Google Cloud Storage and Datastore (now under the Firestore service) often being popular choices. Vertex AI Vector Search stands out as the fastest and most scalable solution for high-performance applications, consistently maintaining latency in the tens of milliseconds range, even with over a billion documents.

Creating the required infrastructure

We create the required architecture in three steps:

1. **Create an index**: The index is the part of the architecture where the embeddings and metadata are stored and structured in a way that makes queries faster.

2. **Create an endpoint**: The endpoint is the **Uniform Resource Identifier (URI)** where our final application will make requests and interact with the index.

3. **Deploy the index**: The index is deployed into an endpoint, where we can choose the type of machine and scaling that our application requires.

You have multiple options for creating the infrastructure, both programmatically (using the `gcloud` tool or various language **software development kits (SDKs)**) and through the Google Cloud console.

To find the approach that best aligns with your workflow and preferences, please consult the official documentation for detailed instructions and guidance [1].

LangChain integration

LangChain offers two distinct VectorStores for integration with Vector Search, each differentiated by the underlying Document Store they utilize. `VectorSearchVectorStore` uses Google Cloud Storage, while `VectorSearchVectorStoreDatastore` leverages a Datastore as the underlying document store.

The choice between these two depends on your specific use case. Generally, Datastore tends to provide lower latency, making it suitable for applications where response time is critical. Conversely, Google Cloud Storage excels in scalability, accommodating a vast number of documents with ease:

```
from langchain_google_vertexai import (
    VectorSearchVectorStore, # GCS Document Store
    VectorSearchVectorStoreDatastore, # DataStore Document store
)
```

Both constructors accept the following parameters:

- `project_id`: The ID of your Google Cloud project.

- `region`: The region of your Google Cloud project.

- `index_id`: The ID of the created index.

- `endpoint_id`: The ID of the created endpoint.

- `embedding`: The embedding model to be used.

- `stream_update` (optional): Whether to use streaming updates for the index. Defaults to `False`. Streaming updates offer faster updating.

We can construct a `VectorSearchVectorStore` instance using the following snippet:

```
vector_store = VectorSearchVectorStore.from_components(
    project_id="my-project-id",
    region="my-region",
    gcs_bucket_name="my-gcs-name",
    index_id="my-index-name",
    endpoint_id="my-endpoint-name",
    embedding=embedding_model,
    stream_update=True
)
```

When using the Google Cloud Storage backend, you must also specify the name of the Google Cloud Storage bucket where the documents will be stored. Documents are stored as a JSON object and a **universal unique identifier (UUID)** is generated for each one of them:

```
vector_store = VectorSearchVectorStoreDatastore.from_components(
    project_id="my-project-id",
    region="my-region",
    index_id="my-index-name",
    endpoint_id="my-endpoint-name",
    embedding=embedding_model,
    stream_update=True,
)
```

If you choose Datastore as your backend, you can use the default constructor arguments or customize them further. You have the option to configure the database name, kind, and other Datastore-specific parameters using keyword arguments.

Regardless of your chosen storage backend (Datastore or Google Cloud Storage), the methods for interacting with the vector store remain consistent. For instance, to add documents to the vector store, you can use the following code snippet:

```
texts = [
    "This is the first document",
    "This is the second document",
    "This is the third document"
]
vector_store.add_texts(texts=texts)
```

Optionally, if you anticipate using filtering later, you can enrich your documents with metadata during the addition process. This metadata will be stored both within Vector Search for efficient retrieval and in your chosen Document Store (either Datastore or Google Cloud Storage) for further processing or analysis:

```
texts = [
    "This is the first document",
    "This is the second document",
    "This is the third document"
]
metadatas = [
    {"page_number": 1, "length": 10},
    {"page_number": 2, "length": 20},
    {"page_number": 3, "length": 5}
]
vector_store.add_texts(texts=texts, metadatas=metadatas)
```

Now that we have documents in our store, we can use the `VectorStore` interface to perform similarity searches:

```
documents = vector_store.similarity_search("first", k=1)
```

To perform filtering, you can provide one or both of the following arguments:

- `filters`: A list of Namespace objects specifying exact match conditions for string metadata attributes
- `numeric_filters`: A list of NumericNamespace objects specifying filtering criteria based on numerical metadata attributes

Both `Namespace` and `NumericNamespace` objects accept an argument called `name`. This argument refers to the specific key within your document metadata that you want to filter on.

In the case of `Namespace`, the other arguments are as follows:

- `allow_tokens`: A list of string values that are allowed for the specified metadata key. The similarity search will only consider documents where the `metadata` field's value matches one of these allowed tokens.
- `restrict_tokens` (optional): A list of string values that are explicitly excluded. If a document's metadata field matches any of these restricted tokens, it will be filtered out, even if it matches one of the allowed tokens.

In the case of `NumericNamespace`, the arguments beyond `name` are as follows:

- `value_float`: The floating-point numerical value to compare against the values in your document metadata. This is the reference point for your filtering condition.
- `op`: The comparison operator, which defines the type of filter you want to apply. Possible values for the op argument include: "EQUAL", "NOT_EQUAL", "GREATER_THAN", "GREATER_THAN_OR_EQUAL", "LESS_THAN" or "LESS_THAN_OR_EQUAL".

The following code snippet shows how to perform a similarity search using both numerical and string comparison filters:

```
from google.cloud.aiplatform.matching_engine.matching_engine_index_
endpoint import (
    Namespace,
    NumericNamespace,
)
filters = [Namespace(name="season",
    allow_tokens=["spring"])]
numeric_filters = [NumericNamespace(name="price",
    value_float=40.0, op="LESS")]
```

```
# Below code should return 2 results now

vector_store.similarity_search("shirt", k=5,
    filter=filters, numeric_filter=numeric_filters
)
```

Vectorstore with pgvector on Cloud SQL

Cloud SQL is a fully managed relational database offered by Google Cloud. It can run PostgreSQL, MySQL, and SQL Server [3].

Cloud SQL, when running with **PostgreSQL** and the **pgvector** extension, can function as both a VectorStore and a Document Store, combining both functionalities in a single service. It also offers the possibility of filtering queries using full SQL syntax, rather than just filtering by metadata.

The first step in using this service is to create a Cloud SQL instance and a database within it.

Creating a CloudSQL instance and database

You have several options for creating these: the Google Cloud console, the gcloud command-line tool, or various SDKs for different programming languages. For detailed instructions on each method, please refer to the official documentation [4].

We will use the gcloud command-line tool to create a new Cloud SQL instance:

```
gcloud sql instances create MY_SQL_INSTANCE_NAME \
--region=MY_REGION \
--database-version=PostgreSQL_14 \
```

You'll need to specify the instance name, region, and database version. It's crucial to select PostgreSQL as the database engine, as the pgVector extension is only compatible with PostgreSQL. After the instance is created, you can proceed to add a new database:

```
gcloud sql databases create  MY_DATABASE_NAME\
--instance= MY_SQLINSTANCE_NAME\
```

Enabling the pgVector extension

To enable the pgVector extension, execute the following SQL statement:

```
CREATE EXTENSION IF NOT EXISTS vector;
```

The pgVector extension introduces a new data type called `vector`, which you can use to define columns within a table to store embeddings. Values can be inserted using a string representation with comma-separated numbers enclosed in square brackets, as illustrated here:

```
CREATE TABLE product_embeddings (
      product_id INTEGER,
      price DECIMAL,
      embedding vector(4)
);

INSERT INTO embeddings VALUES
  (1, 4.1, '[2, 0, -2, 3]'),
  (2, 3.2, '[3, 1, 1, 5]'),
  (3, 1.1, '[4, 2, 54, 1]');
```

Additionally, the `pgVector` extension provides new operators for retrieving similar vectors using different distance metrics, such as the following:

- `<->`: Calculates the Euclidean distance between two vectors
- `<=>`: Calculates the cosine distance between two vectors

As an illustration, the following query retrieves the two most similar products to a given user query embedding, filtering for those with a price less than 3.0 units:

```
WITH vector_matches AS (
    SELECT id,
           1 - (embedding <=> '[1.1, 2, 3, 4]') AS similarity
    FROM product_embeddings
    ORDER BY similarity DESC
    LIMIT 2
)
SELECT product_id
FROM products
WHERE product_id IN (SELECT product_id FROM vector_matches)
  AND price <= 3.0;
```

LangChain integration

To leverage the LangChain integration with Cloud SQL, you'll need to install an additional library alongside `langchain-google-vertexai`. You can accomplish this using `pip`:

```
pip install --upgrade langchain-google-cloud-sql-pg langchain-google-
vertexai
```

The initial step involves constructing the engine object. This object defines the Google Cloud project, location, database, and instance that the VectorStore will interact with. The following code snippet demonstrates how to initialize an engine with the properties we configured in the previous steps:

```
from langchain_google_cloud_sql_pg import PostgresEngine
engine = PostgresEngine.from_instance(
    project_id="my-project-id",
    region="my-region",
    instance="my-instance-name",
    database="my-database-name"
)
```

Making use of the engine object we just created, we can use the `init_vectorstore_table` method to create the necessary table in the database if it doesn't already exist:

```
from langchain_google_cloud_sql_pg import Column
engine.init_vectorstore_table(
    table_name="my-table-name",
    vector_size=768,
    metadata_columns=[Column("PRICE", "FLOAT")],
)
```

This method will take care of generating the appropriate SQL statements to create a table with the required structure for storing vectors and associated metadata with the following standard columns, allowing for custom column naming through keyword arguments:

- `langchain_id`: A primary key (unique identifier) for each document.
- `content`: A text column to store the document content.
- `embedding`: A vector column to hold the embeddings. Ensure the dimension matches that of your embedding model defined by the `vector_size` keyword argument in the preceding code snippet.
- `langchain_metadata`: A JSON column to store metadata associated with the Langchain document.

To enable filtering based on metadata, you can define additional columns using the `metadata_columns` argument. This argument accepts a list of pairs specifying column names and their corresponding data types.

Once the engine and the table are in place, you can proceed to initialize the VectorStore. As with other integrations, you will also need to build an embedding model:

```
from langchain_google_cloud_sql_pg import PostgresVectorStore
from langchain_google_vertexai import VertexAIEmbeddings
embedding = VertexAIEmbeddings(
```

```
    model_name=" textembedding-gecko@003", # This model has embeddings
of dimension 768, as defined in the creation of the table above
    project="my-project-id"
)
store = PostgresVectorStore(
    engine=engine,
    table_name="my-table-name",
    embedding_service=embedding,
)
```

Using the VectorStore object, you can add documents using the `add_documents` or `add_texts` methods. If you've created metadata columns, make sure to include their values when adding documents:

- `add_documents`: This method is typically used when you have a list of Langchain Document objects. Each Document object should contain the text content (`page_content`) and any associated metadata.

- `add_texts`: This method is a convenient way to add raw text strings directly to the `VectorStore`. If you have metadata associated with each text string, you can pass it in as a separate list alongside the texts.

When utilizing metadata columns, ensure that the values provided when adding documents align with the data types specified for those columns.

With the following snippet, you can add records to the vector store:

```
import uuid
all_texts = ["Blue T-shirt", "Spring dress", "Black sunglasses"]
metadatas = [{"PRICE": 21.0}, {"PRICE": 23.0}, {"PRICE": 33.1}]
ids = [str(uuid.uuid4()) for _ in all_texts]

store.add_texts(all_texts, metadatas=metadatas, ids=ids)
```

Additionally, you can remove documents from the VectorStore using the `delete` method, specifying the IDs of the documents you wish to delete:

```
store.delete( ids=ids)
```

Finally, to execute a similarity search, you can utilize the `similarity_search` method. This method accepts the following arguments:

- `query`: A string representing the user's query.

- `k`: An integer specifying the number of relevant documents to retrieve.

- `filter` (optional): A string containing a `WHERE` clause of a SQL statement, referencing the columns created using the `metadata_columns` argument. This enables filtering the search results based on specific metadata criteria.

Here's an example of a similarity search:

```
query = "I want glasses"
docs = store.similarity_search(query, k=2, filter="PRICE <= 10")
```

As a final note, to optimize query performance, this VectorStore also provides a method for creating and applying a vector index to the table, as illustrated here:

```
from langchain_google_cloud_sql_pg.indexes import IVFFlatIndex
index = IVFFlatIndex()
store.apply_vector_index(index)
```

By employing vector indexes, vector similarity queries can be remarkably fast, often taking only tens of milliseconds to process when dealing with less than a million documents. However, it's important to note that this approach may not scale as effectively as specialized solutions such as Vertex AI Vector Search when handling significantly larger datasets.

Vectorstore with BigQuery

BigQuery is Google Cloud's fully managed, petabyte-scale data warehouse designed to handle the most demanding big data analytics workloads.

Expanding beyond structured data analytics, BigQuery's recently introduced Vector Search capability allows for efficient similarity-based search on unstructured data. This functionality is seamlessly integrated into BigQuery, utilizing the same scalable infrastructure and familiar SQL interface.

BigQuery natively supports storing vector embeddings as arrays of floats. Vector search within BigQuery leverages the `VECTOR_SEARCH` function, optionally utilizing a vector index for enhanced performance.

When a vector index is employed, the `VECTOR_SEARCH` function utilizes an **approximate nearest neighbor** (**ANN**) search, improving search speed at the potential cost of slightly reduced recall. Conversely, when a vector index is not available or is explicitly disabled, BigQuery defaults to brute-force search for exact results.

While BigQuery excels at large-scale batch processing of vector similarity searches, it's important to note that its architecture may introduce noticeable latency (in the order of seconds) when used for real-time, single-query searches. Therefore, for applications demanding near-instantaneous responses to individual similarity queries, BigQuery might not be the most optimal solution. However, its strength lies in handling massive volumes of vector data and efficiently processing large batch similarity search requests.

The initial step for using BigQuery is to create a dataset to store your vector embeddings and related data.

Creating a BigQuery dataset, table, and vector index

In the same way as Cloud SQL, BigQuery offers several methods for dataset creation, including the web UI, the bq command-line tool, the BigQuery API, and the Cloud console.

The following snippet demonstrates the use of the Python client to create a new dataset. As with many other services, you must provide a Google Cloud project ID, a region, and the name of the dataset you wish to create:

```
from google.cloud import bigquery
bq_client = bigquery.Client(project="my-project-id", location="my-region")
bq_client.create_dataset(dataset="my-dataset", exists_ok=True)
```

We have the option to create a table to store the documents and their embeddings. If we prefer not to, the LangChain VectorStore integration will automatically create one for us.

The table should include the following columns and types:

- content: A string column to hold the document content
- metadata: A JSON column to store document metadata
- text_embedding: An array of float64 values representing the document's vector embedding
- doc_id: A string serving as a unique identifier for each document

While you can customize the column names, remember to specify these names later when creating the VectorStore. Additionally, we can opt to create an index right away using this SQL statement:

```
CREATE [ OR REPLACE ] VECTOR INDEX [ IF NOT EXISTS ] INDEX_NAME
ON DATASET_NAME.TABLE_NAME(COLUMN_NAME)
OPTIONS(
  index_type = IVF,
  distance_type = COSINE,
)
```

At the time of writing, the only supported index type is the **inverted file index** (**IVF**). This type of index utilizes a k-means algorithm to cluster the vector data and subsequently partitions it based on these clusters. When you employ the VECTOR_SEARCH function, it can use these partitions to narrow down the data it needs to examine to determine a result [5].

LangChain integration

As with other integrations, we must initialize a specialized `VectorStore` class to use VectorSearch in BigQuery. In this case, it is available through `langchain_google_community` under the name `BigQueryVectorSearch`:

```
from langchain.vectorstores.utils import DistanceStrategy
from langchain_google_community.vectorstores import
BigQueryVectorSearch

mbedding_model = VertexAIEmbeddings(
    model_name=" textembedding-gecko@003",
    project="my-project-id"
)
store = BigQueryVectorSearch(
    project_id="my-project-id",
    dataset_name="my-dataset",
    table_name="my-table-name",
    location="my-region",
    embedding=embedding_model,
)
```

In addition to the usual parameters required for initializing a `VectorStore`, the `BigQueryVectorSearch` constructor offers optional parameters for customization:

- `content_field`: Specifies the column name containing the raw text data for embedding and retrieval.

- `metadata_field`: Specifies the column name storing metadata associated with each document, allowing for filtered searches.

- `text_embedding_field`: Specifies the column name where the generated text embeddings will be stored.

- `doc_id_field`: Specifies the column name containing unique identifiers for each document.

- `doc_id`: This is a required parameter for identifying documents, even if the table already has a `doc_id_field` column. It should be the same value as `doc_id_field` if the column exists.

- `distance_strategy`: This parameter determines the distance metric used for similarity calculations during vector search. The available options are euclidean or cosine. However, if a pre-existing index is found in the table, this parameter will be ignored, as the index is built using a specific distance metric and cannot be changed without rebuilding.

During the creation of the `BigQueryVectorSearch` object, a check is performed to confirm whether the specified BigQuery table exists and whether it already has an index. If the table or index is missing, they will be automatically created, ensuring the necessary infrastructure is in place for efficient vector search operations.

The interface for adding texts to `BigQueryVectorSearch` is consistent with other `VectorStore` subclasses. However, it's important to note that metadata, unlike in the Cloud SQL integration, can only be stored within the designated `metadata_field` as a JSON object. This means you'll need to structure your metadata accordingly to leverage it for filtered searches within BigQuery:

```
texts = [
    "Blue T-shirt",
    "Spring dress",
    "Black sunglasses",
]
metadatas = [{"len": len(t)} for t in texts]
store.add_texts(texts, metadatas=metadatas)
```

The methods for performing similarity searches in `BigQueryVectorSearch` are aligned with those in other `VectorStore` subclasses. However, there is a notable distinction regarding the `filter` parameter.

In `BigQueryVectorSearch`, the `filter` parameter exclusively accepts a dictionary containing key-value pairs, where the keys represent metadata field names, and the values represent the desired filter criteria.

For instance, to retrieve documents where the `len` metadata field equals `6`, you would execute the following:

```
docs = store.similarity_search(query, filter={"len": 6})
print(docs)
```

While basic filtering is supported in this way, the `BigQueryVectorSearch` integration does not yet allow full SQL statement filtering. More complex filtering operations may require the use of raw SQL.

Summary

In this chapter, we discussed a vector search architecture. You now understand what role it plays in generative AI applications, especially in RAG, and you can deal with core LangChain interfaces for embedding models and vector stores.

We also learned how to use three different managed vector stores on Google Cloud – Vertex Vector Search, pg_vectors with Cloud SQL, and VectorSearch with Big Query. We discussed how to provision the corresponding Google Cloud services, how to ingest data there, and how to retrieve your results based on queries. We also looked into how to retrieve semantically similar texts with pre-filtering based on text metadata.

References

1. Overview of Vertex AI Vector Search, Google Cloud:

   `https://cloud.google.com/vertex-ai/docs/vector-search/overview`

2. Google Vertex AI Vector Search, LangChain Documentation:

   `https://python.langchain.com/v0.1/docs/integrations/vectorstores/google_vertex_ai_vector_search/`

3. Google Cloud SQL for PostgreSQL:

   `https://python.langchain.com/docs/integrations/vectorstores/google_cloud_sql_pg/`

4. Create Cloud SQL instances, Google Cloud:

   `https://cloud.google.com/sql/docs/mysql/create-instance`

5. Google BigQuery Vector Search:

   `https://python.langchain.com/docs/integrations/vectorstores/google_bigquery_vector_search/`

Get This Book's PDF Version and Exclusive Extras

UNLOCK NOW

Scan the QR code (or go to `packtpub.com/unlock`). Search for this book by name, confirm the edition, and then follow the steps on the page.

Note: Keep your invoice handy. Purchases made directly from Packt don't require one.

5

Ingesting Documents

This chapter explores the range of document parsing capabilities available within Google Cloud and LangChain. Document ingestion is an integral part of RAG applications, providing the knowledge base that will be used to answer questions and generate text.

We'll explain the use of LangChain document loaders to parse documents of different formats, and examine both pre-trained and custom-built Document AI parsers. Additionally, we will cover a variety of out-of-the-box techniques that Vertex AI Agent Builder offers for ingesting content from different external sources.

We will discuss the following main topics:

- Ingesting documents with LangChain
- Document chunking
- Parsing documents with Document AI
- Ingesting data with Vertex AI Agent Builder

Technical requirements

In order to follow the examples of this chapter, in addition to specific requirements for each service mentioned, you will need an active Google Cloud project and a Python environment with the following libraries installed:

```
pip install langchain-google-vertexai langchain_community langchain-
google-community[docai]
pypdf
```

Specifically, for working with Google Drive data, you will need to install these additional libraries:

```
pip install google-api-python-client google-auth-httplib2 google-auth-
oauthlib
```

Ingesting documents with LangChain

The main way of ingesting documents to be used by a generative AI application is using the DocumentLoader interface provided by LangChain.

Document loaders facilitate the extraction of data from various sources, transforming them into LangChain's Document class. As discussed in previous chapters, a Document encapsulates both text content and associated metadata. This versatility allows for the integration of diverse data types, from simple text files and web page content to even transcripts of YouTube videos.

Each document loader features a load method for eagerly loading data as documents from a specified source, and optionally, a lazy_load method for deferred loading to optimize memory usage [1] when dealing with large document collections.

It's important to note that neither the load nor lazy_load methods accept additional arguments. This applies to all DocumentLoader subclasses, as configuration parameters must be provided during the object's initialization.

Plain text documents

The most basic document loader is TextLoader. It takes the file path of a text file as input and loads its entire content into a single Document object:

```
from langchain_community.document_loaders import TextLoader

loader = TextLoader("./text_file.txt")
documents = loader.load()
```

The loader's output is a list containing a single Document, holding the text file's content without any transformations. The document's metadata includes the path to the original file.

Let's now dive into how we can utilize document loaders to effectively load structured data.

CSV documents

We can integrate structured data from various sources using the CSVLoader module. It parses **Comma-Separated Value (CSV)** files and transforms their tabular content into a list of Document instances. Each row within the CSV file is treated as an independent document.

CSVLoader accepts the path to a CSV file and converts the structured data within into a set of documents. Each row of the CSV file is represented as an individual document.

Consider a product catalog stored in a CSV file with the following structure:

product_id	product_name	price
A1	Product A1	50
A2	Product A2	30
A3	Product A3	40

The following Python code snippet shows how to use the CSVLoader to ingest data from a CSV file named data.csv:

```
from langchain_community.document_loaders import CSVLoader
loader = CSVLoader("./data.csv")
documents = loader.load()
```

Upon execution, the load() method returns a list of Document objects. Each Document object encapsulates the content of a single row from the CSV file, along with metadata, such as the source file and row number:

```
loader = CSVLoader(
    "./data.csv",
    csv_args={"delimiter": ";"},
    source_column="Text"
)
documents = loader.load()
```

The csv_args argument is a dictionary of arguments that you can pass directly to Python's built-in csv.DictReader. This is useful for customizing how the CSV file is parsed. In the preceding code snippet, we passed the {"delimiter": ";"} dictionary use to specify a semicolon as the delimiter instead of the default comma.

PDF documents

Raw documents we need to use in our systems are often **Portable Document Format** (**PDF**) documents. Loading them might become a challenge since they vary in quality and layout, and can have a mix of text and image data. To extract data from PDF files, you can either use commercial or open source parsers, and LangChain provides integration for many of them. Let's start with one of the most popular open source PDF parsers: PyPDF. We can use it on LangChain with the PyPDFLoader class. This loader extracts textual content from PDF documents, converting it into a list of Document instances. Each page within the PDF is treated as an independent document.

The `PyPDFLoader` takes the path to a PDF file as input:

```
from langchain_community.document_loaders import PyPDFLoader

loader = PyPDFLoader("./research_paper.pdf")
documents = loader.load()
```

The `PyPDFLoader` offers additional configuration options to customize the loading process. For instance, you can specify a range of pages to extract or apply text processing functions to clean or normalize the extracted content. As mentioned earlier, please keep in mind that you need to re-create a loader class each time you need to load a new document.

GoogleDriveLoader

LangChain facilitates seamless integration with Google Drive through its `GoogleDriveLoader` class, enabling direct file loading.

Prerequisites include enabling the Google Drive API, authorizing desktop app credentials, and installing the following libraries [8]:

```
pip install --upgrade google-api-python-client google-auth-httplib2
google-auth-oauthlib
```

Additionally, be aware that Google services often impose rate limits for certain requests. This may raise issues when working with large datasets or multiple files. It's advisable to consult the Google API rate limit documentation and consider batching requests to avoid hitting these limits.

Basic usage is demonstrated here:

```
from langchain_google_community import GoogleDriveLoader
loader = GoogleDriveLoader(
    folder_id="my-folder-id",
    token_path="/path/to/token.json",
    recursive=False,
)
docs = loader.load()
```

The `GoogleDriveFolder` class allows you to access and load data from Google Drive folders. Here's a breakdown of its key arguments:

- `folder_id`: This alphanumeric string, extracted from the Google Drive folder URL (`https://drive.google.com/drive/folders/{folder-id}`), specifies the target folder.

- `token_path`: This is the path to `credentials.json` for authentication. If absent, the class prompts browser authentication and generates the file.

- `recursive`: Setting this flag to `True` extends loading to subdirectories.

By default, all Google Docs, Sheets, and PDFs within the folder are loaded. However, this can be refined using the `file_types` argument and specifying a list of extensions. Instead of loading an entire document, a specific list of files can be targeted using `file_ids`. These IDs are obtainable from individual file URLs, similar to folder IDs. In such scenarios, any file type can be loaded by specifying a base file loader through the `file_loader_cls` argument. The resulting documents from the load have the same structure as the ones loaded with the underlying DocumentLoader class. For instance, consider a list of XML files in Google Drive with known IDs. Loading them is achieved as follows:

```
from langchain_community.document_loaders import (
    UnstructuredXMLLoader
)


loader = GoogleDriveLoader(
    file_ids=[file_id_1, file_id_2, file_id_3],
    file_loader_cls=UnstructuredXMLLoader,
    file_loader_kwargs={},
    # Loader kwargs can be added using this argument
)


docs = loader.load()
```

Additional types

While we have discussed text, CSV, and PDF formats, it's worth noting that the LangChain ecosystem supports a wide range of loaders for other common data formats, such as JSON, XML, and Markdown, and of course, it allows loading data from various databases. There also exist multiple additional loaders within the Google ecosystem, such as one for GMail or BigQuery. These additional loaders follow similar principles. Please visit LangChain documentation[1] for a full list of loaders and examples.

Loading directories

To allow the ingestion of multiple documents stored within a directory structure, the `DirectoryLoader` module offers a convenient solution. It automates the process of discovering and loading files with specific extensions, consolidating them into a list of `Document` instances.

The `DirectoryLoader` accepts the path to a directory as input. It recursively traverses the directory, identifying files matching the provided glob patterns (e.g., `*.txt`, `*.pdf`).

Consider a directory named `documents` containing a mix of text files, PDFs, and CSV files. To load all the text files, we can use the following code snippet:

```
from langchain_community.document_loaders import DirectoryLoader

loader = DirectoryLoader("./documents", glob="*.txt")
documents = loader.load()
```

Under the hood, the loader uses the `UnstructuredFileLoader` class. This class supports the loading of text files, PowerPoints, HTML, PDFs, images, and more depending on the extension of the file being loaded [9].

This can be customized to an arbitrary loading class using the `loader_cls` keyword argument in the class constructor.

For example, continuing the previous example, let's load all PDF files in the directory with the following snippet:

```
from langchain_community.document_loaders import PyPDFLoader

loader = DirectoryLoader(
    '../', glob="*.pdf", loader_cls=PyPDFLoader)

loader.load()
```

Integrating with Google Cloud Storage

These `DocumentLoaders` would only work for a file stored in the local file system. If we work with Google Cloud Storage as our file storage of choice, we can use the `GCSFileLoader` class:

```
from langchain_google_community import GCSFileLoader

loader = GCSFileLoader(
    project_name="my-gcp-project-id",
    bucket="my-bucket",
    blob="my-file.txt"
)
```

There are only three arguments required:

- `project_name`: Name of the Google Cloud project
- `bucket`: Name of the Google Cloud Storage bucket where the data is stored
- `blob`: Name of the blob that we want to ingest

For specialized file types, you can combine `GCSFileLoader` with other loaders using the `loader_func` argument:

```
from langchain_community.document_loaders import PyPDFLoader

def load_pdf(file_path):
    return PyPDFLoader(file_path)
```

```
loader = GCSFileLoader(
    project_name="my-gcp-project-id",
    bucket="my-bucket",
    blob="my-file.txt",
    loader_func = load_pdf
)
```

In this example, we define a `load_pdf` function that uses the `PyPDFLoader` specifically for PDF files. The `GCSFileLoader` handles the interaction with GCS, while `load_pdf` ensures the content is correctly parsed as a PDF.

To process multiple files within a GCS bucket, the `GCSDirectoryLoader` class provides a convenient solution:

```
from langchain_google_community import GCSDirectoryLoader

loader = GCSDirectoryLoader(
    project_name="your-gcp-project-id",
    bucket="your-bucket-name",
    prefix="path/to/your/directory"
)

documents = loader.load()
```

Let's now explore how we can, once documents are ingested, apply chunking techniques to improve the performance of RAG applications.

Document chunking

LangChain's `TextSplitter` interface helps to break down large documents into smaller chunks for processing. As we discussed in the previous chapter, it's one of the patterns for developing RAG applications (since it helps to keep the input context small). The choice of splitter depends on the document's structure and your specific requirements.

RecursiveCharacterTextSplitter

A versatile option is `RecursiveCharacterTextSplitter`. It intelligently divides text based on natural breaks such as paragraphs, sentences, and individual words:

```
from langchain.text_splitter
import RecursiveCharacterTextSplitter

text_splitter = RecursiveCharacterTextSplitter(
    chunk_size=1000,  # Adjust chunk size as needed
```

```
        chunk_overlap=200 # Optional overlap for context preservation
)
```

In this example, the splitter aims for chunks of approximately 1,000 characters, allowing for a 200-character overlap between chunks. Overlapping chunks ensures that information split between two chunks remains connected, maintaining the context of the original text. Furthermore, without overlapping, information falling at the edges of chunks could be lost or fragmented, leading to incomplete or inaccurate responses.

Other Text Splitters

LangChain offers a variety of other splitters:

- `CharacterTextSplitter`: Splits on a specific character (e.g., newline)
- `MarkdownTextSplitter`: Handles markdown formatting for structured documents
- `PythonCodeTextSplitter`: Preserves the structure of Python code snippets

You can experiment with different splitters to find the best fit for your use case [3].

Applying text splitters

To split a LangChain Document into smaller chunks after initializing the `splitter` class, you need to call the `split_documents` method. It takes a list of documents as input:

```
texts = text_splitter.split_documents(documents)
```

The resulting `texts` variable will be a list of text chunks, each a manageable unit for further processing or embedding.

Parsing documents with Document AI

Instead of using PyPDF for loading and parsing PDF documents, we can use Document AI. Document AI is a managed Google Cloud service that helps with "document processing and understanding" [4]. Document AI is recommended for scanned PDFs, or ones with complex layouts or a mix of images and text. It offers various processors for extracting data PDF files (from generic PDF parsers to specialized expense or invoice parsers). LangChain integrates this Google Cloud service through the `DocAIParser` class:

```
from langchain_google_community import DocAIParser

parser = DocAIParser(
    location=LOCATION,
```

```
        processor_name=PROCESSOR_NAME,
        gcs_output_path=GCS_OUTPUT_PATH
)
```

Before using the class, you need to do the following:

- Create a Document AI processor (choose a pre-trained or custom one). You can read more in the documentation on how to create one (either programmatically or with a few clicks in the Google Cloud console):

  `https://cloud.google.com/document-ai/docs/create-processor`

- Create a Google Cloud Storage bucket to store the processor's output.

General processors

These processors are designed to work with any document type. Examples include the following:

- `Document OCR`: This extracts text from documents, including handwritten text, in over 200 languages.

- `Form Parser`: This extracts key-value pairs and tables from structured and semi-structured forms. Use this processor when you need to extract tables from your PDFs.

- `Layout Parser`: It extracts document layouts and chunks.

Specialized processors

These processors are tailored for specific types of documents commonly used in businesses. Examples include the following:

- `Invoice Parser`: Extracts information such as invoice number, date, line items, and total amount from invoices

- `Passport Parser`: Extracts personal information from passports

Creating a pre-trained processor

A pre-trained processor can easily be created within the Google Cloud console. Navigate to the Document AI homepage and select the desired processor from the **Processor gallery**. Assign a name to the processor and click **Create**. The new processor will immediately appear in the **My Processors** section, where its unique ID can be retrieved.

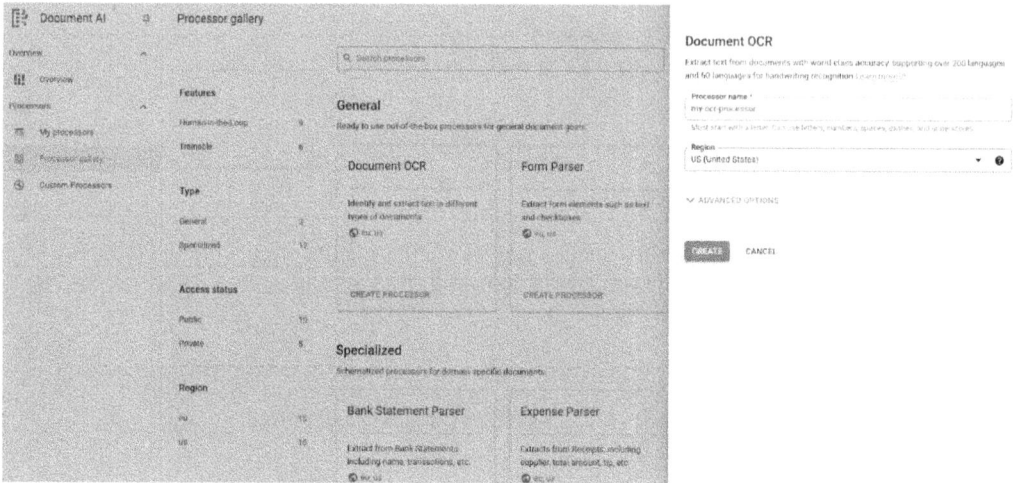

Figure 5.1: Google Cloud console pre-trained processor creation process

Creating a custom processor

Document AI custom processors enable you to create tailored solutions for extracting and analyzing data from documents specific to your business needs.

To get started, you need to create a custom extractor in the console through the **Custom Processors** tab. Once it is created, you can access it in the **My Processors** section.

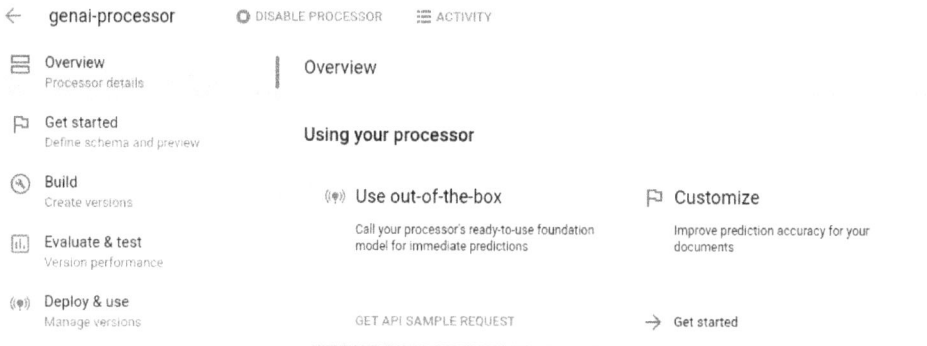

Figure 5.2: Customize a custom processor

The initial step is to define the output schema for the processor. A schema consists of one or more labels, each with its associated data type. For instance, if you're processing passport data, you might define labels such as `passport-number` (plain text), `birth-date` (datetime), and `Nationality` (plain text).

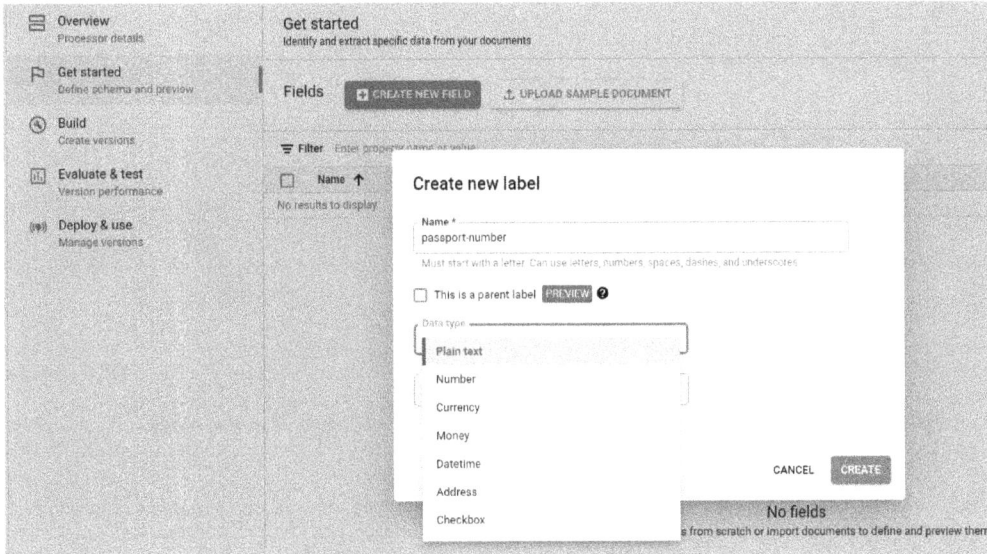

Figure 5.3: Include DocumentAI fields

Once you have defined your output schema, you can immediately utilize a foundational model processor with zero-shot learning to process the documents.

To improve model performance, you can choose one of two options:

- **Fine-tune a foundational model**: Adapt an existing model to your specific task

- **Train a custom model (without generative AI)**: Build a model from scratch tailored to your data

Both options require a labeled dataset of documents, with a minimum of 10 and a recommended minimum of 50 for better performance.

Document AI provides a convenient interface for document labeling, streamlining this process.

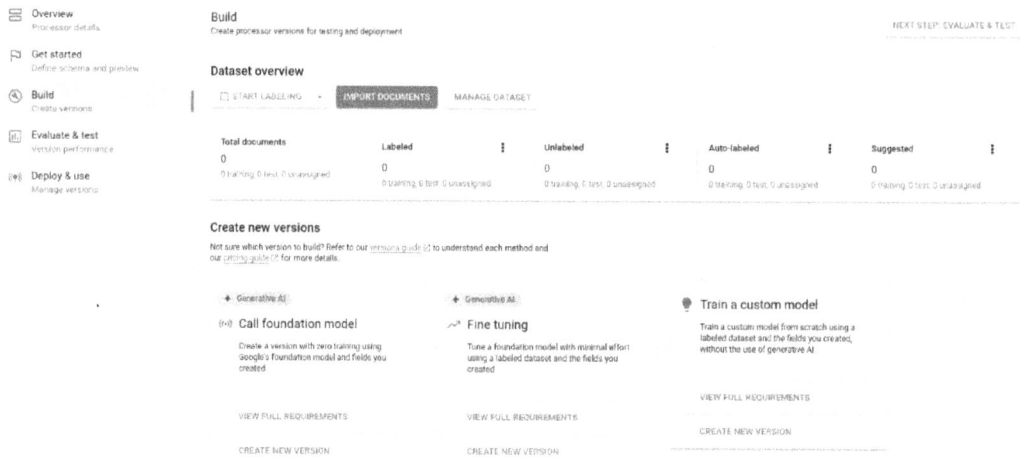

Figure 5.4: Create a new version of a custom model

You can optionally evaluate model performance using the **Evaluation & Test** menu item if you have a labeled dataset available.

Once your custom model is trained, deploy it using the **Deploy & Use** menu item to make it operational.

LangChain usage

Now that you have an operative processor, you can initialize the `DocAIParser` class with the following snippet:

```
from langchain_google_community import DocAIParser
from langchain_core.document_loaders.blob_loaders import Blob

LOCATION = "us"
GCS_OUTPUT_PATH = "gs://BUCKET_NAME/FOLDER_PATH"
PROCESSOR_NAME = "projects/PROJECT_NUMBER/locations/LOCATION/
processors/PROCESSOR_ID"

parser = DocAIParser(
    location=LOCATION,
    processor_name=PROCESSOR_NAME,
    gcs_output_path=GCS_OUTPUT_PATH
)
```

Once the class is instantiated, we can use the `lazy_parse` method to execute the processor and get the documents from a `Blob` in Google Cloud storage:

```
path = "gs://my-bucket/my-folder/my-pdf.pdf"
blob = Blob(path=path)
docs = list(parser.lazy_parse(blob))
```

Rather than executing the end to end pipeline sequentially for all files, we can instead batch the operations to improve scalability with the docai_parse method.

```
operations = parser.docai_parse([blob])
```

PDF parsing happens asynchronously on Google Cloud, and it takes time. Google Cloud has a notion of a **Long-Running Operation** (**LRO**). Please read more in the documentation if you're interested (`https://cloud.google.com/document-ai/docs/long-running-operations`). In short, Google Cloud doesn't block the API response and returns an identifier of such a LRO. You can always check the status of the LRO, and when it's completed, retrieve the output. LangChain integration offers you two options: either block the execution and wait until all PDFs are processed, or split it into steps (first, get LRO identifiers, and when they're ready, use another call to retrieve the results). This method will return a list of executing operations that we can wait for, as shown here:

```
import time
while parser.is_running(operations):
    time.sleep(0.5)
results = parser.get_results(operations)
```

Finally, transform the results into LangChain `Document` instances to use in our pipeline:

```
docs = list(parser.parse_from_results(results))
```

Ingesting data with Vertex AI Agent Builder

Vertex AI Agent Builder offers a managed way to ingest data using a service called DataStore. It automatically ingests and chunks a number of documents with few configuration parameters. In order to create a DataStore, you need to navigate to the **Data Stores** section inside **Agent Builder** in the Google Cloud console.

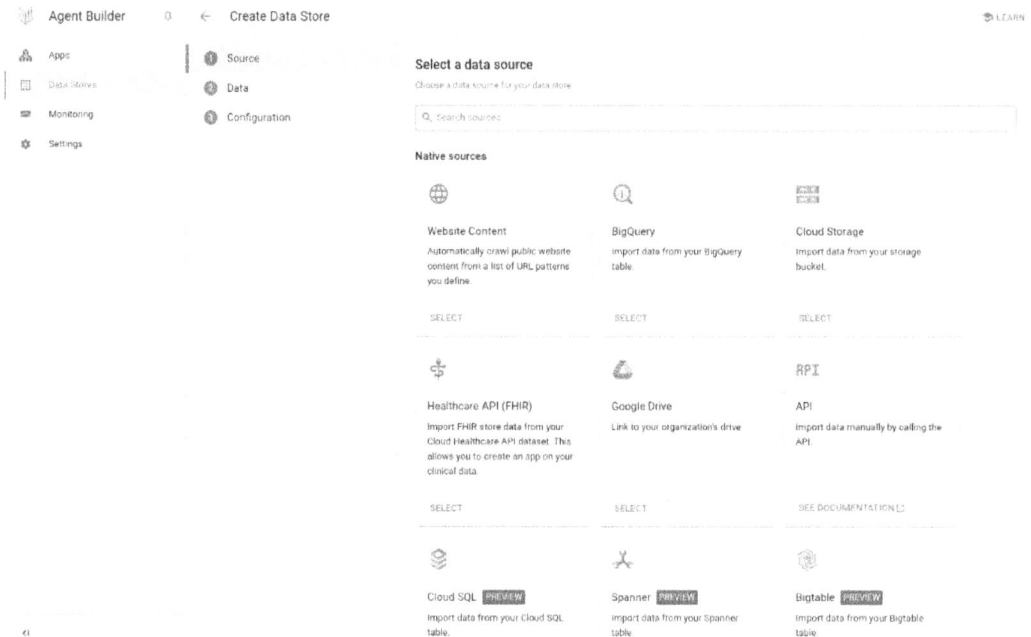

Figure 5.5: Create a new version of a custom model

Agent builder supports several source types, such as the following.

Website data

For website data, it's important to check whether the web pages are blocked by `robots.txt` and verify domain ownership for advanced indexing. Adding structured data such as meta tags and PageMaps can further enhance the indexing process.

Unstructured Data

Unstructured data, such as HTML, PDF, TXT, PPTX, and DOCX files, can be imported from Cloud Storage using the console, API, or streaming ingestion. File size limits apply, with a limit of 2.5 MB for HTML or TXT and 100 MB for PDF, PPTX, and DOCX. **Optical Character Recognition (OCR)** is recommended for non-searchable PDFs, while document chunking enables retrieval-augmented generation. When importing from Cloud Storage with metadata, JSON Lines or NDJSON format is required. If using BigQuery, a specific schema with a `uri` field pointing to Cloud Storage files is necessary.

Structured data

Structured data should be in JSON Lines or NDJSON format, with each file not exceeding 2 GB. Up to 100 files can be imported simultaneously from Cloud Storage. Importing with metadata, including `id` and `jsonData` fields, is recommended for better results. Schema can be auto-detected or provided manually. Specific guidelines exist for structured media data.

In addition to this source, there also exist some connectors to third-party data sources, such as Confluence, Jira, Salesforce, or Slack. Remember to refer to the official Vertex AI documentation for detailed instructions and the most up-to-date information on each data type and ingestion method.

Let's choose, as an example, to create an unstructured data Datastore, selecting **Google Cloud Storage** from the available data sources menu.

In this case, we have stored in the selected bucket a series of `*.html` files to be parsed, so we should select **Unstructured documents** as our type of data.

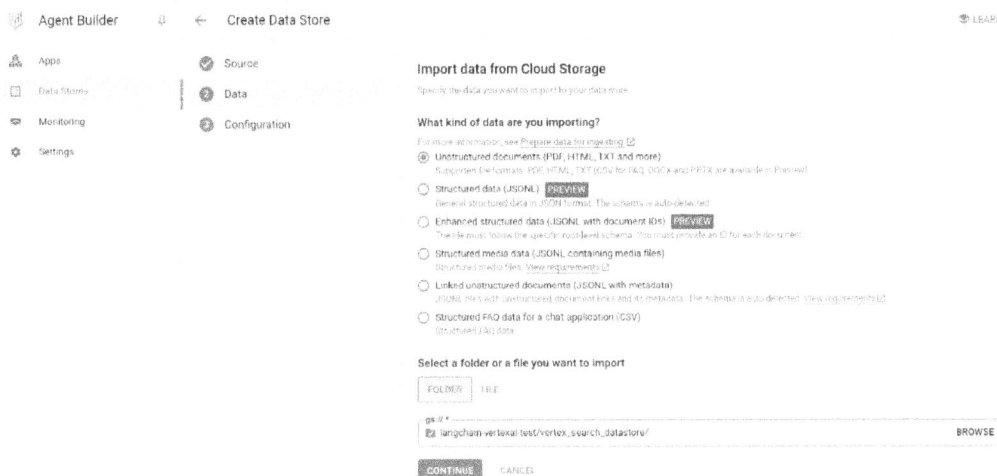

Figure 5.6: Importing data from Google Cloud Storage in the Datastore

Finally, we need to select the parsing and chunking configuration for our datastore.

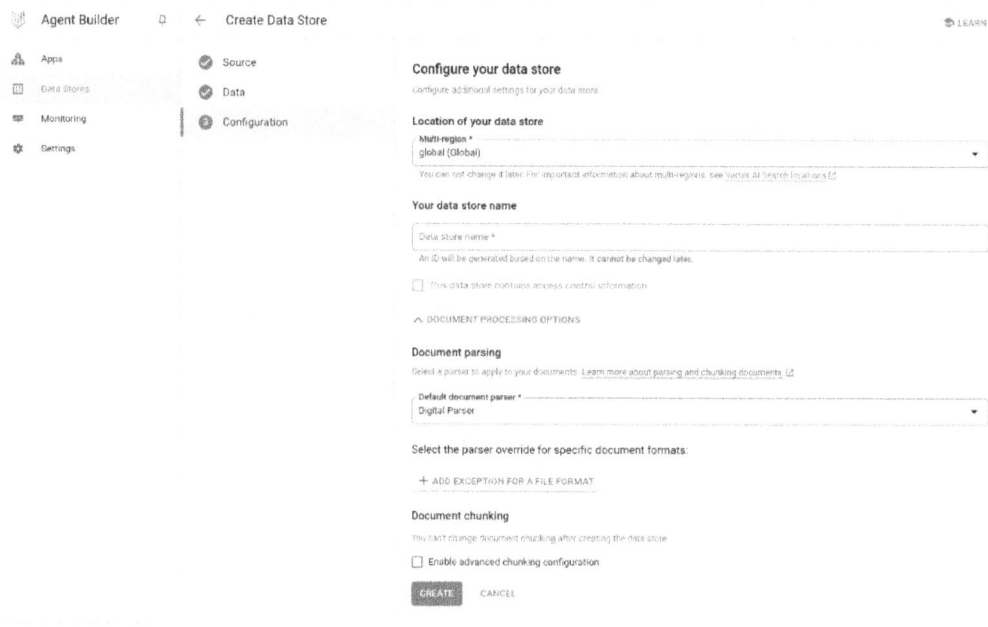

Figure 5.7: Configuring the datastore

Parsing

There are three options here, as follows:

1. **Digital**: Specialized parsers that are designed to extract structured information from specific document types such as HTML, XML, or JSON

2. **Layout-Aware Document Chunking**: This option uses the layout of your documents (headings, paragraphs, etc.) to create meaningful chunks.

3. **OCR Parser for PDFs**: If you're uploading scanned PDFs, it's recommended to configure an OCR parser

Chunking

If you enable advanced chunking, you can set the maximum token size for each chunk (the default is 500, and the supported range is 100-500) and you can choose whether or not to include headings in each chunk.

In our case, we choose a digital parser and the default chunking configuration.

Once we click **Create**, a new DataStore will be generated that can be used in any Agent Builder app or as a `VectorStore`, as explained in previous chapters.

Summary

In this chapter, we explored document parsing capabilities in LangChain and Google Cloud. We discussed using LangChain document loaders such as TextLoader, CSVLoader, and PyPDFLoader to parse various file formats. We also covered Google ecosystem-specific integrations such as GoogleDriveLoader.

We explained how to use Document AI for parsing and extracting structured data from documents, covering both pre-trained and custom processors.

Finally, we demonstrated how to use Vertex AI's Agent Builder to ingest data from various sources such as websites, unstructured data, and structured data.

Links

Here are some important links to further your understanding:

1. Document Loaders, LangChain documentation,

    ```
    https://python.langchain.com/v0.1/docs/modules/data_connection/
    document_loaders/.
    ```

2. Google Cloud Storage File, LangChain documentation,

    ```
    https://python.langchain.com/v0.1/docs/integrations/document_
    loaders/google_cloud_storage_file/.
    ```

3. Text Splitters, LangChain documentation,

    ```
    https://python.langchain.com/v0.1/docs/modules/data_connection/
    document_transformers/.
    ```

4. Document AI, Google Cloud Documentation,

    ```
    https://cloud.google.com/document-ai/docs/.
    ```

5. Google Cloud Document AI, LangChain Documentation

    ```
    https://python.langchain.com/v0.2/docs/integrations/document_
    transformers/google_docai/.
    ```

6. Google Cloud DataStores, Google Cloud Documentation

    ```
    https://cloud.google.com/dialogflow/vertex/docs/concept/data-
    store.
    ```

7. Parse and chunk documents, Google Cloud Documentation

    ```
    https://cloud.google.com/generative-ai-app-builder/docs/parse-
    chunk-documents.
    ```

8. Google Drive, LangChain Documentation

    ```
    https://python.langchain.com/v0.2/docs/integrations/document_
    loaders/google_drive/.
    ```

9. Unstructured File, Langchain Documentation,

    ```
    https://python.langchain.com/v0.2/docs/integrations/document_
    loaders/unstructured_file/.
    ```

Get This Book's PDF Version and Exclusive Extras

UNLOCK NOW

Scan the QR code (or go to `packtpub.com/unlock`). Search for this book by name, confirm the edition, and then follow the steps on the page.

Note: Keep your invoice handy. Purchases made directly from Packt don't require one.

6

Multimodality

Information can be presented in various modalities – for example, text, images, videos, audio, and so on. Typically, **machine learning** (**ML**) models deal with a single modality. For example, they might take a video input and provide a text description of this video as an output. Imagine how great it would be if you could ask a **large language model** (**LLM**) a question about a specific image. In that case, your input would become both a text and an image (or maybe only a text or an image). **Multimodality** is the capability of ML models to take as input or produce as output data of various modalities at the same time (e.g., text, image, video, audio, etc.), and multimodal models can deal with different modalities at the same time (either on the input or output side, or both). [1]

Our documents often contain multimodal input (a very simple example – images or charts in a document that have an important meaning). Imagine how better our **retrieval augmented generation** (**RAG**) could be if it not only accounted for text information but also extracted information from other modalities. You will learn how to build multimodal RAGs, deal with multimodal input (mainly images), use multimodal embeddings, and parse images with LangChain and Google Cloud.

In this chapter, we will cover the following topics:

- Multimodality with Gemini and LangChain
- Using Imagen with LangChain
- Developing multimodal RAGs

Technical requirements

For this chapter, you will need an active Google Cloud project and a Python environment with the following libraries installed:

```
!pip install --upgrade langchain_google_vertexai langchain-community
langchain_google_community google-cloud-vision
```

In order to make unstructured library work, you need to follow the OS-specific instructions (or use a Docker image) described here:

```
https://docs.unstructured.io/open-source/introduction/quick-start
```

If you're using Unix, you need to run the following:

```
apt-get update && apt-get install libmagic-dev
pip install unstructured==0.15.9 unstructured[pdf]==0.15.9  opencv-
python==4.9.0.80
```

Multimodality with Gemini and LangChain

First, what does it mean for a model to be multimodal? It means the model that supports text content as an input (or output). For example, some models can support audio, PDFs, images, and other types of content as input (or they can also generate images, audio, video, etc.).

As of September 2024, Google Cloud exposed the *Gemini 1.0 Pro Vision*, Gemini 1.5 Pro, and Gemini 1.5 Flash models that allowed text, images, audio, video, and PDFs to be included in prompts. Responses are in the form of text or code [2].

Unlike many other models, these models can seamlessly process images and video, together with text, as part of their prompting. This enables them to understand text and visuals and answer questions related to visuals. We will discuss potential use cases later in this chapter. If you need a model to generate text or answer questions based on text (or to perform other text-centric tasks), you can use Gemini Pro 1.0 or other models. If you need a model that can integrate visual information with text for tasks such as image understanding, caption generation, or potentially creating text-visual content, then Gemini Pro Vision or Gemini 1.5 is the better choice.

To create a vision-capable language model using LangChain and Google Vertex AI, we can import the necessary library and initialize the model:

```
from langchain_google_vertexai import ChatVertexAI
chat_vision_model = ChatVertexAI(model_name="gemini-1.0-pro-vision")
```

The main interface for multimodal support on LangChain is a **chat model**. That means that in order to construct a multimodal input, you need to provide it as part of your **message** (the same way we discussed in *Chapter 2*). If we want to interact with the model by providing a text input, nothing changes:

```
from langchain_core.messages import HumanMessage

question1 = HumanMessage(content="Hello. Who are you?")
answer1 = chat_vision_model.invoke([question1])
```

```
question2 = HumanMessage(content="What kind of input and output do you
support")
answer2 = chat_vision_model.invoke([question1, answer1, question2])
```

However, what if we want to add other types of content to the input? Let's add an image, and in this case, we need to construct a message part in a special way:

```
image_message_part = {
    "type": "image_url",
    "image_url": {"url": YOUR_IMAGE},
}
```

You can pass an image as raw base64-encoded bytes, a local path, a web URL, or a path to an object on **Google Cloud storage (GCS)**. If you pass a path to GCS, then your applications won't even fetch this data and just pass the link to Google's API as a parameter. This will reduce both latency and network load. Let's take a look at an example:

```
image_url = "gs://cloud-samples-data/vision/label/wakeupcat.jpg"
image_message_part = {
    "type": "image_url",
    "image_url": {"url": image_url}
}

message = HumanMessage(content=["What is shown in this image?",
    image_message_part])

output = chat_vision_model.invoke([message])
print(output.content)
```

The library handles all the loading image logic for you, but if you prefer, you can interact with a loader directly. You don't need to resize large images (as soon as they fit within the overall prompt's limit of 4 MB) but keep in mind that large images are reduced in size to fit within a 3072 x 3072-pixel boundary, maintaining their original proportions. Let's see how to interact with the image directly, for example, to display it in Jupyter Notebook for inspection purposes:

```
from langchain_google_vertexai._image_utils import ImageBytesLoader
from vertexai.vision_models import Image

image_loader = ImageBytesLoader()
image = image_loader.load_bytes(image_url)
Image(image).show()
```

Please note that the `vertexai` library is pre-installed when you install `langchain_google_vertexai`.

You can pass any media input (such as PDF, audio, video, etc.) with a special `media` type, but in that case, you need to provide a passing `mime_type`. You can even create your text part conveniently as a dict, as you can see here:

```
llm = ChatVertexAI(model_name="gemini-1.5-pro-001")
audio_uri = "gs://cloud-samples-data/generative-ai/audio/audio_
summary_clean_energy.mp3"
audio_message_part = {
    "type": "media",
    "file_uri": audio_uri,
    "mime_type": "audio/mp3",
}
text_message_part = {"type": "text",
    "text": "Describe the attached media in 5 words!"}
message = HumanMessage(
    content=[audio_message_part, text_message_part])
result = llm.invoke([message])
print(result)
```

Instead of a `file_uri`, you can use a data argument in the dictionary and pass the base64-encoded byte string of your media content (but of course, it would create additional network overhead, and it might not work for large content such as videos).

Vertex AI supports PNG and JPEG images (MIME data types should be `image/png` or `image/jpeg`). Your prompt can contain up to 16 images; each image adds 258 tokens to your input context (and you're billed accordingly).

Now that you know how to send your multimodal model to Gemini, let's look at how to use other foundational models for more specific image-related use cases. What if we want a nuanced understanding of an image or even an image generation?

Using Imagen with LangChain

When discussing multimodal tasks, we should mention **Imagen**, a text-to-image diffusion model developed by Google Research and Google Brain [3]. It is available at VertexAI, and we can use it with LangChain.

Let's start with a simple funny image (available as a sample at a public GCS bucket):

Figure 6.1 – Cat Humor

Imagen on VertexAI covers a few use cases, and for each of them ,we need a slightly different model's class on LangChain with a different interface:

- Visual captioning, or generating text description from an image, is one option. It's a common problem statement in ML that generates text descriptions from an image:

```
from langchain_google_vertexai import VertexAIImageCaptioning

response = VertexAIImageCaptioning().invoke(image_url)
print(response)
>> a cat yawning with the caption wake up human
```

- Visual question and answering (Q&A), or answering a question based on image content, is another option. Although LangChain uses the interface of a chat model for visual Q&A, take into account that in this case, only a single-turn chat is allowed. In other words, you can't ask follow-up questions, and all the context from the previous conversation should be within the question itself:

```
from langchain_google_vertexai import VertexAIVisualQnAChat
model_qa = VertexAIVisualQnAChat()

message_qa = HumanMessage(content=[image_message_part,
    "What is shown in this image?"])
answer = model_qa.invoke([message_qa])
print(answer.content)
```

```
message_qa1 = HumanMessage(content=[image_message_part,
    "What is the cat doing?"])
answer1 = model_qa.invoke([message_qa1])
print(answer1.content)
>>cat
>>yawning
```

- Image generation can also be based on a text description of an image:

```
from langchain_google_vertexai import VertexAIImageGeneratorChat
model_generate = VertexAIImageGeneratorChat()

message_gen = HumanMessage(content=["Generate an image with a
yawning cat."])
answer = model_generate.invoke([message_gen])
image_loader = ImageBytesLoader()
image = image_loader.load_bytes(
    answer.content[0]["image_url"]["url"])
Image(image).show()
```

That's what we got (and of course, each time you run it, you might get a different result):

Figure 6.2 – Image generation example

- Image editing allows you to generate an edited image given the original one and a task in a human language:

```
from langchain_google_vertexai import VertexAIImageEditorChat
model_edit = VertexAIImageEditorChat()

message_edit = HumanMessage(content=[image_message_part,
    "Replace a cat with a dog."])
answer = model_edit.invoke([message_edit])
image_loader = ImageBytesLoader()
image = image_loader.load_bytes(
    answer.content[0]["image_url"]["url"])
Image(image).show()
```

It's for you to judge how successful the model was in doing the job:

Figure 6.3 – Image editing result

You can read about the additional parameters that these models accept (that allow you to change the amount of results, add negative examples by describing with natural language what you'd like to omit when generation images, etc.) at the documentation page:

https://api.python.langchain.com/en/latest/google_vertexai/vision_models.html

Now that you know how to use Imagen for various use cases related to image understanding, let's talk about how we can extract images from original documents and use these images to enhance our RAG.

Developing multimodal RAGs

In the previous chapter, we discussed a classic example of RAG: a Q&A application on enterprise data. Often, the source of the data is PDFs that contain images that incorporate important – pie charts, graphs, and other types of visualizations.

We have two problems in front of us – first, we have to determine how to extract images from underlying objects. Second, if we have text and images from the underlying document, we need to know how to prepare the context for the LLM. Let's look at these problems one by one. Of course, you can expand this approach to other types of content.

Extracting images from PDF documents

Ideally, we should have images as a separate source of data for our RAG applications. However, in practice, images are often a part of PDF files and other unstructured data sources, and we'd like our Q&A application to take them into account. That means we need to extract them during the pre-processing.

Let's define a custom function that would process a local file and extract images:

```python
from unstructured.partition.pdf import partition_pdf


def load_pdf(file_path: str):
    """Uses Unstructured library to load pdf and extract images."""
    file_name = file_path.split("/")[-1]
    output_dir = f"./extracted_images/{file_name}"
    return partition_pdf(
        filename=file_path,
        extract_images_in_pdf=True,
        chunking_strategy="by_title",
        extract_image_block_types=["Image", "Table"],
        extract_image_block_to_payload=False,
        extract_image_block_output_dir=output_dir
    )
```

Now we can load a file (or multiple files) from GCS using a custom load function:

```python
from langchain_google_community import GCSFileLoader

project = ...
bucket = "cloud-samples-data"
gcs_path ="gen-app-builder/search/alphabet-investor-pdfs/2022_
alphabet_annual_report.pdf"
loader = GCSFileLoader(
    project, bucket, gcs_path, loader_func=load_pdf)

docs = loader.load()
```

You can take a look at our GitHub code to see how we processed the output from the unstructured parser and extracted tables and images. We extracted tables to a list of LangChain documents, but since parsing takes quite some time, we don't want to repeat it every time. Let's look at how we can serialize almost any object in LangChain (as soon as it inherits from a Serializable, of course):

```
import json

for i, d in enumerate(documents):
    with open(f"./documents/document_{i}.json", "w") as f:
        json.dump(d.to_json(), f)
```

As you can see, we used a `to_json` method, and we can use another procedure to de-serialize objects from a JSON file:

```
import os
import json
from langchain_core.load import loads

documents = []
folder_path = "./documents"
for path in os.listdir(folder_path):
    full_path = os.path.join(folder_path, path)
    with open(full_path, 'r') as f:
        document = json.load(f)
        documents.append(loads(json.dumps(document)))
```

Look at our GitHub samples for more details and a full flow.

Multimodal context

Now it's time to address the second problem – how to retrieve multimodal content as part of a RAG pipeline and how to pass it to the LLM. We have three options:

- Describe each image as a text with a multimodal LLM. Then deal with these texts the same way to deal with the other text chunks – embed them, add to your vector store, retrieve passing ones, and enrich the LLM's context with them. You only need a multimodal LLM for this.

- Do the same as in the preceding list item, but when you have retrieved the chunk from the vectorstore, pass not its description but the image itself to the multimodal LLM's context. You only need a multimodal LLM for this.

- Embed images directly with a multimodal embedding model, and let each image be a separate chunk. Add them to the vectorstore, retrieve passing images (together with text chunks), and enrich a context with them to pass to a multimodal LLM. You need both multimodal embeddings and a multimodal LLM for this.

To demonstrate these approaches to building a multimodal RAG, we selected a question that can only be answered with an image understanding. Our question is: "How many public short views did YouTube have in the last 90 days?", and it can only be answered with an image on page 19 in our example file (it's a publicly available PDF that contains a 2022 Alphabet annual report). The text of the report itself doesn't contain the answer to this question:

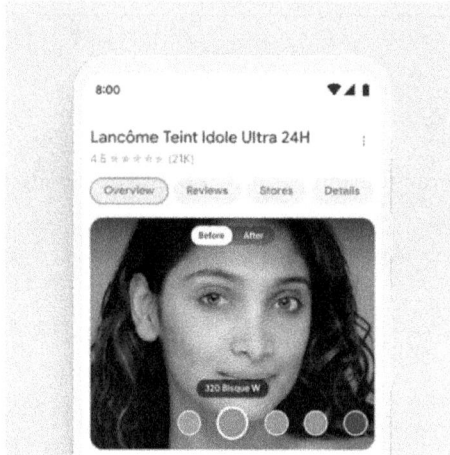

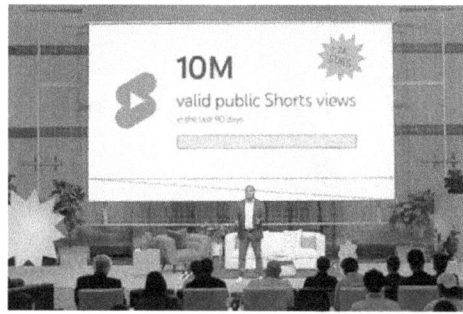

Figure 6.4 – An example of an image from the Alphabet's annual
report that contains the answer to the question

1. We will create three vector indices:

    • One for text documents only

    • One for text documents and text descriptions of images

    • The last one is for only images (embedded with multimodal embeddings)

2. For the sake of saving space, we won't include the code to create and deploy indices and add documents to them, but you can find the full code on our GitHub.

Let's test our initial RAG (which was based only on extracted text) on two questions:

```
chain_rag.invoke("What was Alphabet's revenue in 2022?")
chain_rag.invoke("How many public short views did Youtube have in the
last 90days?")

>> Alphabet's revenue in 2022 was $282.8 billion.
>> The provided context does not mention the number of public short
views on YouTube in the last 90 days, so I cannot answer this question
from the provided context.
```

As we can see, it got the first question right, but it couldn't answer the second question since this subtle piece of information is hidden within an image.

Describing image as text

The first option is relatively straightforward. We need to process our images and convert them to text chunks. Let's put together all we've learned in this chapter so far:

```python
def describe_image(llm: ChatVertexAI, image_path: str) -> str:
    """Describes an image with a multimodal LLM."""

    text_message = {
        "type": "text",
        "text": (
            "Your task is to summarize images for retrieval. "
            "These summaries will be embedded and used to retrieve "
            "the image that is relevant for the query. "
            "Give a concise summary of the image and optimize it "
            "for retrieval.\nIf it's a table, extract all its
elements. "
            "\nIf it's a graph or a chart, explain the findings in the
"
            "graph. Do not include any numbers that are not mentioned
in the "
            "image."
        )
    }

    image_message = {
        "type": "image_url",
        "image_url": {"url": image_path},
    }

    message = HumanMessage(content=[text_message, image_message])
    return llm.invoke([message]).content
```

Let's take a look at our example:

```
describe_image(llm_mm, f"gs://{bucket_name}/{path_example}")

>> Neal Mohan, Chief Product Officer at YouTube, stands in front of a
screen with a graph showing 10M valid public Shorts views in the last
90 days.
```

We got a valid text description that contains all the information we need to answer the question. Now, let's add generated image descriptions as texts to the vectorstore, and test again (please keep in mind that we should use a multimodal LLM):

```
from google.cloud import storage

prefix = ...
storage_client = storage.Client()
bucket = storage_client.bucket(bucket_name)
blobs = bucket.list_blobs(prefix=prefix)
image_docs = []

for blob in blobs:
    full_path = f"gs://{blob.bucket.name}/{path_example}"
    description = describe_image(llm_mm, full_path)
    image_docs.append(Document(
        page_content=description.content,
        metadata={"source": full_path, "element": "image"}
    ))

_ = vectorstore.add_docs(image_docs)
chain_rag.invoke("How many public short views did Youtube have in the
last 90days?")
>> 10M
```

As we can see, we were able to improve the RAG's quality by incorporating the information that is contained only in the images (on top of texts extracted from original documents).

Option 2 – Pass the image directly to the LLM

Option 2 is similar to the option described above. We won't change anything on the indexing and retrieval part, but let's pass an image itself to the RAG instead of its description. In other words, we will still use the generated image description to retrieve a passing image for the query (if any), but we pass the image itself for generation.

The key difference is that with Option 1, you can use a smaller (or faster) model for generation that doesn't have multimodal capabilities. However, if you pass an image itself, a model might take more nuances of the image into account during the generation step.

Let's redefine a function that formats a context for the model. It will create a `HumanMessage` that contains a question part, image parts, and text context parts:

```python
raw_prompt_template_mm = (
    "Use image or text data or both to answer the question:
{question}"
)


def format_mm_docs(docs, question):
    texts = [
        doc for doc in docs
        if doc.metadata.get("doc_type") != "image"
    ]

    images = [
        doc.metadata["source"] for doc in docs
        if doc.metadata.get("doc_type") == "image"
    ]

    context = "\n".join(
        "page: {0}\n{1}".format(
            text.metadata.get("page", 0),
            text.page_content
        )
        for text in texts
    )

    image_messages = []
    for image in images:
        image_message = {
            "type": "image_url",
            "image_url": {"url": image},
        }
        image_messages.append(image_message)

    start_text_message = {
        "type": "text",
        "text": raw_prompt_template_mm.format(question=question),
    }

    text_message = [{
        "type": "text",
        "text": context,
    }] if context else []
```

```
        return [HumanMessage(content=[start_text_message]
            + image_messages + text_message)]
```

Now our RAG composition will look slightly different (we don't need a prompt template anymore, since we will prepare a message while formatting the output of the retriever):

```
chain_rag_example2 = (
    {
        "docs": itemgetter("question") | retriever_mixed,
        "question": RunnablePassthrough()
    }
    | RunnableLambda(
        lambda x: format_mm_docs(x["docs"], **x["question"])
    )
    | ChatVertexAI(
        temperature=0,
        model_name="gemini-1.5-pro-001",
        max_output_tokens=1024
    )
    | StrOutputParser()
)
```

We can test it out:

```
chain_rag_example2.invoke(
    {
        "question": "How many public short views did Youtube have in
the last 90 days?"
    }
)
>> YouTube had **10 million** valid public Shorts views in the last 90
days.
```

Multimodal embeddings

For the next option, we'll need multimodal embeddings. We've discussed what embeddings are in *Chapters 3* and *4*. However, we now want to embed not only text but images too. We can do this with multimodal embeddings.

Generating multimodal embeddings with LangChain is very easy. You use the same class as before, but just change the model's name. Also, instead of providing a text, you can provide a path to the image or its binary representation itself:

```
from langchain_google_vertexai import VertexAIEmbeddings

# Define the model name for multimodal embeddings
```

```
model_name = "multimodalembedding"

# Initialize VertexAI embeddings with the specified model
llm_mm_embeddings = VertexAIEmbeddings(model_name=model_name)

# Generate embeddings for the image URL
emb = llm_mm_embeddings.embed_image(image_url)

# Print the length of the embedding vector
print(len(emb))
>> 1408
```

Please note that embeddings' sizes are different for multimodal and text embeddings (and it's dictated by our choice of embedding model). That's why we can't put the, into a single vectorstore, and why we need to create two retrievals and somehow combine results. That's why we created the third vectorstore, and why we're going to add images there.

An alternative, if we would still like to use a unified vectorstore, would be to reduce the dimension size to 512 (so that text and multimodal embeddings have a common dimension size). Why 512? That's because (at the moment of writing of this book) multimodal embeddings provided by Google supported only the following dimensions: 128, 256, 512, or 1024 (and text embedding sizes are up to 768).

You can do it in the following way:

```
llm1 = VertexAIEmbeddings(model_name="text-embedding-004")
r = llm1.embed(["Hello world"], dimensions=512)
print(len(r[0]))

>> 512
```

Option 3 – Embed images directly

Now let's look at the third option. We want to embed an image and search through image embeddings. So, let's take all images in the folder on GCS and embed them as described:

```
image_paths = [f"gs://{blob.bucket.name}/{blob.name}"
    for blob in blobs]
image_embeddings = [llm_multimodal.embed_image(path)
    for path in image_paths]
documents = [Document(page_content=str(uuid4()),
        metadata={"source": path, "doc_type": "image"}
    ) for path in image_paths]
```

Then we will add these embeddings to a separate vectorstore. You can find the full code on Github. After the index creation is finished, we can try to query it – and we'll see that we get exactly the image we've been looking for:

```
from langchain_google_vertexai._image_utils import ImageBytesLoader
from vertexai.vision_models import Image

results = vectorstore_images.similarity_search(
    "How many users does Youtube have?")
image_loader = ImageBytesLoader()
image = image_loader.load_bytes(
    results[0].metadata["source"])
Image(image).show()
```

Now we can put it all together. We have two different indices, and we'd like to combine documents from both of them. We can achieve it with an `EnsembleRetriever` – a special type of LangChain retriever that combines the output of two or more retrievers. We provide a list of retrievers to it, and also weights for how to combine the output (please note that a combined output is unordered; hence, you should be careful when truncating it if you need `top-k` documents).

A classical use case for such a retriever is a hybrid search (when you combine both dense and sparse embeddings), and another possible use case (out of many) is ours:

```
retriever_raw = vectorstore_raw.as_retriever(search_kwargs={"k": 10})
retriever_images = vectorstore_images.as_retriever(
    search_kwargs={"k": 10})

ensemble_retriever = EnsembleRetriever(
    retrievers=[retriever_raw, retriever_images], weights=[0.5, 0.5]
)
```

Now let's put together a RAG. You can find the full code (including how we construct the prompt) on GitHub. Our message will consist of multiple parts; that's why we define a `format_mm_docs` function:

```
chain_rag = (
    {
        "docs": itemgetter("question") | ensemble_retriever,
        "question": RunnablePassthrough()
    }
    | RunnableLambda(lambda x: format_mm_docs(x["docs"],
**x["question"]))
    | ChatVertexAI(
        temperature=0.5,
        model_name="gemini-pro-vision",
        max_output_tokens=1024
```

```
    )
    | StrOutputParser()
)
```

Let's test it out:

```
chain_rag.invoke({"question": "How many short views does Youtube
have?"})

>> YouTube Shorts are popular, with 10M valid public Shorts views in
the last 90 days.
```

As we can see, this approach also allows us to answer questions that were previously unanswerable with a RAG based only on text.

Parsing an image

> **Note on alternative approaches**
>
> LLMs are great for solving any tasks described in natural language, but sometimes it makes sense to use a custom model (especially since they're already available) for specific tasks. These models can be faster and cheaper, as well as provide better quality.

An example of such a case might be parsing an image when images are just texts (e.g., scans or photos of hand-written text). In this case, it might be easier to pass them through the Vision API directly, extract the text, and use it as a `Document` to be indexed by the vector store. LangChain allows us to do it easily:

```
from langchain_google_community import CloudVisionParser
parser = CloudVisionParser()

parser.load(image_url_text)

>> Document(page_content='This is a hand written message\nto use with
Google Cloud\nPlatform, To demonstrate the capabilities\nof the Cloud
Vision API to detect\nhandwritten text,', metadata={'source': 'gs://
cloud-samples-data/vision/handwritten.jpg'})
```

You can even incorporate an additional image understanding step into your indexing pipeline – for example, you can ask a multimodal LLM to classify an image as a scanned text, and if the answer is yes, pass it to the `CloudVisionParser` for text extraction.

On our GitHub, you can find the full sample, including another example of how to render this image (so that you compare the output with it). As a last note, sometimes (e.g., when you use document parsing chains) you need to use a `CloudVisionLoader` instead. The only difference between these two integrations is that it implements a different interface – `BaseLoader` instead of `BaseBlobParser` – and that it takes the path to the image as a parameter during initialization.

Summary

In this chapter, we discussed how to construct a multimodal input on LangChain. We also learned how to use Google's Imagen foundational model on LangChain for various image-related use cases (such as visual question answering or visual captioning).

Then, we looked into multimodal RAGs. We learned about multimodal embeddings and ways to extract images from raw documents. We also discussed various options that exist to include images in the RAG (from finding the passing images up to adding them into the context).

Finally, we explored parsers available for image understanding on LangChain based on Google Vision API.

In the previous few chapters, we discussed various aspects of building RAG, deepened our understanding of how to use LLMs for various scenarios, and learned how to develop applications with LangChain. In the next chapter, we'll look at other generative AI use cases. We'll start with summarization one, and we'll talk about how to build an application that works with long input (which exceeds the LLM's context window). Of course, these techniques could also be adapted to RAG workflows.

References

1. Overview of multimodal models, Google Cloud,

   `https://cloud.google.com/vertex-ai/generative-ai/docs/multimodal/overview`

2. Gemini: A Family of Highly Capable Multimodal Models, Google, Google Deepmind,

   `https://storage.googleapis.com/deepmind-media/gemini/gemini_1_report.pdf`

3. Imagen, Google Research, Brain Team,

   `https://imagen.research.google/`

Part 3: Common Generative AI Architectures

Many LLMs have limitations on how many tokens they can process. If the size of the input document exceeds the token limit of the model, additional steps need to be taken to bypass this limit. Even though many models increase their token limits and larger and larger texts could be fed into the model to generate a summary, the techniques described in this part are still relevant to optimize your applications for speed and performance.

This part has the following chapters:

- *Chapter 7, Working with Long Context*
- *Chapter 8, Building Chatbots*
- *Chapter 9, Tools and Function Calling*
- *Chapter 10, Agents in Generative AI*
- *Chapter 11, Agentic Workflows*

7

Working with Long Context

In the previous chapter, we discussed how you can work with text in LangChain. We also briefly discussed context windows, and how they limit the amount of data that you can process in **large language models** (**LLMs**). Unfortunately, your users do not accept this limitation and expect you to build applications that can give them concise summaries and answer their questions on documents that might span hundreds of pages!

The most common way of addressing this limitation is to summarize documents. This will enable your LLM to either process more context or process that same context more efficiently within its limited context window. Luckily, due to their architecture, LLMs excel at summarizing long documents and extracting relevant information. In this chapter, we will discuss how you can answer user questions by summarizing documents in LangChain and even how you can leverage the newest long-context LLMs to skip the summarization step altogether!

We will cover the following main topics:

- Basics of summarization
- Using loaders to get text into LangChain
- MapReduce pattern
- Using long-context LLMs to answer questions on documents

Technical requirements

For this chapter, in addition to the specific requirements for each service that is mentioned, you will need an active Google Cloud project and a Python environment with the following libraries installed:

```
pip install -qU langchain langchain-google-vertexai langchain_
community langchain_google_community[speech] langchain-text-splitters
```

This will install the LangChain base functionality, LangChain on Google Cloud Vertex AI, and the LangChain splitters for working with long texts. It will also install the LangChain Community package, which includes community-maintained packages, such as document loaders, and the LangChain Google Community package, which includes some Google Cloud features, such as the Speech-to-Text API.

What is summarization?

Summarization is one of the common natural language processing tasks. The goal of this task is to condense a long original piece, (text, audio, video, etc.) into a shorter text version while retaining important information from the original one.

The same limitations of **retrieval-augmented generation** (**RAG**) that we have discussed in the previous chapters apply to summarization tasks: hallucinations, lack of "real" reasoning capabilities, and challenges with processing complex formatting. Paying close attention to the input document, and, for example, implementing a rewriting step to improve legibility may help you generate better results.

In practice, when we work on summarization tasks, we typically want to control for a few factors:

- Tone of voice
- Formatting output (either using tables or lists with bullet points with multiple indentations, or just a concise text, etc.)
- Keeping the most important points of the original documents and rewriting them (**abstractive** summarization) versus identifying the most important points out of the text (**extractive** summarization)
- Length of the output (being concise versus generating long summaries)
- Avoiding hallucinations

Such adaptation can be achieved with prompt engineering and adding additional steps to your summarization chain, and we're going to discuss such techniques in this chapter. But keep in mind that if you have a dataset with a few hundred examples of summarization tasks from your domain, you might consider fine-tuning the LLM for your specific task first [1].

Summarizing documents

In this section, we will discuss two ways of summarizing long documents. The first way uses traditional MapReduce patterns to summarize documents across multiple LLM calls, while the second makes use of the long-context windows and multimodal capabilities of the latest LLMs to create summaries more efficiently. We will also quickly cover loaders to get documents into your chain, and then go deep into MapReduce patterns to give you a good understanding of what is going on under the hood.

Summarizing text

We'll start by summarizing text. Since most advanced modern LLMs have a long-context window, we can just put the whole text in the model's context and wrap it with additional instructions about what kind of summary we aim for. In practice, we use zero-shot learning for summarization tasks since examples are typically long. We can achieve better domain adaptation with fine-tuning (as mentioned previously) or with more complex pipelines with a few refinement steps in the chain. Let's start with Gemini release updates (https://gemini.google.com/corp/updates) and ask Gemini to create a summary. For your convenience, we don't include the full release in the book, but you can find it in our samples on GitHub:

```
from langchain.chains.summarize import load_summarize_chain
from langchain_google_vertexai import ChatVertexAI
from langchain_core.documents import Document

google_gemini_release_updates = """LONG TEXT HERE"""
llm = ChatVertexAI(temperature=0, model_name="gemini-1.5-pro-001")
chain = load_summarize_chain(llm, chain_type="stuff")

doc = Document(page_content=google_gemini_release_updates)
result = chain.invoke([doc])
print(result["output_text"])
>> Google is significantly expanding access to its advanced AI
chatbot, Gemini, in India and several other countries. This includes
launching the Gemini mobile app, integrating Gemini into Google
Messages, and providing access to the more powerful Gemini 1.5 Pro
model with enhanced features, such as document analysis and a larger
context window. This expansion aims to make AI more accessible across
languages and devices.
```

Let's discuss what happens here.

LangChain provides factory methods to create chains for basic tasks (see the section on LangChain primitives in *Chapter 1* for an explanation of chains). In this example, we leverage `load_summarize_chain`, which comes with a prebuilt function for "stuffing" long context into a summarization function [2]. A `stuff` chain is a vanilla summarization that puts all the context for summarization into the prompt and sends it to the underlying LLM. This returns a `StuffDocumentsChain` object inherited from `Chain`, which in turn inherits from a `RunnableSerializable` object.

`StuffDocumentsChain` then takes all the documents we pass to it and formats them into one single document (or, to be precise, a dictionary with `text` combined from all documents and other arguments specified) with a default template. As always, LangChain is transparent about its inner workings and lets you inspect the template:

```
print(chain.document_prompt)
>> PromptTemplate(input_variables=['page_content'], template='{page_
content}')
```

Let's see how two simple documents are combined to be passed to the next step:

```
doc1 = Document(page_content="text1")
doc2 = Document(page_content="text2")
chain._get_inputs([doc1, doc2])

>> {'text': 'text1\n\ntext2'}
```

Finally, it passes the combined input dictionary to the summarization chain. We can explore the default summarization prompt:

```
print(chain.llm_chain.prompt)
>> PromptTemplate(input_variables=['text'], template='Write a concise
summary of the following:\n\n\n"{text}"\n\n\nCONCISE SUMMARY:')
```

Good news: All default values can be redefined when we instantiate the object, which means that we can have full control over the behavior of our chain! This is one of the key benefits of LangChain – you get a default skeleton of a chain (a pipeline of transformations) for your use case with some good enough defaults, but you can always adjust them if needed.

Let's use a custom prompt and add additional customization. As you can see, we redefined a lot of default parameters:

```
from langchain_core.prompts.chat import ChatPromptTemplate
prompt = ChatPromptTemplate.from_messages(
    [("system", "Create an extractive summary in simple English with
no more than {max_length} words"),
    ("human",
        "Use the following context for the summary: \n{context}")]
)

chain = load_summarize_chain(
    llm, chain_type="stuff", document_separator="\n",
    prompt=prompt, document_variable_name="context")

result = chain.invoke(
    input={"input_documents": [doc], "max_length": 20})
```

```
print(result["output_text"])
>> Gemini's advanced features, including the mobile app, are now
available in India and other countries.
```

Now, we have control over the length of the output. Note that to provide additional arguments to the chain, we need to provide a full dictionary to the input key argument during invocation instead of providing a list of documents:

```
result = chain.invoke(
    input={"input_documents": [doc], "max_length": 50})
print(result["output_text"])
>> Google is launching more Gemini AI features in India, including the
advanced 1.5 Pro model and the Gemini app. Users can now access Gemini
in Google Messages, upload documents, and enjoy expanded language
support. This expansion aims to make AI more accessible.
```

Using loaders

We don't always get our input as cleanly formatted text. Luckily, LangChain provides plenty of loaders [3] that help you load information from various sources, such as PDFs, Markdown, HTML, and so on, as text into Documents (see *Chapter 5*).

Let's look at a practical example: You want to learn about all the amazing new concepts in the world of generative AI, but you simply don't have the time to read through the many papers published each day. How about building a LangChain agent that can help you quickly summarize complex papers in simple English? We can use WebBaseLoader to load the HTML version of any arXiv paper (such as the following example on multi-agent systems) and then pass it to the model:

```
from langchain_community.document_loaders import WebBaseLoader
loader = WebBaseLoader("https://arxiv.org/html/2312.10256v1")
docs = loader.load()

chain = load_summarize_chain(
    llm, chain_type="stuff", document_separator="\n",
    prompt=prompt, document_variable_name="context")

result = chain.invoke(
    input={"input_documents": docs, "max_length": 50})
print(result["output_text"])
>> Multi-agent reinforcement learning (MARL) teaches multiple
agents to make optimal decisions in a shared environment. This
survey explains key concepts of MARL, including stochastic games,
game theory, and deep learning. It highlights the benefits of MARL,
such as enabling complex applications and its challenges, including
computational complexity, non-stationarity, and coordination issues.
```

MapReduce pattern

What should we do if our document doesn't fit into the model's input window? We have a classic answer – MapReduce! This is a big data processing technology that has been with us for around 15 years. The idea is to split the original task into smaller ones that can be processed independently (Map phase) and then combine task outputs together (Reduce phase) [5]. Originally, this allowed you to reduce the memory footprint on every independent task worker and to scale across a large cluster of such workers. We can apply the same paradigm to summarization tasks – breaking down the document into smaller chunks, summarizing each chunk individually, and then combining the summaries into a final, comprehensive summary. *Figure 7.1* shows how this approach works under the hood.

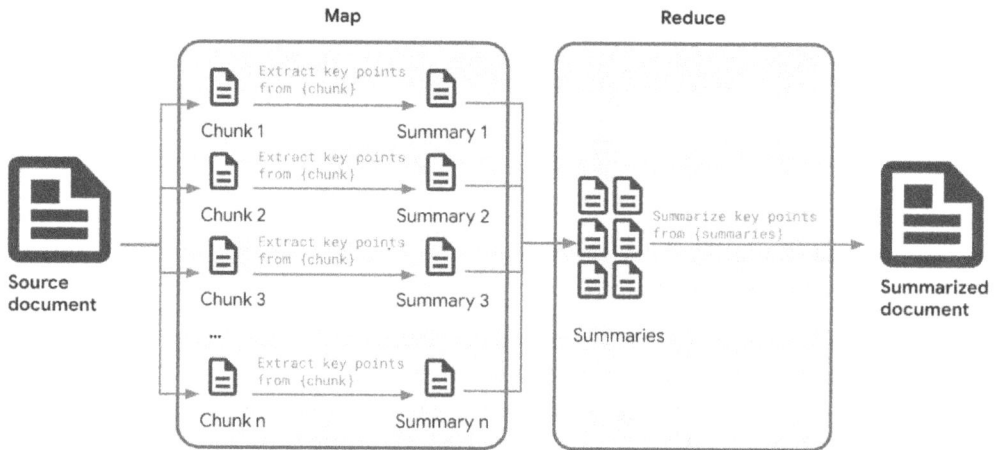

Figure 7.1: MapReduce documents chain

First, we need to load our long PDF and split it into smaller chunks:

```
from langchain_text_splitters import RecursiveCharacterTextSplitter

loader = WebBaseLoader("https://arxiv.org/html/2312.10256v1")
doc = loader.load()

text_splitter = RecursiveCharacterTextSplitter(
    chunk_size=2000, chunk_overlap=100,
    length_function=len, is_separator_regex=False)
docs = text_splitter.split_documents(doc)
print(len(docs))
>> 104
```

Next, we want to create the summary:

```
from langchain_core.prompts import PromptTemplate

prompt = PromptTemplate.from_template(
    "Collapse this content: {text}"
)
chain_mr = load_summarize_chain(
    llm, chain_type="map_reduce", collapse_prompt=prompt)

result = chain_mr.invoke(docs)
print(result["output_text"])
>> ## Concise Summary:
This collection of research explores **Multi-Agent Reinforcement
Learning (MARL)**, focusing on key challenges and advancements in:
* **Exploration:** Using curiosity to drive learning in multi-agent
settings.
* **Cooperation:** Developing algorithms for effective agent
collaboration.
* **Scalability & Applications:** Building platforms like SMARTS for
training autonomous driving agents.
* **Communication:** Investigating the role of communication in MARL.
```

What happens here? Let's go step by step. First, by using the `load_summarize_chain` factory method with `chain_type="map_reduce"`, we created a `MapReduceDocumentsChain` [6] document object. This chain automatically performs the MapReduce process described earlier. Let's look at the default prompt to understand how it "maps" documents to summaries:

```
print(chain_mr.llm_chain.prompt)
>> PromptTemplate(input_variables=['text'], template='Write a concise
summary of the following:\n\n\n"{text}"\n\n\nCONCISE SUMMARY:')
```

Next, we group the processed documents after the map step together and pass them to the `reduce` step. If the output is still too large, we repeat both steps.

As usual, we can redefine all parameters if we wish – for example, we can have different instances of LLMs for different phases, such as map or reduce, and we can change prompts, the collapse limit, and much more.

You can apply the same approach to other modalities, such as audio and video.

Summarizing other modalities

The previous option summarized text. Now, what about documents that contain both text and image (i.e., multimodal) information? Every time we want to summarize input from other modalities than text, such as images, audio, or video, we have two options:

- Use multimodal models (such as Gemini 1.5) that can take multimodal input and process it within the model's context

- Transform the input into text by using loaders

The easiest way to process content is to pass the PDF version directly into a model such as Gemini and leverage its multimodal capabilities. By loading files directly into the LLM, you do not need to worry about processing, formatting, and storing text data. On the other hand, you need to trust the capability of the LLM to process your content and will not be able to troubleshoot what happens "inside" of the multimodal LLM. If you decide to leverage a loader, you will have full control over every step of the process. You may also spend a little bit less on processing, as text is generally cheaper to process than multimodal content. On the other hand, you may miss out on powerful multimodal capabilities and incur lower-quality results.

Let's look at how we would process the arXiv paper we analyzed in the previous section using multimodal capabilities. This time, we will get a `.pdf` file from a public Google Cloud storage bucket and construct a `HumanMessage` that has two (or more) pieces of content. You can find the full code in our GitHub repository:

```
from langchain_core.messages import HumanMessage, SystemMessage
pdf_message = {
    "type": "image_url",
    "image_url": {
        "url": "gs://arxiv-dataset/arxiv/arxiv/pdf/2312/2312.10256v1.
pdf"
    },
}
summarize_message = {
    "type": "text",
    "text": "Create an extractive summary in simple English with no
more than 50 words of the following documents.",
}

message = HumanMessage(
    content=[pdf_message, summarize_message])
result = llm.invoke([message])
print(result.content)
>> Multi-agent reinforcement learning (MARL) is a type of AI where
multiple agents learn to work together in a shared environment.
MARL is challenging because it involves coordinating the actions
```

of multiple agents, which can lead to complex and unpredictable behaviors. Despite the challenges, MARL has the potential to solve complex problems that are difficult or impossible for single agents to solve.

Let's look at another example of using a loader for processing multimodal information: Google Cloud speech services help us to transcribe audio or video into text that can be processed by any LLM [4]. For the following example, assume you want to transcribe and process a recording of a presentation given by a colleague:

```
from langchain_google_community import SpeechToTextLoader

# First we load a speech file from the public domain
! wget https://upload.wikimedia.org/wikipedia/commons/a/ae/Rep._Vance_
McAllister_on_Increasing_the_Mississippi_River_MRT.flac

# Then we create a speech loader for this file
speech_loader = SpeechToTextLoader(
    project_id = PROJECT_ID,
    file_path="""Rep._Vance_McAllister_on_Increasing_the_Mississippi_
River_MRT.flac""",
    is_long=False)

audio_recording_docs = speech_loader.load()
# Let's print out how long it is
print(len(docs[0].page_content))

>> 1974
```

Now, we can work with these documents as usual:

```
chain = load_summarize_chain(
    llm, chain_type="stuff", document_separator="\n",
    prompt=prompt)

result = chain.invoke(
input={"input_documents": audio_recording_docs, "max_length": 50})
print(result["output_text"])

>> Despite the ongoing Padam Canal expansion project, continuous
investment in data resources is crucial. These waterways are vital
to our nation, and their significance outweighs any single finding.
The committee deserves commendation for their diligent work on this
complex challenge.
```

Another option is to pass the whole audio (or video) content directly to the model. In this case, we need to construct a special type of media message pointing to the Google Cloud storage path and mentioning the `mime` type of the content:

```python
import base64


# We first need to encode our audio to base64 so we can pass it to the LLM
with open("audio.flac","rb") as f:
audio = base64.b64encode(f.read()).decode('utf-8')


# Then just construct a media message, making sure to give the correct mime_type
media_message = {
    "type": "media",
    "data": audio,
    "mime_type": "audio/flac",
}


message = HumanMessage(
    content=[summarize_message, media_message])


output = llm([message])


print(output.content)


>> The Mississippi River and its tributaries are vital for commerce
and are currently experiencing flooding. The amendment proposes
increasing funding for the Mississippi River and Tributaries project
by $47 million to restore it to FY14 levels. This investment is
crucial, especially with the Panama Canal expansion underway, and
reducing funding would be detrimental to the nation.
```

Answering questions on long documents

Summarization is just the first step in achieving the goal of our users: Answering questions on long documents! No one has time to read these long documents, and while summaries are helpful, what users really want is a clear, concise answer to a question. In this section, we will discuss how you can use the long-context window of modern LLMs to efficiently answer questions on long documents.

With the introduction of Gemini 1.5 Pro, Google was able to significantly expand the context available for processing one message to the LLM. Imagine that you can perform Q&A on a 132-page long document with a single call! To easily enable you to work with long context, LangChain introduced new types of messages:

```
# Don't be confused by image_url when loading pdfs--this started as an
image loader
pdf_message = {
    "type": "image_url",
    "image_url": {"url": "gs://arxiv-dataset/arxiv/arxiv/
pdf/2312/2312.10256v1.pdf"},
}

text_message = {
    "type": "text",
    "text": "What is the biggest challenge with MARL? Respond in 10
words or less.",
}

# We simply add the pdf message to the model
message = HumanMessage(content=[pdf_message, text_message])

output = llm.invoke([message])
print(output.content)
>> Non-stationarity from other agents' adapting behaviors.
```

To work with long context in a single message, create a message of type image_url and pass it a link to an item on Google Cloud storage. Don't be confused by the types; since long context was born out of multimodal model capabilities (processing images and text in the same invocation), the message type for PDF messages is image_url. You can also provide multiple PDFs and ask more advanced questions:

```
pdf_message_1 = {
    "type": "image_url",
    "image_url": {"url": "gs://arxiv-dataset/arxiv/arxiv/
pdf/2312/2312.10256v1.pdf"},
}
pdf_message_2 = {
    "type": "image_url",
    "image_url": {"url": "gs://arxiv-dataset/arxiv/arxiv/
pdf/2410/2410.01706v1.pdf"},
}

text_message = {
    "type": "text",
```

```
    "text": "What are the key differences between MARL and Sable?
Respond in 50 words or fewer.",
}

# We simply add the pdf message to the model
message = HumanMessage(
    content=[pdf_message_1, pdf_message_2, text_message])

output = llm.invoke([message])
print(output.content)

>> MARL (Multi-Agent Reinforcement Learning) involves multiple agents
learning in a shared environment, while Sable is a specific MARL
algorithm that uses a memory-efficient sequence modeling approach with
retention instead of attention.
```

There you go; it's as easy as that! Of course, you can do a lot more interesting experiments by passing multiple long messages into a single LLM invocation.

Summary

This chapter explores document summarization techniques using LangChain, building upon the previous chapter's discussion of text processing and context windows. It covers various summarization methods, including the `stuff` method for short documents, loaders for different data sources, and MapReduce patterns for handling long documents. The chapter also provides guidance on prompt engineering and discusses the use of multimodal models, such as Gemini 1.5, for summarizing multimodal content. Finally, it examines the future relevance of MapReduce patterns considering advancements in LLMs with large context windows. We also provided many examples to help you get started – check out our GitHub!

After witnessing the power of Q&A in context, you might wonder whether MapReduce patterns for summarization will still be relevant in the future. We believe that the answer is "yes," but for more specific use cases. Specifically, when working with (less advanced, resource-constrained) open-source models, such as Gemma-2B, you may not have the ability and token throughput for processing in context.

In the next chapter, we will look at how you can further enhance the Q&A systems you built in this chapter with memory, turning them into powerful, interactive chatbots.

References

1. *About supervised fine-tuning for Gemini models*, Google Cloud.

    ```
    https://cloud.google.com/vertex-ai/generative-ai/docs/models/
    gemini-supervised-tuning
    ```

2. *.load_summarize_chain*, LangChain.

    ```
    https://api.python.langchain.com/en/latest/chains/langchain.
    chains.summarize.chain.load_summarize_chain.html
    ```

3. *Document loaders*, LangChain.

    ```
    https://python.langchain.com/v0.1/docs/modules/data_connection/
    document_loaders/
    ```

4. *Speech-to-Text documentation*, Google Cloud.

    ```
    https://cloud.google.com/speech-to-text/docs/
    ```

5. *MapReduce*, Wikipedia.

    ```
    https://en.wikipedia.org/wiki/MapReduce
    ```

6. *.MapReduceDocumentsChain*, LangChain.

    ```
    https://api.python.langchain.com/en/latest/chains/langchain.
    chains.combine_documents.map_reduce.MapReduceDocumentsChain.html
    ```

8

Building Chatbots

In the previous chapters, we discussed how to answer questions on long documents using summarization techniques. However, answering a single question may not be enough for your users. Enterprise question-answering is one of the most popular use cases these days, and users expect multiple turns in their conversation. In this chapter, we will discuss how we can leverage the power of LangChain to add memory to our LLM system, turning it into a powerful chatbot. Before we dive into the nuts and bolts, let's discuss the experience our users would like to have with a chatbot.

ChatGPT and other GenAI-powered chatbots have shaped user experience expectations toward chatbots. Most chatbots have a specific purpose and are designed to help users reach a specific goal such as booking a flight, making a restaurant reservation, or answering difficult questions. Users also want their chatbot to be conversational, with a friendly and approachable demeanor. And finally, users expect their chatbot to have some form of memory that enables it to have a conversation that also takes previous messages into account.

This chapter will first give you a brief introduction to the concept of conversation engineering and then teach you key concepts for building a chatbot using the LangChain framework.

We will cover the following main topics:

- A brief introduction to conversation engineering
- Key concepts of building a chatbot using the LangChain framework with practical examples
- Routing between user intents and chatbot functions

Technical requirements

For conversation history, we require a CloudSQL instance running in a Google Cloud project that the user or service account that executes your LangChain code is authenticated with. Look at the Google Cloud documentation for more information about setting up and connecting to CloudSQL instances [1].

```
# Base components for using LangChain on Google Cloud
pip install -qU langchain-google-vertexai
```

```
# LangGraph enables creation of graph-based chat agents
pip install -qU langgraph httpx
# Grandalf is a tool to visualize graphs (like LangGraph)
pip install -qU grandalf # for visualizing the graph
# Enables LangGraph to use SQLite for memory handling
pip install -qU langgraph-checkpoint-sqlite # for chatbot memory
```

These libraries contain the core components of LangChain, as well as the ability to handle memory in a local MySQL database.

Introduction to conversational design

Conversational design predates the new concepts introduced by Gen AI and has been around for many years to make the chatbots that have replaced customer service representatives across industries perform better. It involves crafting and refining the conversation flow, prompts, and responses to create natural, engaging, and goal-oriented interactions between the chatbot and its users. The key challenge of conversational design has been to predict the behavior (intent) of human users and model possible responses in advance to give the perception of an intelligent conversation partner. With Gen AI, this step has gotten a lot easier, as LLMs are able to effectively identify intents and craft suitable responses. LangChain as a framework has expanded on these capabilities by giving engineers the ability to craft sophisticated systems with developer-friendly instruction and state handling.

There are two different types of chatbots:

- Intent-based chatbots follow a predefined conversational flow and meet specific user needs by wrapping a set of end user scenarios through a conversational interface that ends with a function that triggers real-world behavior (e.g., a chatbot that helps you initiate a bank transaction or order a pizza).

- Open-ended chatbots enable divergent conversations with LLMs. This includes employee assistants that help employees answer questions about the company (grounded by the company's data), write drafts of emails, summarize or translate documents, etc. These chatbots are a convenient interface over LLM capabilities (that adds additional enterprise features such as security, grounding, logging, etc.).

Often, users want to have both; they want to use the same interface for enterprise question-answering (grounded on internal data) and, at the same time, they want this tool to utilize LLM capabilities to answer open questions or fulfill tasks described in natural language. We'll discuss how to combine these two different tasks together through a semantic router.

Our focus is on the second use case. We will briefly touch on three components of conversation engineering that you need to build these chatbots: intent identification, conversation flow design, and entity extraction.

Intent identification

Everything begins with understanding the possible intents of our users. As they enter the workflow, what could they possibly try to achieve? Let's take the help desk of a bank as an example. Users might be looking to trigger a business process, such as resetting the password of their online banking or blocking a credit card that they lost. Or they may just look for information, for example, on the opening hours of their branch. With LLMs, we can map user intents to lists of predefined intents even if the specific words that are being used differ. We can also identify unmatched intents and give good answers out of the box (e.g., "I am sorry, I cannot help you with that."). However, reaching user goals will still require additional steps, such as pulling information from a trusted source (see ref: grounding) or triggering a business process (see ref: c10.tools). Having clearly defined user intents enables you to understand what your users are looking for and ensure that you build a chatbot that is both useful and user-friendly.

So, what is an intent? The format of an intent is very similar to the format of a user story in Agile: "As a banking customer, I want to learn about the right loan product, so I can finance my purchase." You start with a description of the persona, define the task they need to perform, and then map the final outcome of their activity. You will need to do some user research (i.e., speak to some real users) to identify this information.

Your users will have more than one intent. Mapping out all personas, their goals, their intents, and also the relationships between those intents is crucial to building a successful chatbot. It is very important that you do not forget about common intents that should exist in all conversations, such as the welcome intent, the conversation restart intent, or the escalation intent. You will use these intents in the routing functions and edge definitions in LangChain and LangGraph.

When we get into building the chatbot with LangChain, we will have examples for some of these intents. You will also see that LangChain comes with many pre-built agents that can handle many intents out of the box, such as question-answering and summarization chains.

Conversation flow design

Once intents have been identified, we need to understand how they relate to each other. For example, users may want to learn about our loan products first before starting a process to contract a loan. Before LLMs, the relationship of intents, the dialogue flow, had to be largely hardcoded, as "open" intents (where the chatbot would not know which user input to expect) were time-intensive to design and implement. Consequently, the industry standard even today is routing systems with hardcoded decision trees in their chatbots (such as "Press 1 if you have questions about your credit card bill") at the cost of user experience. With powerful LLMs orchestrated by LangChain, we can detect even complex intents in milliseconds, enabling a far more natural conversation flow. Still, informing your LLM about which intents are valid and which intents should be blocked (such as "Say something bad about this famous person") is key to creating a good chatbot experience.

As part of the dialogue flow design, we will also identify which agents and tools we want to use to respond to questions. We may have intents that require a more friendly, conversational, and creative response. For example, the user may ask us to tell a joke or tell them about the weather. Depending on the nature of our chatbot, its branding, and the desired tone of voice, we may choose to respond differently. What's important is that we have these so-called "fallback intents" in place to ensure users cannot trick us or derail our conversation.

This is also a good time to talk about security. While the focus of this book is not on agent security (an entire book could be written about this), it's important to harden the prompt to ensure that users cannot "trick" the LLM into divulging confidential information, such as its system prompt or tool messages. If you are interested in this topic, Litmus is a good starting point for testing and hardening prompts [2].

Entity extraction

Once the conversation has been designed, we will also know which information our agent needs to help users fulfill their intents. For example, for our banking customers interested in a consumer loan, we may need to know their customer ID to inform them about loans they are eligible for. Requesting this information and then extracting it from user messages is called "entity extraction." Entity extraction is not trivial. Users may respond in many ways, and our agent needs to be able to make sense of their responses and ensure that it has everything it needs to give a good response. The agent also needs to be able to store user information in its session state and must be instructed to collect all necessary information.

There are two ways to store entity information in your agent. First, you can leverage the session state of the conversation, extract entities from conversations, and store them explicitly in a database or the filesystem of the instance running your agent. The advantage of this is that you have clearly defined each entity and its value, and can easily leverage them for running an API call to retrieve additional information from backend systems, for example. The other way is to store entities in an unstructured form in the memory of your session. This way is much easier to implement, as you can leverage LangChain's native memory capability. Unfortunately, this approach is more prone to hallucinations if you have multiple similar entities in agent memory.

In the section on detecting intents and routing messages in this chapter, you will see simple examples of an agent that extracts multiple entities from user conversation.

Conversational design workflow

The conversational design workflow has five steps: data collection and analysis, conversation design, prompt and response crafting, testing and iteration, and continuous improvement. *Figure 8.1* shows the detailed conversation engineering workflow.

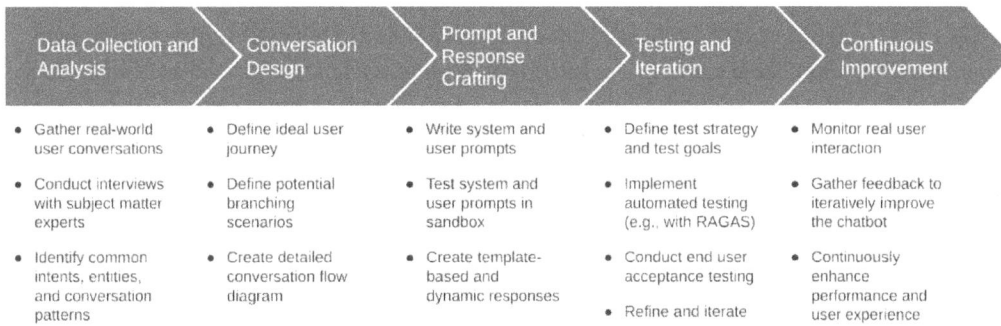

Figure 8.1 - Conversation engineering workflow

Let us look at the benefits of conversational design. We will see an increased task success rate, as we effectively guide users toward their goals and completing tasks. This is coupled with improved user experience by creating natural and engaging conversations that meet user expectations. We also significantly lower development effort, as we can significantly reduce the number of iterations and feedback loops by starting with a clear definition of what good looks like.

You can see that by investing time and effort in conversation engineering, you can create chatbots that not only fulfill their intended purpose but also deliver exceptional user experiences.

Building chatbots with LangChain

Now that you have created a clear concept for your conversation, it is time to implement it. LangChain offers a powerful framework for building chatbots using LangGraph for modeling the conversation flow. By providing pre-built components and abstractions that address diverse aspects of chatbot creation, LangChain empowers developers to focus on the unique components of their application while leaving the heavy lifting of managing models and integrating different components to the framework.

Building a basic chatbot with LangChain messages

Building a basic chatbot requires three things: human messages, AI messages, and a memory of the history, which allows the chatbot to respond to what has been said before. Deceptively simple, right?

Adding memory to a chatbot comes with a lot of challenges. First, storing and persisting memory across multiple invocations of LLMs requires knowledge of application engineering and application memory. With serverless architectures such as AWS Lambda and Google Cloud Run, handling session states and ensuring that users have persistent access to the memory of their session usually requires leveraging external data stores. At the same time, host-based implementations, where multiple users may share the same machine, bring the risk of users accessing sessions of other users and potentially extracting confidential information.

Complexities do not stop there. For a long time, LLMs were limited by the size of their context window and, even today, large contexts can incur high costs and latency for each LLM invocation. If we include the full memory of the conversation in each subsequent invocation, LLMs quickly become expensive, less performant, and may even stop functioning entirely if the context becomes too large. Consequently, reducing the size of the conversation memory, for example, by compressing the conversation using map-reduce approaches (see the previous chapter on working with long context) is a common component of most chatbot implementations.

Let's start with the basics first and have a full conversation using human and AI messages:

```
from langchain_google_vertexai import ChatVertexAI
model = ChatVertexAI(model="gemini-1.5-flash-001")
```

We can start chatting with the LLM after instantiating the model by sending a `HumanMessage` using the `model.invoke` function. However, we will not be able to have a conversation with this model, since our chatbot does not have memory. You can try it out yourself:

```
from langchain_core.messages import HumanMessage
model.invoke([HumanMessage(content="Hello, my name is Max!")])
>> "Hello Max, how can I help you?"
model.invoke([HumanMessage(content="What is my name?")])
>> "I am sorry, I do not know your name."
```

You can work around this by manually passing the chat history to the chatbot using an array of `HumanMessage` and `AIMessage`. See the following code block for a simple example:

```
from langchain_core.messages import HumanMessage, AIMessage

model.invoke([
    HumanMessage(content="Hello, my name is Max!"),
    AIMessage(content="Hello Max, it's a pleasure to meet you. How can
I assist you today?"),
    HumanMessage("What is my name?")
    ])
```

What do you think will happen if you run this code? If you guessed something along the lines of `"Your name is Max, is there anything else I can help you with?"`, you would be right. Theoretically, you could already implement a chatbot by implementing the full conversation flow in an array and passing the entire conversation every time you run the bot. Unfortunately, as discussed before, this would be inefficient and computationally expensive.

There's a very important point to mention. LLMs don't store any conversation's history on their side. If you use any client SDK (a **software development kit** or **SDK** is a library that helps to use a specific API with a given programming language instead of calling `http` or `grpc`), the client's SDK is just storing a history in memory on the client side. And when the LLM is preparing an answer, It just gets an input such as the following:

```
Human: Hello, my name is Max!

  AI: Hello Max, it's a pleasure to meet you. How can I assist you
  today?

Human: What is my name

  AI:
```

It then continues this input. The reality is a little bit more complex (it might be wrapped with a system message and other instructions), but that's what is happening on the LLM side. Typically, all modern LLMs are chat-tuned, too (i.e., they're fine-tuned on large amounts of such dialogues, and hence, they can continue the conversation nicely). The good thing is that you typically don't need to care about all these details as they are handled by the LLM provider (but you might need to handle chat-tuning yourself if you are using an open source LLM such as Gemma-2B).

Adding memory to your chatbot

If the history is stored in some form of local memory (e.g., a Python array), this makes your application stateful (and it's an anti-pattern for web applications since you can't scale horizontally), and users can continue the conversation if the local client instance has been deleted. Recognizing these limitations, LangChain introduced the concept of memory to their framework. In LangChain, memory plays a crucial role in maintaining context and continuity in chatbot interactions. It functions as a stateful component within chains, enabling them to retain information from past executions and incorporate that context into future interactions. The best part? You do not have to worry about handling format, summarization, and similar challenges. However, you still need to decide where you want to store your memory. You can either store it in the compute resource that runs your application, you can use a dedicated application store such as Google Cloud Firestore, or you can use any MySQL or PostgreSQL database.

We begin by connecting to our MySQL instance and instantiating a `MySQLChatMessageHistory` object using LangChain:

```
from langchain_google_cloud_sql_mysql import MySQLEngine
from langchain_google_cloud_sql_mysql import MySQLChatMessageHistory
engine = MySQLEngine.from_instance(
    project_id="my-project-id",
    region="my-region",
    instance="my-instance",
```

```
    database="my-database"
)

# Creates the structure of the history table in the database
engine.init_chat_history_table(table_name="my-table-name")
session_id = "1"
history = MySQLChatMessageHistory(
    engine,
    session_id=session_id,
    table_name="my-table-name"
)
history.add_user_message("Hi Gemini!")
history.add_ai_message("Hi user! How can I help you?")
```

Interacting with the MySQLChatMessageHistory object is straightforward. You can use add_
user_message and add_ai_message, as in the preceding simple example. Using an external
message history brings many advantages. By setting session_id, such as the session_id = "1"
variable in the preceding example, you can cleanly separate user conversations, log user conversations,
and enable users to resume their conversations. The MySQLChatMessageHistory object will
only return the history connected to the UUID.

If you do not want to manage your own MySQL database, we have also prepared managed offerings
using Google Cloud AlloyDB [3] or Google Cloud Firestore [4]. They follow the same structure as
MySQL memory but free you from managing the underlying resources.

Handling memory using Runnables

In the preceding example, we handled memory by manually adding messages to our history table.
Luckily, LangChain introduced the concept of RunnableWithMessageHistory to abstract the
task of handling chat memory [5], enabling you to develop applications quicker and without having
to worry about manually adding messages to the message history object:

```
from langchain_core.runnables.history import (
    RunnableWithMessageHistory (
from langchain_core.prompts import (
    ChatPromptTemplate, MessagesPlaceholder )
from langchain_google_vertexai import ChatVertexAI
from langchain_google_cloud_sql_mysql import MySQLEngine
from langchain_google_cloud_sql_mysql import MySQLChatMessageHistory

engine = MySQLEngine.from_instance(
    project_id="my-project-id",
    region="my-region",
```

```
    instance="my-instance",
    database="my-database"
)

system_prompt = ChatPromptTemplate.from_messages(
    [
        (
        "system",
            """You are the dread pirate captain Sally Bloodhair.
            You talk like a pirate.
            You tell users stories about your pirate adventures.
            """
        ),
        ("placeholder", "{history}"),
        ("human", "{input}"),
    ]
)
model = ChatVertexAI(model="gemini-1.5-pro-001")
chain = system_prompt | model

history_chain = RunnableWithMessageHistory(
        chain,
        lambda session_id: MySQLChatMessageHistory(
            engine,
            session_id=session_id,
            table_name="my-table-name"
        ),
        input_messages_key="input",
        history_messages_key="history",
        output_messages_key="answer",
    )

history_chain.invoke("Tell me about your adventures, Sally!".
    config={"configurable": {"session_id": "1"}}
)
```

Using RunnableWithMessageHistory is straightforward. After you have defined your chain in LCEL, you equip the runnable with a lambda function to retrieve the history for the session_id passed in the invocation. The runnable will handle the retrieval of messages for you and automatically attach new messages to the message history. Just remember to include the session_id when you invoke the chain to make sure you retrieve messages from the right session.

You can replace the definition of the `lambda` function with all compatible LangChain memory stores (for example, AlloyDB), which is a much more scalable database implementation in the Google Cloud platform:

```
from langchain_google_alloydb_pg import AlloyDBChatMessageHistory

#[...]

history_chain = RunnableWithMessageHistory(
        chain,
        lambda session_id: AlloyDBChatMessageHistory.create_sync(
            chat_memory.engine,
            session_id=session_id,
            table_name="my-table-name",
        ),
        input_messages_key="input",
        history_messages_key="history",
        output_messages_key="answer",
    )
```

You can use `RunnableWithMessageHistory` for other purposes, too. Sometimes your conversation might become too long. With modern models with long context windows, this is not a big deal, but if you are using smaller models on the edge, it might become a problem since the input length is limited. Long history might also confuse the model and degrade answer quality, especially if the user has been asking completely unrelated questions.

You see, handling memory for your chatbot is simple and straightforward with LangChain runnables. In the next section, we will look at an even easier way to handle memory – the inbuilt memory state of LangGraph!

Automatically handling memory with LangGraph

LangGraph offers a new solution to implement memory in your bot. Unfortunately, that means that we will need to learn LangGraph first – but don't worry, it's as easy as everything else in LangChain! Let's delve into a practical example of building a simple chatbot using LangChain and LangGraph. LangGraph is a library that is part of the LangChain ecosystem and facilitates designing and implementing stateful multi-actor applications. LangGraph allows you to define and execute a flow of actions and conditions. Imagine it as a flowchart for AI: it will guide your AI system through various stages, keeping track of its current state, and initiating the next steps based on events. For example, if you build a chatbot that answers user questions on the loan products of your bank, you will want to start with a friendly introduction and a question. If a user enters a question on a loan product, you will want to give a response, and you will want to give responses until the user either doesn't have questions anymore or is ready to make a purchasing decision. At the point of the purchasing decision, you hand the user off to a human agent.

LangGraph simplifies the visual design and orchestration of this conversation flow. You create a graph of nodes (representing actions or states) and edges (defining transitions between nodes) using an intuitive and expressive programming language.

Let's get started!

First, we begin with defining the state of our chatbot. As you can guess, the state of a chatbot is defined by the messages that go into it, so it's a `TypedDict` of messages. We then create a `StateMachine`. The `StateMachine` is the class that will host our chatbot and its various states, as defined in our conversation engineering process. Within the `StateMachine`, we begin with defining the memory by setting `self.memory = SqliteSaver.from_conn_string(":memory:")`. This adds memory to our chatbot instance using a connection string to a `SqliteSaver` instance that runs on our local machine. If you use `SqliteSaver` on your local machine, you also need to specify a `thread_id` using `self.thread={"configurable": {"thread_id": "2"}}`. You should, of course, specify a dynamic value for your thread to ensure that user conversations do not cross, for example, by passing a session ID or UUID to the conversation. As you learned before, there are many other ways in which we can store memory, for example, by connecting to a remote database. LangGraph calls this memory a checkpoint. Check the LangGraph documentation for more details [6].

Now it's time to define your chatbot. First, we need to define a `system_prompt` that instructs the chatbot to act in a certain way. Note that the `system_prompt` also expects a placeholder of messages (the previous conversation) and a new human message called `{input}`, which will prompt it to give a response. We then bind this `system_prompt` into our model using the `system_prompt | model` function. Next, we can define any number of functions that will make up our graph. For example, we may want to insert tool calling, function calling, and various system prompts into these functions depending on the user intent. In this very simple example, we only have a function called `chatbot`, which simply invokes the chatbot model on the messages in the previous conversation.

Finally, it's time to build our graph. We do this by creating a `StateGraph(State)` and adding nodes to this `StateGraph` using the `add_node()` function. In this example, we just have one node, our chatbot. Finally, we use the `set_entry_point()` and `set_finish_point()` functions to define the entry and finish points of our chatbot – easy as that! There are many other nodes and conditions that you could add to your `StateGraph`. Check the LangGraph documentation [6] for all options and many tutorials and examples. Note how we set the check pointer to our previously created memory!

This concludes the initiation of our `StateMachine`. Of course, we also want to ensure that we get responses in a format that fits our needs. For this, we define a `respond(self,USER_MESSAGE:str)` function that returns the `AIMessage` for any given user input.

Now all we need to do is initialize our `StateMachine`. Note that with the `chatbot.chain.get_graph().print_ascii()`, we can create a nifty graphical representation of our graph to see whether we configured it correctly. Check it out in the following code! All we do is open a command line where users can send any number of inputs to our chatbot:

```python
# Import necessary langgraph classes to define the chatbot and handle
memory for you
from langchain_core.prompts import ChatPromptTemplate
from langchain_google_vertexai import ChatVertexAI
from langgraph.checkpoint.memory import MemorySaver
from langgraph.checkpoint.sqlite import SqliteSaver
from langgraph.checkpoint.sqlite.aio import AsyncSqliteSaver
from langgraph.graph import StateGraph
from langgraph.graph.message import add_messages

from typing import Annotated
from typing_extensions import TypedDict

# Create the agent
class State(TypedDict):
    # Update add_messages to append messages, not overwrite
    messages: Annotated[list, add_messages]

class StateMachine:
    def __init__(self, memory):
        model = ChatVertexAI(model="gemini-1.5-pro")

        # Define a system prompt that defines how the agent should
interact with users
        system_prompt = ChatPromptTemplate.from_messages(
            [
                (
                    "system",
                    """You are an expert advisor in a bank. Your name
is Terry.
                    You advise users on the three loan products of the
bank:
                    1/ Short term loan, 6 month duration, 5% interest
rate, up to USD 10000. Great for making quick payments.
                    2/ Mid-term loan, 24 month duration, 3% interest
rate, up to USD 20000. Great for buying used cars.
                    3/ Long-term loan, 60 month duration, 2% interest
rate, up to USD 50000. Great for buying a new car or a cheap house.
                    Only respond to user questions on these loans.
                    """
```

```
                ),
                ("placeholder", "{messages}"),
                ("human", "{input}"),
            ]
        )

        # Bind the system_prompt to the model
        sally = system_prompt | model

    def chatbot(state: State):
        return {"messages": [sally.invoke(state["messages"])]}

# Create the state graph
graph_builder = StateGraph(State)
graph_builder.add_node("chatbot", chatbot)

# Set a finish point. This instructs the graph "any time this node is
run, you can exit."
graph_builder.set_finish_point("chatbot")
graph_builder.set_entry_point("chatbot")

# If you use memory, you need to provide a thread id to the chatbot
self.thread = {"configurable": {"thread_id": "2"}}
self.chain = graph_builder.compile(checkpointer=memory)

def respond(self, USER_MESSAGE: str):
    result = self.chain.invoke({"messages": ("user", USER_MESSAGE)},
    self.thread)

    # Need to cut off the first 80 characters, which say "AI Message"
    return result["messages"][-1].pretty_repr()[80:]

# Create memory for the bot
with SqliteSaver.from_conn_string(":memory:") as memory:
    # Initiate the memory
    chatbot = StateMachine(memory)

    # Draw the graph
    chatbot.chain.get_graph().print_ascii()

print("Agent will keep going until you say 'STOP'")
```

```
question = ""
while "STOP" not in question:
    question = input("User: ")
    answer = chatbot.respond(question)
    print("Bot: " + answer)

>> Grandalph output
+-----------+
| __start__ |
+-----------+



+---------+
| chatbot |
+---------+



+---------+
| __end__ |
+---------+
```

While these might be a few lines of code, this is also a scalable scaffold that enables you to add any number of nodes and tools to your chatbot. Want to give Terry access to a document containing hundreds of banking products? Give her a tool node that is connected to a knowledge base.

Optimizing your RAG for memory

Implementing **retrieval-augmented generation (RAG)** with memory can be challenging. While your underlying chatbot will be able to respond based on its message history, your retriever will usually only retrieve information for the latest user input. The naive way to handle this challenge is to include the chat history in the search string. While this is easy to implement, it may not lead to good results. Most retrievers operate based on semantic similarity, and matching to a long collection of messages may not retrieve the most relevant information.

The best solution is to leverage an LLM to create a matching search string that takes your history into account. Since you might be rewriting your search string from the user question anyway to increase RAG results, this should not affect the responsiveness of your application:

```
from langchain_core.prompts import (
    ChatPromptTemplate, MessagesPlaceholder )
```

```
# Define the System Instruction to condense the user prompt
condense_prompt = (
    """
    System Instruction:
    You are an assistant to another agent. Your task is to condense
    the user's follow-up question into a standalone question using the
    Chat History.
    The standalone question must be in the same language as the
    conversation.
    If the chat history is empty, ONLY REPEAT the follow-up question.
    ```

    CHAT HISTORY:
    ```

    {chat_history}
    ```

    FOLLOW-UP QUESTION:
    ```

    {input}
    ```

    CONDENSED PROMPT:
    """
)

# Create a ChatPromptTemplate; we will pass through history and input
condense_question = ChatPromptTemplate.from_messages(
    [
        ("system", prompt.condense_prompt),
        MessagesPlaceholder(variable_name="chat_history"),
        ("human", "{input}"),
    ]
)

# Include the prompt in our history-aware retriever
history_aware_retriever = create_history_aware_retriever(
    llm, retriever, condense_question
)
```

LangChain has a special retriever call called `history_aware_retriever` to handle this issue. You create a history-aware retriever using the `create_history_aware_retriever` function with an LLM and a retriever of your choice. Make sure that you define a prompt with a system instruction for summarizing the history in line with your goals. We have given a sample function in the preceding code. You should modify it to match the specific requirements of your use case. For example, if your chatbot needs to reply to specific information such as medical conditions, you should instruct it to focus on listing the relevant conditions in the summary.
```

Caching memory in context

For applications that require a large context, potentially encompassing thousands of tokens including images and media files, the Gemini family of models offers a caching mechanism. This approach reduces response latency and the associated costs [5].

Leveraging the LangChain integration, you can create a context cache with the following code snippet:

```
from langchain_core.messages import SystemMessage, HumanMessage
from langchain_google_vertexai import (
    create_context_cache, ChatVertexAI )

model_name = "gemini-1.5-pro-001"

system_instruction = """
    - You are a machine learning researcher.
    - You always answer in accordance with the documents provided.
    - You never make up new facts.
    Now have a look at these research papers, and answer the following
questions.
    """

cached_content = create_context_cache(
    ChatVertexAI(model_name=model_name),
    messages=[
        SystemMessage(content=system_instruction),
        HumanMessage(content=[
            {"type": "image_url",
                "image_url": {"url": "gs://cloud-samples-data/…"}},
            {"type": "image_url",
                "image_url": {"url": "gs://cloud-samples-data/…"}},
        ]),
    ],
)
```

In this example, we create a cache that includes a system prompt instructing the model on its role and behavior and the content of two large PDF documents (represented here by placeholder image URLs).

The cache is identified by a unique ID, which we can then use to create a new model instance that is pre-loaded with this context on the API side so you don't need to send the context again, only the incremental content such as follow-up questions. While it looks deceptively simple, the `create_context_cache` function triggers a lot of magic in the API to ensure the LLM makes optimal use of your context [7].

This new model instance can be used just like a regular model:

```
chat = ChatVertexAI(model_name=model_name,
    cached_content=cached_content)
model.invoke(HumanMessage(content="Whats the title of the first
paper?"))
```

If you are using LangGraph for orchestration, you could simply pass this model to your `StateMachine` to ensure that LangGraph benefits from the cached context.

Detecting intents and routing messages

Your chatbot now has memory, and it's able to retrieve information that matches its memory. What else do you need? Well, you might want to route messages based on the intent of the user. In LangChain, there are two ways for routing messages: a custom routing function and routing based on semantic similarity. While setting up a custom routing function is easy and quick, semantic routing requires using an additional embedding function to achieve better routing results. Let us show you how to do it!

Custom routing functions

First, we need to define the intentions of our users. Let's start with a simple example. Our bank offers loans, credit cards, and other stuff. Depending on what customers want to buy, they need to be routed to a different sales agent. Let's see how we build this with a routing function:

```
from langchain_core.prompts import PromptTemplate
from langchain_google_vertexai import ChatVertexAI
from langchain_core.runnables import RunnableLambda

llm = ChatVertexAI(model="gemini-pro")

classifier = (
    PromptTemplate.from_template("""Given the user input below,
        identify if they want to buy 'loan', 'credit card', or 'other'
items.
        Do not respond with more than one word.
        INPUT:
        {prompt}
        CLASSIFICATION:"""
    )
    | llm
)
```

```
def router(prompt):
    loan_chain = PromptTemplate.from_template("You sell loan
products...") |    llm
    credit_chain = PromptTemplate.from_template("You sell credit
cards...") | llm
    fallback = PromptTemplate.from_template("You sell banking
products...") | llm

    if "loan" in prompt["topic"].lower():
        return loan_chain
    elif "credit card" in prompt["topic"].lower():
        return credit_chain
    else:
        return fallback

routing_chain = {"topic": classifier, "prompt": lambda x: x["prompt"]}
| RunnableLambda(router)

routing_chain.invoke = ({"prompt": "I would like to learn about a loan
for my new car."})
```

Routing functions are pretty straightforward. We first define an LLM-based classifier to identify the topic of a message based on a prompt. In the preceding example, this function is called `classifier`. We then create a routing function, which, based on the topic passed to it, will select the appropriate prompt and return it to the model. To execute this function, we create a `RunnableLambda` object in our routing chain. When we invoke the chain, it will first run our input through the classifier and then invoke the chain that matches the output of the classifier. Make sure to include a fallback chain in case your classifier cannot match it to any of the scenarios. While this approach is simple to implement, it requires an additional (costly) LLM call that will increase the latency of your application.

Semantic routing

A different approach is semantic routing. While it is not as straightforward as routing functions, this approach uses cheaper embedding models to identify the intent of user input based on its semantic similarity to different prompts. To determine semantic similarity, we can use the LangChain `cosine_similarity` function:

```
from langchain.utils.math import cosine_similarity
from langchain_core.prompts import PromptTemplate
from langchain_core.runnables import RunnableLambda,
RunnablePassthrough
from langchain_google_vertexai import VertexAIEmbeddings
from langchain_google_vertexai import ChatVertexAI
```

```
llm = ChatVertexAI(model="gemini-pro")
loan_seller = """You sell loans. \
    You advise customers on which loans are right for them \
    Here is the customer input:
    {input}"""

credit_seller = """You sell credit cards. \
    You advise customers on which credit cards to subscribe\
    Here is the customer input:
    {input}"""

embeddings = VertexAIEmbeddings()
prompt_templates = [loan_seller, credit_seller]
prompts = embeddings.embed_documents(prompt_templates)

def router(prompt):
    query = embeddings.embed_query(prompt["query"])
    similarity = cosine_similarity([query], prompts)[0]
    most_similar = prompts[similarity.argmax()]
    return PromptTemplate.from_template(most_similar)

routing_chain = (
    {"query": RunnablePassthrough()}
    | RunnableLambda(router)
    | llm
)

routing_chain.invoke = ({"prompt": "I would like to learn about loans
for buying a car."})
```

That's it! So what did we do here? First, we defined our prompt strings. We then created `VertexAIEmbeddings()` for the prompt strings. Next, we defined the routing function, which created embeddings of the input string, before performing a `cosine_similarity` match between the query and the embedded prompts. We then selected the prompt with the highest similarity. What's great is that this is not limited to a choice of two prompts. You can add as many prompts as you want to the function. Since you need to only embed each prompt once, this is an efficient way to perform routing. In `routing_chain`, you will recognize the familiar `RunnableLambda` object. The same limitations that apply to cosine similarity apply to routing in this use case. It's a quick and efficient way to match text, but it's not always the most reliable. So, make sure that you use clear words in each prompt, and that the prompts have low cosine similarity between each other.

Summary

This chapter provided a comprehensive guide to building chatbots using LangChain. It covered fundamental concepts such as conversation engineering, intent identification, dialogue flow design, and entity extraction. You learned about the importance of understanding user intents and designing effective dialogue flows to create natural and engaging chatbot interactions. We also provided practical examples for building chatbots with memory, routing messages based on user intent, and integrating RAG for context-aware responses. After reading this chapter, you should now have the knowledge and tools to build effective and user-friendly chatbots using LangChain.

References

1. Connect to Cloud SQL for MySQL from Cloud Shell, Google Cloud documentation:

    `https://cloud.google.com/sql/docs/mysql/connect-instance-cloud-shell`

2. Litmus: A comprehensive LLM testing and evaluation tool designed for GenAI Application Development. Google GitHub:

    `https://github.com/google/litmus`

3. Use Pgvector on AlloyDB with LangChain, Google Cloud GitHub:

    `https://github.com/googleapis/langchain-google-alloydb-pg-python?tab=readme-ov-file#chat-message-history-usage`

4. Use Firestore Chat Message History with LangChain, LangChain documentation:

    `https://v02.api.js.langchain.com/classes/langchain_community_stores_message_firestore.FirestoreChatMessageHistory.html`

5. Runnable With Message History, LangChain documentation:

    `https://api.python.langchain.com/en/latest/runnables/langchain_core.runnables.history.RunnableWithMessageHistory.html`

6. Using memory in LangGraph, LangChain documentation:

    `https://langchain-ai.github.io/langgraph/reference/checkpoints/`

7. Context caching in Google Cloud, Google Cloud documentation:

    `https://cloud.google.com/vertex-ai/generative-ai/docs/context-cache/context-cache-create`

9

Tools and Function Calling

As we discussed in *Chapter 1*, **large language models** (**LLMs**) have demonstrated outstanding reasoning abilities. Nevertheless, there's not enough evidence that scaling models alone will be sufficient to "*achieve high performance on challenging tasks such as arithmetic, commonsense, and symbolic reasoning*" [1].

In this chapter, we will discuss some modifications in the ways we interact with LLMs that demonstrate a large improvement in such complex tasks.

We'll start with discussing advanced prompt techniques, such as **chain-of-thought** (**CoT**), before covering what tools and functions are in the context of LLMs. We'll investigate examples of giving a model information about recent events and the outside world by giving it access to Google Search and improving its mathematical capabilities with a calculator. Finally, we'll discuss different ways of defining your custom tools on LangChain and briefly discuss the ReACT pattern since it's the foundation of agentic workflows, which we're going to discuss in the next chapter.

In this chapter, we will cover the following topics:

- Examples of advanced prompting techniques (such as CoT)
- Using function calling (tool calling) with LangChain
- Wrapping APIs as tools and using Google Search for LLM grounding

Technical requirements

You need to enable Vertex AI Search API on your Google Cloud project and install the following libraries:

```
pip install langchain-google-vertexai langchain-google-
community[search] langgraph
```

To use Google Search with the LLM, you also need to create your own programmable search engine here: `https://programmablesearchengine.google.com/about/`. Follow the instructions on the LangChain documentation page: `https://python.langchain.com/v0.2/docs/integrations/tools/google_search/`.

Advanced prompt design

As your generative AI applications become more complex, vanilla zero-shot or few-shot prompting might not be enough. The next few chapters will look at the various aspects of developing more complex solutions that allow us to enhance LLMs and use their reasoning capabilities to solve complex tasks.

First, we will start with a few prompt design techniques. There is still a lot of confusion between prompt engineering and prompt design in the industry, and the distinction is not always clear. However, you can think about prompt engineering as a way to formulate more efficient prompts (or, in other words, to describe your specific task in natural language), and prompt design as a way to create prompt templates that improve the performance of a wide variety of tasks (each of them would still need a specifically engineered prompt). We will look into a few prompt design techniques in this chapter.

Let's start with a simple math problem:

```
math_problem1 = (
    "John had 1097 candies. They ate 14 yesterday, bought 18 today and
shared 341 more with "
    "their classmates. How many candies to they have left? "
    "Give a short answer (a single number only)"
)
```

Let's see how well a LLM performs:

```
from langchain_google_vertexai import ChatVertexAI
from langchain_core.messages import SystemMessage, HumanMessage

llm = ChatVertexAI(
    model_name="gemini-1.5-pro-001",
    temperature=0.)
result = llm.invoke([
    SystemMessage(
        content="Give a short answer (a single number only)."),
    HumanMessage(content=math_problem1)])
print(result.content)
>> 704
```

As you can imagine, the correct answer was 1097-14-18-341=724. By the way, I added such a strange number on purpose – to compose a math equation that LLM didn't exactly observe during the training process. How can we improve the LLM's reasoning? First, we can try a technique called **sampling** – we increase the temperature (to make LLM less deterministic) and sample from many attempts (with an assumption that the right answer has a higher probability, hence we can get it with a higher probability). After that, we'll look at the distribution of answers and pick the most probable one:

```
from collections import Counter

answers = Counter()
llm_high_temperature = ChatVertexAI(
    model_name="gemini-1.5-pro-001",
    temperature=0.7)

for _ in range(20):
answer = llm_high_temperature.invoke([
    SystemMessage(
        content="Give a short answer (a single number only)."),
    HumanMessage(content=math_problem1)
]).content
answers[answer] += 1

print(answers)
>> Counter({'704 \n': 18, '724 \n': 2})
```

We're close but not quite there. Maybe the issue is that we retrieve the answer immediately, and ask the model to shorten it.

Naive controlled generation

So, let's remove our initial system message:

```
print(llm.invoke([
    HumanMessage(content=math_problem1)
]).content)


>> Here's how to solve the problem step-by-step: * **Step 1: Find
the total eaten.** 14 candies (yesterday) + 18 candies (today) = 32
candies * **Step 2: Find the total given away.** John gave away 341
candies. * **Step 3: Find the total gone.** 32 candies (eaten) + 341
candies (given away) = 373 candies * **Step 4: Subtract to find the
remaining amount.** 1097 candies (start) - 373 candies (gone) = 724
candies **Answer:** John has 724 candies left.
```

What happened? You can see some reasoning traces in the LLM output, and the quality of the answer has improved. But what if you need an answer only? (That's what we wanted to achieve in our previous version of the prompt.) Let's add another step and try to parse the output with a regular expression. Our answer can appear in any text form, so let's adjust the system message a little bit:

```
from langchain.output_parsers.regex import RegexParser

result = llm.invoke([
    SystemMessage(
        content="Always give a final answer in a form
FINAL_ANSWER=..."),
        HumanMessage(content=math_problem1)
]).content
print(result)
>> Here's how to solve the problem: * **Total eaten:** 14 + 18 = 32
candies * **Total given away:** 341 candies * **Total gone:** 32 +
341 = 373 candies * **Candies left:** 1097 - 373 = 724 candies FINAL_
ANSWER=724
```

Now, let's parse the output. We will use a specific implementation of a LangChain parser – it parses output based on a provided regular expression:

```
parser = RegexParser(
    regex="FINAL_ANSWER=(\d+)",
    output_keys=["answer"])
print(parser.invoke(result))
```

What's the problem with our code? We always need to prepend specific system messages, hence it's difficult to run the prompt. That's where ChatPromptTemplate can help:

```
from langchain_core.prompts import (
    ChatPromptTemplate, PromptTemplate, MessagesPlaceholder )

prompt = ChatPromptTemplate(
    [("system",
        "Always give a final answer in a form FINAL_ANSWER=..."),
    ("human", "{user_input}")]
)
chain = prompt | llm | parser
chain.invoke(math_problem1)
>> {'answer': '724'}
```

What happened here? We created a template that prepares input for a chat model, and since it has a single input variable (user_input), it will automatically convert any input string to a HumanMessage with corresponding content inside:

```
assert prompt.invoke({"user_input": "test"}) == prompt.invoke("test")
```

You can read more about this in the LangChain documentation: `https://api.python.langchain.com/en/latest/prompts/langchain_core.prompts.chat.ChatPromptTemplate.html`

It's a very naive example of a controlled generation, and you can improve it (e.g., by using `RetryWithErrorOutputParser` on top of it). It's a parser that will try to parse your output, and if it fails, it'll retry the request to the LLM by appending the parsing error to the end (and asking the LLM to consider parsing errors with a specific prompt). (We'll discuss it in more detail later in this chapter.) You can learn more about the parser in the following documentation: `https://api.python.langchain.com/en/latest/output_parsers/langchain.output_parsers.retry.RetryWithErrorOutputParser.html`

This is a way of forcing an LLM to generate an answer following a certain pattern (ask to follow a template or generate valid JSON or an even more complex object). Now, let's get back to the reasoning traces we observed in the output.

Chain-of-Thought (CoT)

As we saw in the previous section, once the LLM started generating longer output, it was able to get the answer right. This is the key idea behind the simple prompting technique called CoT, which was suggested by researchers from Google Research in 2022 [1]. More complex prompting techniques have been developed since, but we're not going to discuss them in this book. However, we'd like to demonstrate the idea of using such advanced prompting techniques with CoT.

A funny note is that when we started writing this book, many LLMs couldn't solve the simple math problem defined earlier. These days, more and more of them perform better (from our point of view, mainly because training datasets have been improved, or, in other words, many models have been fine-tuned to follow CoT without being prompted for it), and it makes it more difficult to demonstrate core principles such as CoT. However, it's important to mention that these principles remain the same, and the moment you face a complex reasoning problem that wasn't presented in the training data, you might find all of them useful.

The idea is relatively simple – we just ask the LLM to think step by step and explain its reasoning. Then, it changes the generation and the output. Let's look at the example system message that will call for CoT (but there are multiple modifications possible):

```
cot_prompt = (
    "Always think step-by-step. Explain your reasoning."
    " Split a problem into sequence of reasoning steps and try to
solve it."
    " Always give a final answer in a form FINAL_ANSWER=..."
)
```

Now, let's test it:

```
print(llm.invoke([
    SystemMessage(content=cot_prompt),
    HumanMessage(content=math_problem1)
]).content)
>> **1. Calculate the total number of candies eaten:** * Yesterday: 14
candies * Today: 18 candies * Total eaten: 14 + 18 = 32 candies **2.
Calculate the total number of candies given away or eaten:** * Eaten:
32 candies * Shared: 341 candies * Total given away: 32 + 341 = 373
candies **3. Subtract the total given away from the initial amount:**
* Initial amount: 1097 candies * Total given away: 373 candies *
Remaining candies: 1097 - 373 = 724 candies **FINAL_ANSWER=724**
```

You might ask yourself this: CoT is a zero-shot approach, but how can we combine it with a few-shot learning? The issue might be that when you use CoT, answers are relatively long, hence examples would consume much more space in the input. So, you'll need to reduce the number of input examples, and you can keep your examples in a separate database, use embeddings to find the closest ones to your input, and use a `FewShotPromptTemplate` [2] interface on LangChain to pick examples according to the user input [3].

Now, as we've seen how to control a generation to be easily parsed and how to improve an LLM's output to improve its performance on complex tasks, let's go a step further. What else can we do to improve LLMs' capabilities on reasoning tasks even more?

Enhancing LLMs' capabilities with tools

What is a tool? Let's continue asking an LLM to solve a mathematical problem. An obvious way to improve the quality is to collect some examples and add them into training (or a fine-tuning dataset). But are there any easier ways? Now, let's ask it a different question:

```
math_problem2 = "How much is 23*2**2+156/4-18?"
```

As we've mentioned earlier, these days, even smaller LLMs (such as Gemma 2 2B or Llama 3.1 8B) do a surprisingly amazing job on such mathematical examples. But still, for the sake of an argument, let's discuss what else we can do besides improving our datasets.

What if instead of teaching LLMs how to solve mathematical problems, we give them access to a calculator that was designed exactly to solve such problems? This logic can be applied to any specific instruments (we will call them tools) that are developed for certain tasks (such as creating weather forecasts, using CRM systems, or scheduling calendar invites).

Let's take a look at the following prompt:

```
calculator_prompt = (
    "You have access to calculator that can solve mathematical
problems. "
```

```
    "If you want to ask a calculator, start with CALCULATOR: and
generate an experssion "
    "to be evaluated by a calculator (it should have only numbers and
mathematical operators)."
    "If you ask CALCULATOR, don't do anything else."
    "If you think you have a final solution, start it with FINAL_
ANSWER=.\n"
)

calculator_prompt_template = ChatPromptTemplate(
    [("system", calculator_prompt),
        MessagesPlaceholder(variable_name="messages")]
)
```

First, what is `MessagesPlaceholder`? It's a special instruction to accept a list of messages and add them to the chat input (in other words, we're just creating a chat template that will prepend a system message to any chat history we get as input). Let's call it:

```
step1 = (calculator_prompt_template | llm).invoke(
    [HumanMessage(content=math_problem2)])
print(step1.content)
>> CALCULATOR: 23*2**2+156/4-18
```

Now, let's evaluate this output (**note**: please don't do this in a production application; evaluating any randomly generated expressions might be dangerous):

```
step2 = eval(
    step1.content.replace("CALCULATOR", "").strip(" \n:"))
print(step2)
>> 113
```

Now, let's finalize our answer by actually telling the LLM the result of an evaluation:

```
from langchain_core.messages import AIMessage

print((calculator_prompt_template | llm).invoke(
    [HumanMessage(content=math_problem2),
        step1,
        HumanMessage(content=str(step2))]
).content)
>> FINAL_ANSWER=113
```

To recap, what have we just done? We actually used an LLM only to generate an expression (input) to be evaluated by a calculator. This pattern is called **tool calling**. We tell the LLM about external APIs it can use and instruct it on how to generate input to these APIs.

We augmented the LLM with an external tool. Instead of relying only on data it has memorized during the training process, it can now use a tool to interact with the external world. It can decide to invoke it and generate a payload to this tool instead of a response to the user [3]. We can also call this **function calling** [4].

Typically, tool calling requires **multi-step reasoning**; to generate the final answer, an LLM performs a few reasoning steps. In our case, it generates a request to a tool, gets a response from the environment, and incorporates both the generated request and a received response to generate a final answer. Of course, an LLM can perform more than one step, and there are different techniques on how to orchestrate multi-step reasoning that we'll explore in this and the following chapters [5, 6].

Tool calling has been shown to be a very powerful technique that expands the capabilities of LLMs and allows them to interact with external systems. It has been shown that LLMs' performance on various reasoning benchmarks improves significantly when augmented with the correct set of tools [3].

So far, we imitated the tool calling manually. Now, let's discuss how we can do the same in a programmatic manner.

Constructing tools

How can we construct tools programmatically? In this section, we explore various methods for constructing tools to enhance LLM capabilities, providing flexibility in how you interact with external systems or data. Each method offers unique advantages, allowing you to choose the best fit based on your project requirements

BaseTool

The most obvious way is to inherit from the LangChain BaseTool interface: `https://api.python.langchain.com/en/latest/tools/langchain_core.tools.BaseTool.html`. If you look at the documentation and click on **Source**, you'll see that this interface has a single abstract `_run` method that you need to define. Let's do this:

```
from pydantic import BaseModel, Field
from langchain.tools import Tool

class CalculatorInput(BaseModel):
    """Input to the Calculator."""

    expression: str = Field(
        description="evaluates mathematical expressions"
    )
```

```
class CalculatorTool(BaseTool):
    name = "Calculator"
    args_schema: Optional[Type[BaseModel]] = CalculatorInput
    description = (
        "Useful for when you need to evaluate a mathematical
expression."
    )

    def _run(
        self, expression: str,
        run_manager: Optional[CallbackManagerForToolRun] = None
    ) -> str:
        """Run the Calcualtor tool."""
        return eval(expression)

calculator_tool = CalculatorTool()
```

Let's now call our LLM by giving it access to tools:

```
step2a = llm.invoke(math_problem2, tools=[calculator_tool])
print(step2a.tool_calls)
>> [{'name': 'Calculator', 'args': {'expression': '23*2**2+156/4-18'},
'id': '4ae45a58-c362-4889-a8bd-3a8a6f473e6e', 'type': 'tool_call'}]
```

Our generated output now has a specific field called `tool_calls`, and if we inspect it, we actually see that the LLM told us to query the calculator tool (by adding its name to the response) and which arguments should be passed to this tool. After we evaluate the expression, we can send the result back to the LLM:

```
from langchain_core.messages import ToolMessage

print((calculator_prompt_template | llm).invoke(
    [HumanMessage(content=math_problem2),
     step2a,
     ToolMessage(
        content="113", tool_call_id=step2a.tool_calls[0]["id"])
    ]).content)
>> FINAL_ANSWER=113
```

Here, we used a new interface – `ToolMessage`. It's a specific way to tell the LangChain model that we return the result of a tool execution (and it should have a reference to tools previously called by `tool_call_id`).

Decorator

The preceding code is complex. Can we do it in a simpler manner? What if we have a Python function that we'd like to use as a tool? Then, we can just use a Python decorator:

```
from langchain.tools import tool

@tool
def calculator(expression: str) -> str:
    """Evaluates mathematical expressions."""
    return eval(expression)

step2b = llm.invoke(math_problem2, tools=[calculator])
print(step2b.tool_calls)
>> [{'name': 'calculator', 'args': {'expression': '23*2**2+156/4-18'},
'id': '24d622af-63f9-42c1-82a3-9ba652d0d57e', 'type': 'tool_call'}]
```

As we can see, LangChain has inspected the function we provided and constructed an appropriate tool schema automatically (it also inherited the tool description from the docstring). Please take into account that providing a rich docstring and a good tool description is essential since that is the information the LLM relies on when reasoning which tool to call and how to do it.

OpenAPI specification

Another way to construct is to provide its OpenAPI specification. Please note that we don't need to define a Python class (with a corresponding _run method) anymore; LangChain will take care of everything just by looking at the specification. It can be useful if you'd like to query HTTP APIs, and in our toy example, the specification will look like the following:

```
calculator_declaration = {
    "name": "Calculator",
    "description": " Useful for when you need to evaluate a
mathematical expression.",
    "parameters": {
        "properties": {
            "expression": {"type": "string", "title": "expression"}
        },
        "title": 'CalculatorInput',
        "required": ["expression"],
        "description": 'Input to the Calculator tool.',
        "type": "object"
    }
}
step2c = llm.invoke(
    math_problem2,
```

```
        tools=[{"function_declarations": [calculator_declaration]}])
print(step2c.tool_calls[0])
>> {'name': 'Calculator', 'args': {'expression': '23*2**2+156/4-18'},
'id': 'cd6e2bc3-9599-46b3-a3e8-484bb45a3d56', 'type': 'tool_call'}
```

Please note that we have defined a specification in OpenAPI format (as a dictionary). We explicitly described a name, description, and all the parameters of our API schema. Then, we simply provided this specification as a tool (but we added a special hint by defining it as a `function_declarations` object).

Pydantic models

Sometimes, you'd like your output to be a specific object, for example, a Pydantic model. The main use case where it might be useful is when LLM generation is part of a larger algorithm, and its output is used by some other program. We will talk in more detail about controlled generation in the next chapter, where we'll be discussing agents in depth.

Let's look at how you can use a specific data structure as a tool. Let's imagine we want a LLM to generate an action plan that is a list of steps. How can we do this? First, let's describe a Pydantic model (please, note that we paid special attention to docstrings, and also to documenting each field of the model, hence we're using the `Field` interface from Pydantic and type hints). Then, we simply provide this Pydantic `BaseModel` class to the LLM as a tool, and it generates the workload that can be used to instantiate a corresponding Pydantic `BaseModel` instance itself:

```
from typing import List
from pydantic import BaseModel, Field

class Plan(BaseModel):
    """Plan to execute a task."""

    steps: List[str] = Field(
        description="a plan with steps"
    )
output = llm.invoke("Prepare a plan how to solve the following task:
Learn German as a foreign language. It should be an enumerated list of
actions.")
output1 = llm.invoke(output.content, functions=[Plan])
print(output1.tool_calls[0]['args'])
>> {'name': 'Plan', 'args': {'steps': ['Define your "Why?"', 'Set
realistic goals', 'Choose your learning resources', 'Focus on the
fundamentals', 'Establish a routine', 'Immerse yourself gradually',
'Expand your vocabulary and grammar', 'Practice speaking regularly',
"Don't be afraid to make mistakes", 'Stay motivated', 'Deepen your
grammar knowledge', 'Expand your vocabulary range', 'Consume authentic
content', 'Immerse yourself further', 'Never stop learning']}, 'id':
'ce64f8a9-4ea9-4b08-9059-08eb08025df2', 'type': 'tool_call'}
```

Now, we can execute this output and get a valid Pydantic object that we can further use programmatically:

```
plan = Plan(**output1.tool_calls[0]['args'])
print(type(plan))
print(plan.steps)
>> <class '__main__.Plan'> ['Set Realistic Goals', 'Choose Learning
Resources', 'Establish a Learning Routine', 'Focus on Core Skills',
'Seek Out Opportunities for Practice', 'Track Your Progress and Stay
Motivated']
```

Now, let's put it all together and see how we can call tools in a simpler manner.

ReACT pattern

What we did before is a sequence of steps:

1.   We call a model

2.   It decides to call one of the available tools (a calculator) and generates a payload (input) for this tool

3.   We call the tool and give results back to the model (please note that we send the whole history of our interactions with an LLM since it doesn't cache it server-side, although sometimes it's done client-side on the SDK level)

4.   These steps continue until the model decides to generate a final output that can be passed to a user

In other words, we continuously asked an LLM to reason and then we acted on this reasoning. It is a so-called ReACT pattern. ReACT stands for Reason+Act, and this pattern was introduced in the famous paper published by Google Search and Princeton University (the project resulted from an internship at Google) [7].

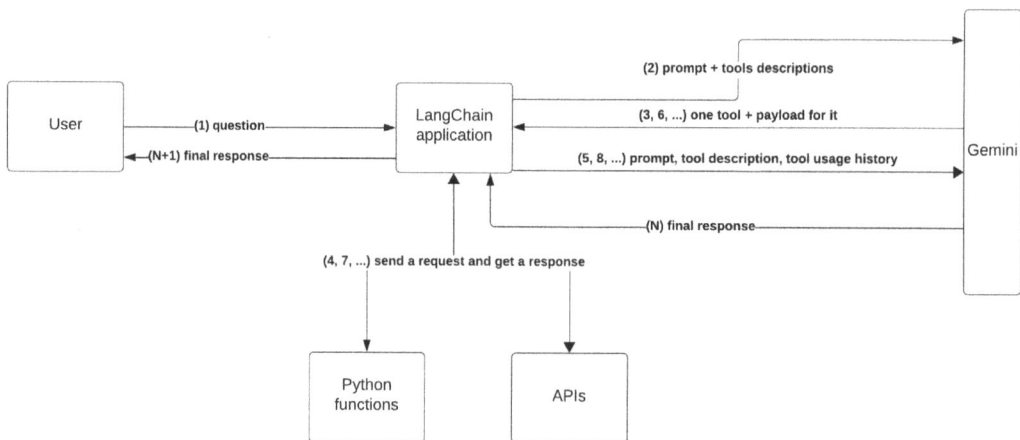

Figure 9.1 – ReACT pattern

Let's look at a very simple example:

```
react_prompt = ChatPromptTemplate(
    [("system", (
        "You are a helpful assistant. Try to use available tools "
        "when appropriate to better answer the question."
    )),
      MessagesPlaceholder(variable_name="messages"),
    ]
)
llm_with_calculator = llm.bind_tools(tools=[calculator])
chain = react_prompt | llm_with_calculator
```

First, we composed a prompt that follows the ReACT pattern, we created a model that has access to the calculator tool, and we chained together the prompt and the model. In other words, this chain will first substitute the prompt with the input message (or messages) and then send these messages as input to the LLM.

Now, let's use it with a simple problem:

```
input_message = HumanMessage(content="how much is 45546*123213")
message1 = chain.invoke([input_message])

if message1.tool_calls and message1.tool_calls[0]["name"] ==
"calculator":
    calculator_result = calculator.invoke(
        message1.tool_calls[0]["args"])
    tool_message = ToolMessage(content=calculator_result,
        tool_call_id=message1.tool_calls[0]["id"])
    final_message = llm_with_calculator.invoke(
        [input_message, message1, tool_message])
else:
    final_message = message1

print(final_message.content)
>> The answer is 5611859298.
```

We parsed the output of the LLM, and since it asked us to invoke the tool, we invoked it ourselves and sent the whole input (initial message, response from the model, and response from the tool) back to the LLM to prepare the final answer. But what if we want to use more tools? Or, what if the model decides to invoke tools a few times? Our code will get more and more complicated. The good news is that you usually don't need to implement the ReACT pattern yourselves; LangChain has a predefined **agent** (and we'll talk more about what an agent is in the next chapter; for now, let's just assume it's a simple workflow orchestrated by LangChain that uses an LLM) that can do it for you.

Let's take a look at an example:

```
from langgraph.prebuilt import create_react_agent

react_agent = create_react_agent(
    llm, [calculator], messages_modifier=react_prompt)
result = react_agent.invoke(
    {"messages": [("user", "how much is 45546*123213-2")]})
print(result["messages"][-1].content)
>> The answer is 5611859296.
```

We invoked the ReACT agent literally with one line of code, and the result is the sequence of messages that was sent back and forth. LangChain took care of orchestrating the whole chain (invoking appropriate tools and sending the responses back to the LLM).

Using ToolConfig

But what if you're using multiple tools, and you'd like to have some control over how the LLM calls the tools? Let's take a look at how you can control tool calling with Gemini (other models might have slightly different parameter naming, but LangChain interfaces remain the same).

By default, Gemini is in the AUTO mode (i.e., it decides itself whether it should call a tool or respond in a natural language). With Gemini 1.5, you can force the model to always use one of the predefined tools [8].

Let's look at the first example. Let's assume we have two tools – search and maps (one is performing a search on Google Search, and another is searching on Maps). Sat we call our LLM like the following:

```
response = llm.invoke(
    "What is the capital of Germany?",
    tools=[{"function_declarations": [search_declaration,
        maps_declaration]}])
```

Then, it decides to call the search tool.

What if we want the model to always call a tool (in other words, perform a forced function calling)? Then, we can specify the ANY mode and provide one or more tool calls. The model will be forced to use one of the tools provided (and not predict the final output):

```
response1 = llm.invoke(
    "What is the capital of Germany?",
    tools=[{"function_declarations": [search_declaration,
        maps_declaration]}],
    tool_config={"function_calling_config": {"mode": "ANY",
        "allowed_function_names": ["Search"]}})
```

This is fully equivalent to using a standard LangChain `tool_choice` parameter (just a little bit easier syntax):

```
response1 = llm.invoke(
    "What is the capital of Germany?",
    tools=[{"function_declarations": [search_declaration,
        maps_declaration]}],
    tool_choice={"mode": "ANY", "allowed_function_names": ["Search"]})

Now, what if we'd like to avoid calling a tool at all and generate a
response to the user using LLM's inherited knowledge? Then we should
use None mode:
response2 = llm.invoke(
    "What is the capital of Germany?",
    tools=[{"function_declarations": [search_declaration,
        maps_declaration]}],
    tool_config={"function_calling_config": {"mode": "NONE"}})
```

Again, it's fully equivalent to the following:

```
response2 = llm.invoke(
    "What is the capital of Germany?",
    tools=[{"function_declarations": [search_declaration,
        maps_declaration]}],
    tool_choice="none")
```

It's useful for two reasons. First, you can force the model to use a tool (and it gives you more control over its behavior). Second, LangChain has a useful method called `bind_tools`, which allows you to create a `Runnable` instance from your LLM that uses the tools provided. You can think about it as a small wrapper that always calls the underlying LLM but adds a tool parameter to each invocation. In that case, it becomes really useful to have a control whether to use or not use a tool:

```
llm_with_tools = llm.bind_tools(tools=tools)
response = llm_with_tools.invoke("What is the capital of Germany?")
```

All `bind_tools` is doing is copying the `Runnable` instance (`ChatVertexAI` in our case) and automatically adding additional arguments related to tool calling by each invocation.

When using multiple tools, it's important to keep in mind a few things:

- Use unique tool names and clear tool descriptions (so that the LLM can easily distinguish one tool from another)

- Try to help the LLM by reducing the number of available tools across your workflow by controlling the flow

- Provide additional instructions on how to use tools in your prompt

Now that we know how to deal with tools, let's take a look at the variety of additional tools you can use.

Tools provided by Google

Almost any Google product has an API, hence you can wrap it as a tool and enhance it with LLMs. Most Google products and services – such as Drive, Maps, Gmail, and so on – have an API, hence you can use them as a tool to build great applications. You can find a full list of tools on the documentation page: `https://python.langchain.com/api_reference/google_community/index.html`

You can wrap any Google Cloud API to make it a tool (and we've already learned how to develop custom tools). Some Google APIs are already integrated into `langchain-google-community`, for example:

- `TextToSpeechTool`: This allows you to transform text into speech with the Google Cloud Translation API.

- `GmailCreateDraft`: This creates Gmail drafts and `GmailSendMessage` sends messages.

- `GooglePlacesAPIWrapper`: This interacts with Google Maps and the Google Places API.

- `VertexAISearchSummaryTool`: This allows you to generate answers with the Vertex AI Agent Builder API.

Of course, if you come up with a nice new tool based on Google APIs that might be useful for developers, don't hesitate to contribute to the library and send a pull request!

However, the tool that is extremely important in keeping an LLM's knowledge of the latest events fresh is Google Search, and we'll explore this in more detail.

Using Google Search

During inference, LLMs have access only to information that they have seen during the training. As we found in *Chapter 4*, it makes it challenging to update an LLM's information on new events. However, a natural way for us to get information on new events is to ask Google Search. Let's give the LLM the same ability!

First, you need to create an API key in the Google Cloud console and create your own Programmable Search Engine [9].

Now, we can go and get results from Google Search:

```
from langchain_google_community import GoogleSearchAPIWrapper
search = GoogleSearchAPIWrapper(
    google_api_key=api_key, google_cse_id=cse_id)
result = search.run("What is the weather in Munich tomorrow?")
```

We got a string that is composed of the results you see on Google Search. We can also retrieve the top-ranked websites:

```
result = search.results("What is the weather in Munich tomorrow?",
    num_results=3)
print(len(result))
print(result[0])
>> 3
{'title': 'Munich, Bavaria, Germany Weather Forecast | AccuWeather',
'link': 'https://www.accuweather.com/en/de/munich/80331/weather-
forecast/178086', 'snippet': 'The air has reached a high level of
pollution and is unhealthy for sensitive groups. Reduce time spent
outside if you are feeling symptoms such as difficulty\xa0...'}
```

Each result is a dictionary that has the title of the web page, its link, and a short snippet describing the content (the one you see on the Google Search page).

Another useful application (out of many) of a tool that queries Google Search is the increased factuality of the LLM's responses (you make them grounded on the Google Search results).

Let's now add Google Search as a tool to the ReACT agent we built in the previous section:

```
from langchain_google_community import GoogleSearchRun

search_tool = GoogleSearchRun(api_wrapper=search)
agent_executor = create_react_agent(
    llm, [calculator, search_tool], messages_modifier=prompt)
result = agent_executor.invoke(
    {"messages": [("user", "how much is distance from Earth to Moon
multiplied by 2?")]})
```

Here, we created a tool from a Search API wrapper and added two tools to the agent. If we inspect the result, we'll see the following chain of events:

- AIMessage with a tool call for the google_search tool and the following payload: 'args': {'query': 'distance from Earth to Moon'}

- The agent called Google Search itself and added results from Google Search to the history

- Then, it created another AIMessage with the second tool call, and this time, the calculator was called with the following payload: {'expression': '384400*2'}

- Results were also added to the queue, and finally, the LLM generated the answer: "FINAL_ANSWER=768800 kilometers"

Search grounding with Gemini

If you want to ground LLM on Google Search, Gemini has a built-in capability for doing this. With any other LLM, you need to use ReACT or another agent that uses Google Search as a tool. Using search grounding with the Vertex AI Search API is a little bit more convenient (you don't need to set up any additional API keys, and your code becomes easier since you don't need to make any additional calls as Vertex AI takes care of it under the hood):

```
from vertexai.generative_models import grounding
from vertexai.generative_models import Tool as VertexTool

tool = VertexTool.from_google_search_retrieval(
    grounding.GoogleSearchRetrieval())

response = llm.invoke("How far is moon from the Earth?", tools=[tool])
```

You get an LLM response (in `response.content`) that is grounded on Google Search results, and you can also explore grounding metadata. For example, that's how you can take a look at which search queries were used to generate a context for the LLM call:

```
print(
    resp.response_metadata[
        "grounding_metadata"
    ]["web_search_queries"]
)
>> ['how far is the moon from the earth']
```

Summary

In this chapter, we discussed examples of prompt techniques, such as CoT, that demonstrate an improvement in an LLM's reasoning abilities. We also discussed that we can take it a step further. If LLMs are not very good at math, what if instead of trying to teach them math, we give them access to a calculator?

We learned about the various ways to define a tool with LangChain from Python functions, by defining your own classes that implement the specific logic of a tool, defining them as Pydantic models (it's useful when you need to parse your output into a specific structure), or providing a direct OpenAPI specification of your API.

In the next chapter, we'll look at how we can use tool calling to develop more sophisticated applications to solve complex tasks with LLMs.

References

1. *Chain-of-Thought Prompting Elicits Reasoning in Large Language Models*, J. Wei et. al., 2022.

    `https://arxiv.org/abs/2201.11903`

2. *Few shot prompting on LangChain.*

    `https://python.langchain.com/docs/how_to/few_shot_examples/`

3. *Chain-of-Thought Prompting.*

    `https://www.promptingguide.ai/techniques/cot`

4. *Tool calling with LangChain*, LangChain blog, 2024.

    `https://blog.langchain.dev/tool-calling-with-langchain/`

5. *TALM: Tool Augmented Language Models*, A. Parisi et. al, 2022.

    `https://arxiv.org/abs/2205.12255`

6. *A Real-World WebAgent with Planning, Long Context Understanding, and Program Synthesis*, I. Gur et. al., 2023.

    `https://arxiv.org/abs/2307.12856`

7. *ReAct: Synergizing Reasoning and Acting in Language Models*, S. Yao et. al, 2022.

    `https://arxiv.org/abs/2210.03629`

8. *Function calling*, Vertex AI documentation.

    `https://cloud.google.com/vertex-ai/generative-ai/docs/multimodal/function-calling`

9. *What Is Programmable Search Engine?*, Google developer's documentation.

    `https://developers.google.com/custom-search/docs/overview`

10

Agents

In the previous chapter, we explored how **large language models** (**LLMs**) leverage tools to enhance their responses and expand their capabilities. This chapter delves into the fundamental concept of an **agent** within the domain of generative AI applications. Agents possess the ability not only to utilize tools but also to strategically plan which tools to employ, the order of their use, and how many times they should be applied.

We will approach agent construction from two distinct perspectives: first, by using LangChain and LangGraph on Google Cloud with the Gemini SDK, where we will explain how to build agents on the Google Cloud platform and provide illustrative implementation examples. Second, we will briefly touch on the use of managed services like **Vertex AI Agent Builder** to create agents that are ready for deployment.

We will cover the following main topics in this chapter:

- What is an agent?
- Agents in LangChain
- Vertex AI Agent Builder

Technical requirements

To follow the examples of this chapter, in addition to specific requirements for each service mentioned, you will need an active Google Cloud project and a Python environment with the following libraries installed:

```
pip install langchain-google-vertexai langgraph
```

What is an agent?

The fundamental concept behind an agent in the context of generative AI applications is the use of a language model as a reasoning mechanism to select a sequence of actions to perform to achieve a goal.

The core distinction between these agent-based systems and traditional generative AI applications lies in their approach to task execution. Traditional generative AI applications usually rely on predefined chains of actions, executing them sequentially in a rigid manner. This limits their adaptability to user input or varying contexts.

Conversely, agent-based systems can dynamically interpret user intent and autonomously select the most appropriate actions and their order of execution. This flexibility allows them to handle complex tasks that require adaptability and decision-making capabilities.

Components of an agent

An agent consists of several essential components that collaborate to enable its intelligent behavior. The following diagram shows the components of an agent:

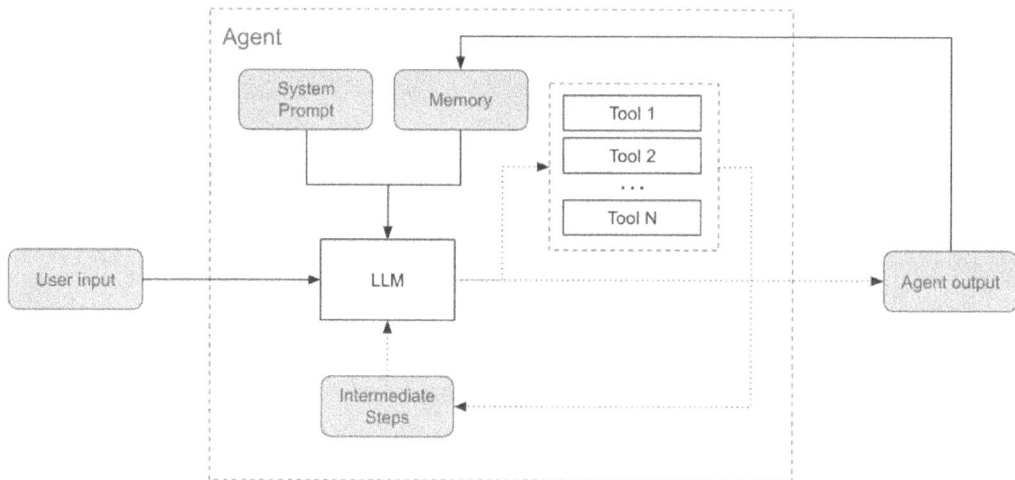

Figure 10.1: Components and workflow of an agent

The LLM serves as the core "brain" of the agent, responsible for understanding and processing natural language inputs. It empowers the agent to interpret user requests, generate meaningful responses, and make informed decisions. Essentially, the LLM provides the underlying intelligence that drives the agent's actions.

The system prompts serve as the guiding principles for the LLM, shaping its behavior and responses. They define the agent's overall personality, knowledge base, communication style, and approach to tasks. Prompt instructions are crucial for aligning the LLM's outputs with the desired outcomes.

Memory stores information from past interactions, outcomes of previous actions, and other relevant data. This allows the agent to maintain a coherent conversation, recall earlier steps, and build upon previous knowledge.

Agents often break down complex tasks into smaller, more manageable steps. These intermediate steps might involve data analysis, calculations, or queries to external tools. The results obtained from these steps are then used to inform subsequent decisions. It functions as a sort of short-term memory for the agent.

As we discussed in the previous chapter, an agent can be provided with a variety of tools to allow it to perform actions. This tool set might include:

- **Code interpreters**: To execute code snippets and utilize programming logic
- **Search engines**: To access up-to-date information from the web
- **Calculators**: To perform mathematical operations
- **APIs**: To interact with external services (e.g., translation, image generation)

How agents work

An agent's workflow can be conceptually understood as a sequence of the following steps:

1. **User Input**: The user initiates interaction with the agent by providing a request or instruction.
2. **LLM interpretation**: The LLM analyzes the user input to understand the intent and desired outcome of the request.
3. **Planning**: Based on the LLM's interpretation, the agent creates a plan of action. This plan may involve either directly generating a response for the user or using one or more tools to gather additional information or perform specific actions.
4. **Action (optional)**: If the plan involves the use of tools, the agent executes the necessary actions. These tools could be anything from calculators and code interpreters to search engines and database queries. The results of these actions are then fed back into the system.
5. **Memory update**: The agent updates its internal memory with the outcomes of any actions taken and any other pertinent information gathered during the process. This updated memory serves as a context for subsequent interactions.
6. **Response**: Finally, the agent formulates a response for the user. This response is based on the cumulative information obtained through the previous steps, including the LLM's interpretation, the results of any tool-based actions, and the updated memory.

Now that we know about the concept, components, and how an agent works, let's explain how they can be implemented.

Agents in LangChain

Let's explore how to build an agent using LangChain with a practical example. Our goal is to create an agent capable of managing a user's bank accounts. This agent should be able to retrieve the balance of each account and execute transactions between them.

While in a production environment, we would interact with dedicated banking systems via APIs, let's craft a simple mock framework for our example. To keep the code limited, the implementation of the methods is available in the code repository.

```
from pydantic import BaseModel

class Account(BaseModel):
    """Represents a bank account with a name and balance."""
    name: str
    balance: float

class UserAccounts(BaseModel):
    """Represents a collection of bank accounts for a user."""

    accounts: list[Account]

    def get_account_names(self) -> list[str]:
        """Returns a list of the names of all accounts."""
        return [account.name for account in self.accounts]

    def get_account(self, account_name: str) -> Account:
        """Returns the account with the given name.

        Raises:
            ValueError: If no account with the given name exists.
        """
        ...

    def transfer_money(
        self, amount: float, source_acc_name: str, dest_acc_name: str
    ):
        """Transfers money from one account to another.

        Raises:
            ValueError: If the source account does not have enough
funds.
        """
        ...
```

This implementation exposes three methods:

- `get_account_names`: This method returns a list of the names of the accounts associated with the user.

- `get_account`: This method retrieves a specific account by its name. If the account doesn't exist, it raises a `ValueError` with a clear message indicating the issue and available account options.

- `transfer_money`: This method allows transferring funds between accounts. It takes the amount, source account name, and destination account name as arguments. It includes error handling to ensure sufficient funds in the source account before executing the transfer.

Let's use this implementation to define the tools for the agent.

Tools

To define the tools available to our agent effectively, we'll employ the `tool` decorator. As discussed in the preceding chapter, remember that comprehensive docstrings are essential, providing the LLM with the context necessary to determine the appropriate tool to call in any given situation.

Let's first create a global `UserAccounts` object holding user account information as a practical example:

```
USER_ACCOUNTS = UserAccounts(
    accounts=[
        Account(name="checking-account", balance=100),
        Account(name="savings-account", balance=3_000)
    ]
)
```

Then, we can proceed to define the tools:

```
from langchain_core.tools import tool
@tool
def list_accounts() -> str:
    """List the names of the user's accounts."""
    return USER_ACCOUNTS.get_account_names()


@tool
    def get_account_balance(account_name: str) -> str:
        """Get the balance of one of the user accounts by its exact
name."""
        try:
            account = USER_ACCOUNTS.get_account(account_name)
            return f"${account.balance}"
        except ValueError as error:
            return f"{error}"

@tool
def transfer_money(
    amount: float, source_account: str, destination_account: str
) -> str:
    """Transfer money between two accounts."""
```

```
    try:
        USER_ACCOUNTS.transfer_money(
            amount, source_account, destination_account
        )
        return "Successful transaction"
    except ValueError as error:
        return f"{error}"
tools = [list_accounts, get_account_balance, transfer_money]
```

Having defined our toolkit, we will next specify the model responsible for orchestrating their use. This model will select the most suitable tool for each interaction and generate contextually relevant responses.

Model

For that, we instantiate a `ChatVertexAI` object, which provides an interface to the Gemini 1.5 Pro model. We set the `temperature` parameter to 0 to encourage the model to produce more focused and consistent responses, which is generally beneficial when working with agents that rely on function calling. Remember that you can further customize this instantiation with additional parameters to fine-tune the model's behavior according to your specific requirements, such as the safety settings or the maximum number of output tokens:

```
from langchain_google_vertexai import ChatVertexAI

MODEL_NAME = "gemini-1.5-pro-002"

model = ChatVertexAI(
    model_name=MODEL_NAME,
    temperature = 0
)
```

Let's now try to refine the behavior of the model by creating a prompt for it.

Prompt template

Now, let's refine the model's behavior by designing an effective prompt. We'll utilize the `ChatPromptTemplate` class for this purpose. This class requires two components:

- `SystemPromptTemplate`: This component contains the general instructions for the model, guiding its overall behavior. For this example, a `SystemPrompt` would be enough because we don't have any template parameters, but it is a good idea to have it in place in case we want to include some later.

- `MessagesPlaceholder`: This component includes a list of messages, encompassing both the conversation history and the user's current query.

Let's examine the following code snippet to see how this can be implemented:

```python
from langchain_core.prompts import (
    ChatPromptTemplate,
    MessagesPlaceholder,
    SystemMessagePromptTemplate,
)


prompt_template = ChatPromptTemplate.from_messages([
    SystemMessagePromptTemplate.from_template(
        """
        You are an agent that helps the user manage their accounts in
a Bank.
        Users may not refer to their account by the exact name, so try
to get a list of valid names
        before getting a balance or executing a transaction.
        """
    ),
    MessagesPlaceholder(
        variable_name="messages",
        optional=True
    )
])
```

The core of this system prompt lies in the message provided within `SystemMessagePromptTemplate`.

This message instructs the language model to assume the role of a banking agent. It explicitly tells the model to prioritize identifying the correct account names before proceeding with any balance inquiries or transactions. This is very important because users might use colloquial or imprecise names to refer to their accounts.

Now that we have all the components of the agent built, let's create the actual object.

Agent creation

To create the agent, we'll use the `langgraph` library introduced in the previous chapter. The `langgraph.prebuilt` module provides the `create_react_agent` function, which simplifies building the agent architecture. In the next chapter, we'll explore how to build cognitive architectures from scratch.

```python
from langgraph.prebuilt import create_react_agent

agent = create_react_agent(
    model=model,
    tools=tools,
```

```
    state_modifier=prompt_template
)
```

Note that the prompt is included using the `state_modifier` parameter. Besides a prompt template, this argument can be any `Runnable` that can be chained to the model and takes the state as an input.

The graph created by this function looks like the following figure:

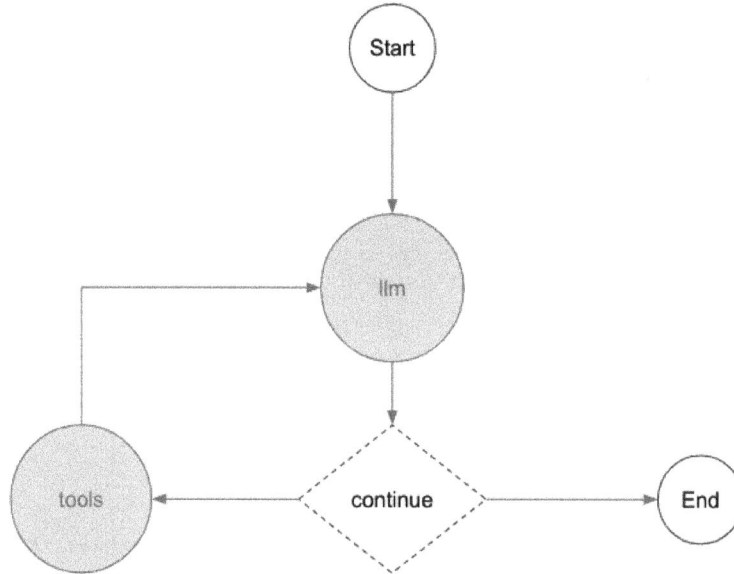

Figure 10.2: LangGraph agent architecture

Upon receiving input, the agent evaluates whether to generate a response directly or employ a tool. If a tool is deemed necessary, a loop is initiated. The output from the tool is then fed back into the model, prompting a reevaluation of the situation. This iterative process allows the agent to call any number of tools, as many times as required, before formulating a final response.

Let's now use the agent we just created in different scenarios.

Agent usage

LangGraph primarily uses the `invoke` method to execute a graph. This method requires an initial state object containing a `"messages"` key. This key holds the conversation history between the user and the agent, encompassing human and agent messages, along with any intermediate tool calls and their corresponding responses. The `invoke` method processes this information, runs it through the graph, and returns an updated state object, which includes any newly generated messages appended to the conversation history.

Let's try it with the following code snippet:

```
state = {
    "messages": [
        ("human", "Hello, what can you help me with?")
    ]
}

new_state = agent.invoke(state)
for message in new_state["messages"]:
    message.pretty_print()

=== Human Message ====
Hello, what can you help me with?
===Ai Message ===
I can help you check your account balances and transfer money between
your accounts.
```

Here, we have asked a simple question to the agent, so no function calls are present in its response, and it has just generated it without using any tools.

Let's ask a specific question where we know the agent must utilize one of the tools provided, such as asking for an account balance:

```
state = {
    "messages": [
        ("human", "Whats the balance in my savings account?")
    ]
}
new_state = agent.invoke(state)
for message in new_state["messages"]:
    message.pretty_print()

=== Human Message ===
Whats the balance in my savings account?
=== Ai Message ====
Tool Calls: list_accounts
Args:
=== Tool Message ===
Name: list_accounts
["checking-account", "savings-account"]
===Ai Message ===
Tool Calls: get_account_balance
Args: account_name: savings-account
=== Tool Message ===
```

```
Name: get_account_balance
$3000.0
=== Ai Message ===
Your savings-account balance is $3000.0.
```

In this scenario, the agent first used the `list_accounts` tool to identify the user's available accounts. After retrieving the list, it correctly determined that the user was referring to the `savings-account` and used the `get_account_balance` tool with the appropriate argument to retrieve the balance. Finally, it generated a response to the user, including the account balance.

The provided tools enable the agent to execute complex tasks, including conditional transactions between accounts, verification of sufficient funds, and balance-dependent transactions.

To illustrate these capabilities, you can experiment with the following prompts available in the code repository:

- *"Transfer $10 from checking to savings please."*

- *"Transfer $1,000 from checking to savings please."*

- *"If my checking account has more than $50, transfer $30 from checking to savings please. Then tell me the starting and final balances in both accounts."*

Having a functional agent, let's next explore how we can deploy it on Google Cloud in a managed runtime, using Reasoning Engine.

Deploying with Reasoning Engine

The **Reasoning Engine API** in Google Cloud's Vertex AI provides a managed runtime environment for deploying your generative AI agents. This offers built-in security, observability, and scalability. It seamlessly integrates with LangChain, allowing you to wrap an agent within a custom application class. To illustrate this process, let's deploy the agent we previously created.

First, initialize Vertex AI with your project, region, and a staging bucket for the Reasoning Engine API:

```
import vertexai
from vertexai.preview import reasoning_engines

PROJECT_ID = "your-project-id"
LOCATION = "us-central1"
STAGING_BUCKET = "gs://your-staging-bucket-name"

vertexai.init(project=PROJECT_ID, location=LOCATION, staging_
bucket=STAGING_BUCKET)
```

Next, create a class to encapsulate the agent. This class should have two methods:

- `set_up`: Handles any necessary class setup. Typically, this involves building and compiling the graph.

- `query`: Takes a message as input and returns the final output.

Here's an example snippet. Note that, for demonstration purposes, we're referencing the agent instead of building it within the `set_up` method, as would be standard practice:

```
class AgentApp:
    """Represents an application that can be deployed in Reasoning
Engine"""
    def __init__(self, project_id: str, location: str) -> None:
        """initializes the agent"""
        self.project_id = project_id
        self.location = location

    def set_up(self):
        """Set ups the agent."""
        self._agent = agent

    def query(self, message: str) -> str:
        """Query the agent"""
        state = {"messages": [("human", message)]}
        new_state = self._agent.invoke(state)
        return new_state["messages"][-1].content
```

With the class defined, you can use the `reasoning_engines` SDK to create your remote application:

```
remote_agent = reasoning_engines.ReasoningEngine.create(
    AgentApp(project_id=PROJECT_ID, location=LOCATION),
    requirements=[
        "google-cloud-aiplatform[langchain,reasoningengine]",
        "cloudpickle==3.0.0",
        "pydantic==2.7.4",
        "langgraph",
        "httpx",
    ],
    display_name="Banking account Agent",
    description="This is an agent that helps you managing your
accounts",
    extra_packages=[],
)
```

This code snippet serializes your application and uploads it to the Reasoning Engine. After deployment, you can query it using the SDK:

```
remote_agent.query(message="What's the balance on my savings account?")
```

To delete a deployed application, simply call the `delete` method:

```
remote_agent.delete()
```

Now that we know how to create an agent from code, let's explore how to build an agent with Google Cloud with a no-code/low-code tool such as Vertex AI Agent Builder.

Vertex AI Agent Builder

Vertex AI Agent Builder is a managed platform that enables the development of AI agents and applications using either the console or a code-first approach. It simplifies the process of grounding these agents or apps in enterprise data, offering various integration options. This platform serves as a central hub for developers, providing all the necessary tools and interfaces to streamline the creation of AI agents and applications (`https://cloud.google.com/products/agent-builder`).

To recreate the agent, we just built using LangChain, let's begin by creating an app within the platform and designating its type as **Agent**. The default screen will prompt you to provide a name, goal, and instructions, and select a generative model version (*Figure 10.3*).

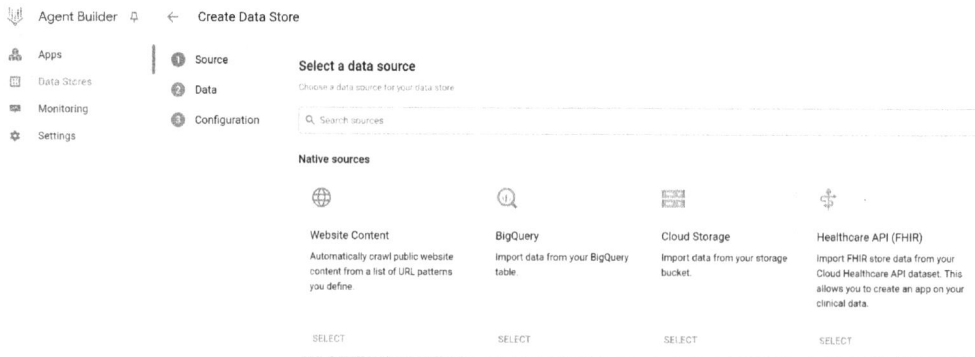

Figure 10.3: Generative agent settings in Vertex AI Agent Builder

The goal and instructions serve as the initial prompt for the base LLM, the "brain" of the application. You can also enhance the agent's performance by including examples using a few-shot strategy in the **Examples** tab.

To specify the tools that the agent can use, you can go to the **Tools** section, as seen in *Figure 10.4*. Here, you can specify which tools to use with a user description.

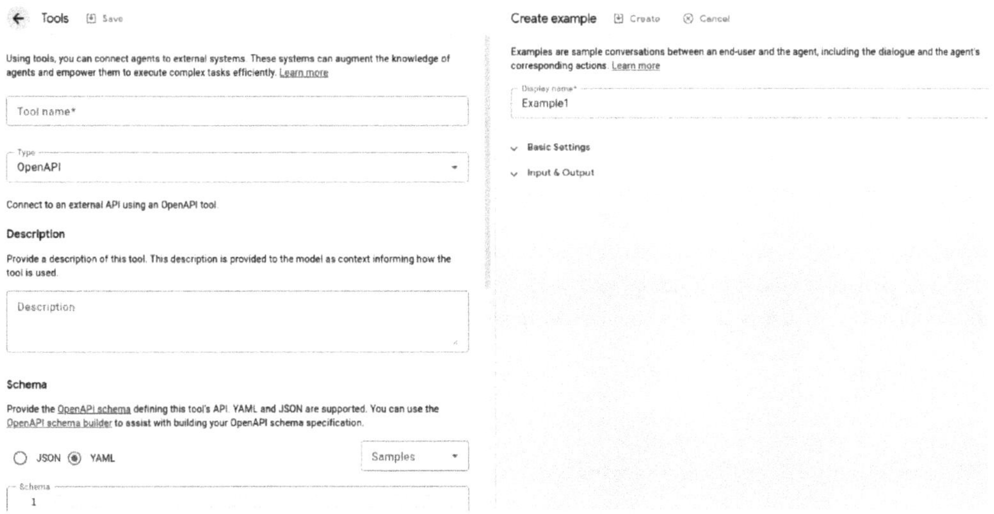

Figure 10.4: Tools definition in Vertex AI Agent Builder

Tools should be available through an external API. We can build one with the tools used previously using Python:

```python
from fastapi import FastAPI

app = FastAPI()

@app.get("/list_accounts")
def list_accounts() -> str:
    """List the names of the user's accounts."""
    return USER_ACCOUNTS.get_account_names()

@app.get("/get_account_balance")
def get_account_balance(account_name: str) -> str:
    """Get the balance of one of the user accounts by its exact
name."""
    try:
        account = USER_ACCOUNTS.get_account(account_name)
        return f"${account.balance}"
    except ValueError as error:
        return f"{error}"

@app.get("/transfer_money")
def transfer_money(amount: float, source_account: str,
                   destination_account: str) -> str:
    """Transfer money between two accounts."""
```

```
try:
    USER_ACCOUNTS.transfer_money(amount, source_account,
        destination_account)
    return "Successful transaction"
except ValueError as error:
    return f"{error}"
```

For the agent to be able to call these tools, you need to specify the API schema using the OpenAPI format (`https://spec.openapis.org/oas/v3.1.0`). Conveniently, we can get the specification for the application we just built with the following snippet:

```
import json

app.openapi_version = "3.0.2"
json.dumps(app.openapi(), indent=4)
```

Vertex AI Agent Builder also provides ready-to-use tools called extensions. For example, we can use a Python code interpreter or even data stores to power our agent (*Figure 10.5*).

Available tools

This agent can use selected tools to generate responses. You can also call other tools, including 3P, directly in steps. Create a data store tool to allow this agent to answer questions using data store content.

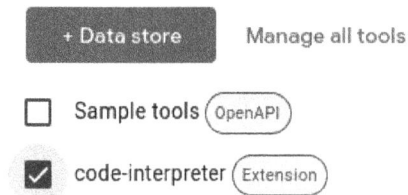

Figure 10.5: Extensions in Vertex AI Agent Builder

Selecting one or more tools from the menu will cause the agent to have access to and be able to utilize these tools.

Summary

This chapter explored the core concept of "agent" in generative AI applications. We delved into how agents utilize tools, strategically planning their use to achieve goals. We explored the components of an agent: LLMs, prompt instructions, memory, intermediate steps, and tools.

LangChain's agent implementation was demonstrated, illustrating the building of agents using LangGraph and tool integration.

Finally, we introduced Vertex AI Agent Builder, detailing its features and how to create agents using it. The chapter concluded with a brief overview of extensions in Vertex AI Agent Builder, showcasing its ready-to-use tools, such as code interpreters and data stores. In the next chapter, we will explore how an agentic workflow works and give some examples of them, such as natural language to SQL and agentic retrieval-augmented generation.

Get This Book's PDF Version and Exclusive Extras

UNLOCK NOW

Scan the QR code (or go to packtpub.com/unlock). Search for this book by name, confirm the edition, and then follow the steps on the page.

Note: Keep your invoice handy. Purchases made directly from Packt don't require one.

11

Agentic Workflows

In this chapter, we will explore agentic workflows. They are essential for building applications that exhibit dynamic behavior, responding intelligently to changes in the application state.

To grasp the concepts of agentic workflows, we will explore workflow state management, learning how applications transition through different states within a graph. You will then investigate controlled generation techniques, enabling you to specify the desired format for responses from **large language models (LLMs)**.

Then, you will implement agentic RAG, a powerful approach that leverages agents to enhance traditional **retrieval augmented generation (RAG)** pipelines.

Finally, you will learn how to build agents capable of translating natural language into SQL queries, allowing you to interact with databases using conversational language.

Technical requirements

To implement the examples in this chapter, you'll need an active Google Cloud project and a Python environment with the following libraries:

```
pip install langchain-google-vertexai langgraph
```

These libraries provide the necessary components for interacting with Google Cloud's Vertex AI services and constructing the LangGraph-based agentic architecture. Please refer to the specific subsections for any additional requirements beyond these core libraries.

Workflow state management

A **cognitive architecture** can be thought of as a connected graph, with designated entry and exit points. Each *node* within the graph represents a specific task, ranging from simple post-processing to a complex, self-contained agent. The *edges* of the graph represent the transitions between two different tasks.

The application begins with an initial state, which is fed into the entry point of the graph. Each node processes and potentially modifies this state as it travels through the graph. Finally, upon reaching the exit point, the final state is returned as the output. In most applications, the state is represented as a list of messages, but it can be any data structure based on the application's specific needs.

To create dynamic behavior that responds to the application's state, we can use **conditional edges**. These structures guide the flow to different nodes based on the application's current state when it reaches that point in the process.

Let's clarify these concepts with a simple example, illustrated in *Figure 11.1*. This application depicts a basic agent with a single tool, sum_numbers, designed to perform addition. The state of this application is represented by a list of messages.

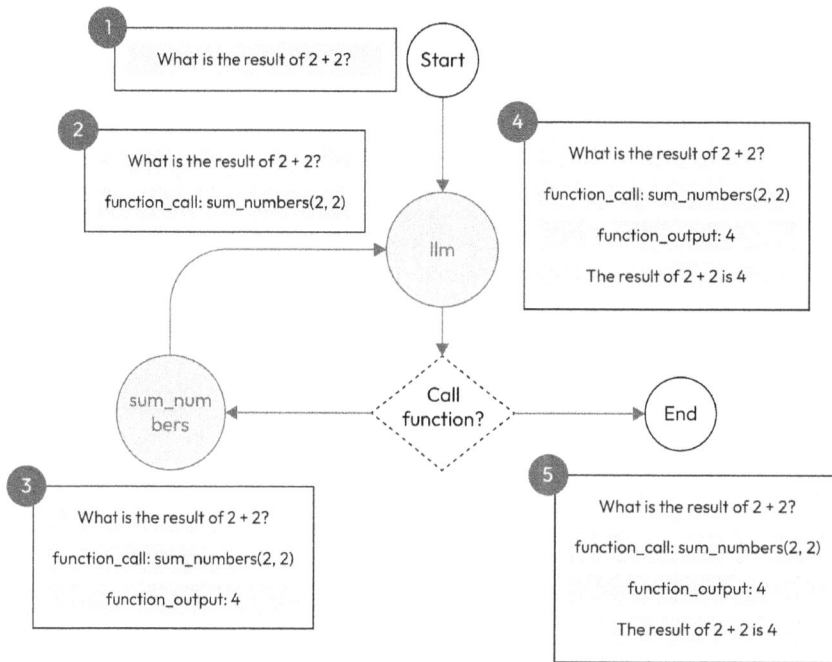

Figure 11.1 - Example of application state modification

As we can see, the following steps are involved:

1. The initial state only contains the user's query, which is immediately sent to the LLM node.

2. The LLM decides to call the tool to perform the addition operation. It adds the message **function call** to the state list. Recognizing the last message as a function call, the conditional edge directs the flow to the sum_numbers node.

3. The sum_numbers node performs the addition and updates the state with the result. The flow is then directed back to the LLM node.

4. The LLM generates an answer based on the calculation, adding it to the state. Since the final message isn't a function call, the conditional edge directs the flow to the end node.

5. The end node returns the final state.

Now that you understand how a cognitive architecture works and how to manage its state, let's explore how you can leverage an LLM to generate structured output to standardize the structure of its responses.

Controlled generation

To ensure consistent communication between different nodes and standardize the structure of responses from an LLM, Gemini models allow you to specify the desired response format as a JSON string.

You can achieve this by setting the `response_schema` parameter to an OpenAPI (https://spec.openapis.org/oas/latest.html) dictionary and the `response_mime_type` parameter to "application/json". This can be done either in the constructor of the `ChatVertexAI` class or within the `invoke` method.

In the following example, we'll instruct the model to structure its response as an array of objects, each containing the `city_name` and `population` properties:

```python
from langchain_google_vertexai import ChatVertexAI

model = ChatVertexAI(
    model_name="gemini-1.5-flash-001",
    response_schema = {
    "type": "array",
    "items": {
        "type": "object",
        "properties": {
            "city_name": {
                "type": "string",
            },
            "population": {
                "type": "number"
            }
        },
        "required": ["city_name"],
    },
    },
    response_mime_type = "application/json",
)

model.invoke("What are the 3 biggest cities in france")
```

```
>> AIMessage(content='[{"city_name": "Paris", "population": 2140526},
{"city_name": "Marseille", "population": 862352}, {"city_name":
"Lyon", "population": 516092}] ', response_metadata={...}, ...)
```

The model relies on the schema's field names to understand what data to fill in. Therefore, ensure field names are brief and clear. If you need to provide additional context for certain fields, you can do this within the prompt.

By default, field values are optional, meaning the model might leave them blank. While you can specify required fields in the schema, be aware that if the model lacks sufficient information to populate them, it may use values from its training data instead.

Next, let's explore how you can leverage a cognitive architecture to solve different scenarios in the real world, such as agentic RAG and **natural language to SQL (NL2SQL)**.

Agentic RAG

As discussed in *Chapter 3*, RAG pipelines serve to anchor responses to a knowledge base, allowing LLMs to generate responses based on actual, dynamic data. *Figure 11.2* shows a standard RAG workflow as a series of steps.

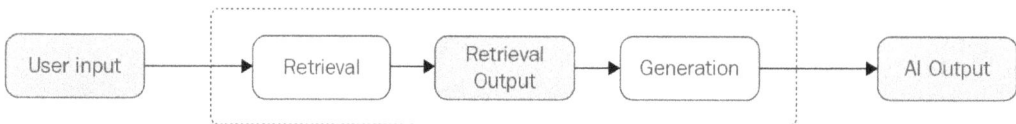

Figure 11.2 - Example RAG pipeline

In real-world conversations, the standard chain workflow doesn't always meet our needs. Sometimes, we may need to make multiple calls to the knowledge base to adequately answer a user's question, or perhaps no calls at all. Agentic RAG addresses this challenge by allowing you to define an agent with a cognitive architecture capable of handling these scenarios, as shown in *Figure 11.3*.

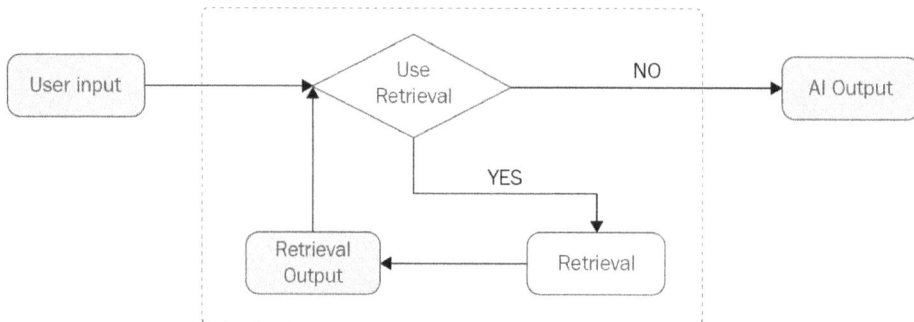

Figure 11.3 - Agentic RAG simple workflow

To illustrate the construction of this type of agentic architecture, let's begin by creating a knowledge base. In this scenario, we will create a clothing item catalog and use a **generative model** to populate it with data:

1. The following prompt provided to Gemini will yield a list of items that we can use as the foundation for our data:

   ```
   Generate a json list of 20 clothing descriptions.
   Make sure there are no duplicate items.
   Each item must have the following attributes:
    - name: Name of the item
    - type: Type of item. Items can only be "t-shirt", "pants" or
   "coat"
    - color: "red", "blue", "black" or "white"
    - season: "summer", "winter" "fall" or "spring"
    - price: Price in dollars.
    - description: At least 30 words description of the items.
   Include color
       and season.
   Output it as a json list.
   ```

2. We will save the generated data in a file called `data.json`, which should look like this:

   ```
   [
    {
      "name": "Red T-shirt",
      "type": "t-shirt",
      "color": "red",
      "season": "summer",
      "price": 15,
      "description": "This vibrant red t-shirt is perfect for
   summer days...."
    },
    {
        "name": "Winter Jeans",
        "type": "pants",
        "color": "blue",
        "season": "winter",
        "price": 45,
        "description": "Stay warm and stylish this winter with
   these blue..."
    },
    ...
   ]
   ```

3. Let's now proceed to load the data and construct `Document` items suitable for use within LangChain. This can be accomplished using the following Python code snippet:

```python
import json
from langchain_core.documents import Document

with open("data.json") as input_file:
    items = json.load(input_file)

documents = [
  Document(f"{item['name']}: {item['description']}") for item in
items
]
```

This code transforms the raw data from the JSON file into a list of `Document` objects, each containing both the name and description of a clothing item.

4. Next, let's build a vector store capable of retrieving these documents based on similarity. For simplicity, we'll utilize Chroma, an in-memory vector store. *Chapter 4* provides a more comprehensive exploration of the various vector stores offered by Google Cloud and their respective capabilities. To use Chroma, ensure you have the necessary package installed by executing the following command:

```
pip install langchain_chroma
```

5. The following code constructs a vector store and a retriever, and exposes it as a tool to be used in a LangChain workflow. It initializes the `VertexAIEmbeddings` model for text embeddings, constructs the `Chroma` vector store from the prepared documents, and configures the retriever instance to return the top three most relevant documents. Finally, the `create_retriever_tool` function packages this retriever as a tool:

```python
from langchain_chroma import Chroma
from langchain_google_vertexai import VertexAIEmbeddings
from langchain.tools.retriever import create_retriever_tool


embedding_model = VertexAIEmbeddings(
    model_name="textembedding-gecko@003")
vector_store = Chroma.from_documents(
    documents=documents,
    embedding=embedding_model
)
retriever = vector_store.as_retriever(k = 3)
retriever_tool = create_retriever_tool(
    retriever=retriever,
    name="retrieve_items",
```

```
    description="Retrieves clothing item descriptions from the
knowledge base."
)
```

When defining a tool, providing a precise and informative description is crucial. The generator model relies on this description to assess the tool's relevance and determine appropriate usage scenarios within the context of user queries.

6. We can now invoke the tool:

    ```
    response = retriever_tool.invoke(
        "I want a black coat for winter")
    print(response)
    ```

    This is expected to return the most relevant documents, as follows:

    ```
    - This classic black wool coat is perfect for fall. The warm,
    insulating...
    - This classic black wool coat is a timeless investment piece.
    The sleek...
    - Stay stylish and warm this fall with this sleek black leather
    jacket. The...
    ```

7. To bring our agent to life, we'll define a cognitive architecture using LangGraph. In this example, we'll establish a structure akin to the one outlined in *Chapter 10*. However, we'll substitute the conditional edge that determines tool usage and the tool node itself with a retriever tool node. *Figure 11.4* provides a diagram of the architecture.

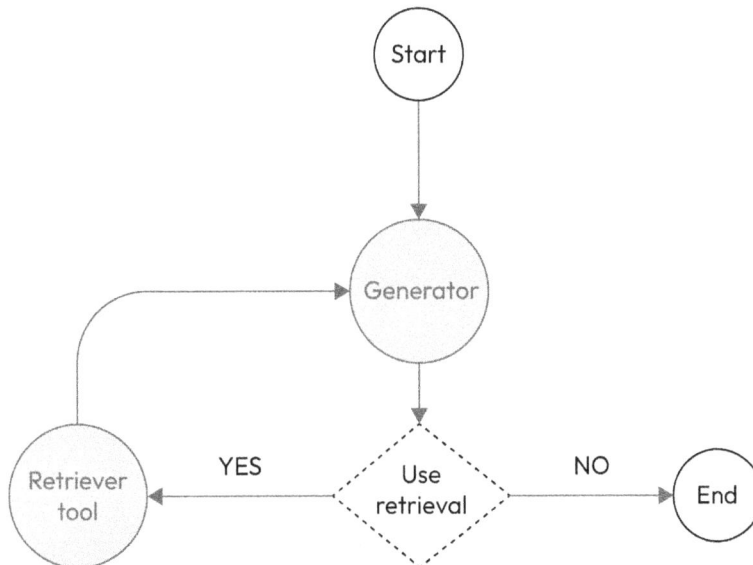

Figure 11.4 - LangGraph agentic RAG cognitive architecture

Let's now proceed to implement the cognitive architecture using the following code.

First, we will need the following imports from LangChain and LangGraph:

```python
from typing import Literal
from langchain_google_vertexai import ChatVertexAI
from langchain_core.messages import (
    AnyMessage, HumanMessage, SystemMessage)

from langgraph.graph import StateGraph, MessagesState, END
from langgraph.prebuilt import ToolNode
tools = [retriever_tool]
```

Next, we can move to implement the logic of each of the nodes:

```python
generator = ChatVertexAI(
    model_name="gemini-1.5-pro-001",
    temperature = 0
).bind(tools=tools)

def invoke_generator(state: MessagesState) -> None:
    """ Represents the generator node.
    """
    print("---")
    for message in state["messages"]:
        message.pretty_print()
    response = generator.invoke(state["messages"])
    state["messages"].append(response)

def use_retrieval(
    state: MessagesState
) -> Literal["retriever_tool", END]:
    """"Represents the use_retrieval conditional edge."""
    if not state["messages"]:
        return END
    if state["messages"][-1].tool_calls:
        return "retriever_tool"
    return END

tool_node = ToolNode(tools)
```

Finally, we define the graph structure by adding the nodes and edges:

```
graph = StateGraph(MessagesState)
graph.add_node("generator", invoke_generator)
graph.add_node("retriever_tool", tool_node)
graph.set_entry_point("generator")
graph.add_conditional_edges("generator", use_retrieval)
graph.add_edge("retriever_tool", "generator")
agentic_rag = graph.compile()
```

Once the graph is compiled, we need to provide a suitable prompt for the generator node. Since we're building an assistant capable of retrieving items and answering questions about them, here's a simple example of such a prompt:

```
GENERATOR_PROMPT = """
  - You are a useful assistant that help users navigate a catalog of
    clothing items.
  - You can retrieve clothing items from the catalog using a natural
    language query.
  - Answer in natural language and format your output using paragraph
    or bullet points if necessary.
  """
```

With the prompt set, let's test the agent with a simple question:

```
messages = [
    SystemMessage(GENERATOR_PROMPT),
    HumanMessage("Hello! How can you help me?")
]

stream_generator = agentic_rag.stream(
    {"messages": messages}, stream_mode="values")

for state in stream_generator:
    state["messages"][-1].pretty_print()
```

In this case, we intuitively know that the agent should use the retriever tool, but only use information contained in the prompt. As such, if we print the steps of the response, we get the following output:

```
=== Human Message ===
Hello! How can you help me?


===Ai Message ===
I can help you navigate a catalog of clothing items. For example, you
can ask me to find a red dress or a pair of blue jeans.
```

Conversely, let's explore how the agent handles a query that needs to retrieve live data from our clothing catalog. This will reveal how the agent dynamically integrates tool usage into its response generation process:

```
messages = [
    SystemMessage(GENERATOR_PROMPT),
    HumanMessage("Do you have any yellow t-shirts?")
]
stream_generator = agentic_rag.stream(
    {"messages": messages}, stream_mode="values")

for state in stream_generator:
    state["messages"][-1].pretty_print()
state["messages"][-1].pretty_print()
```

As shown in the following output, the agent has now opted to use the `retrieve_items` tool:

```
=== Human Message ===
Do you have any yellow t-shirts?


=== Tool Message ===
Name: retrieve_items


- Sunny Day Tee: This vibrant yellow t-shirt...
- Summer Solstice Tank: Stay cool and comfortable...
- Blossom Blouse: Embrace the beauty of spring with...


=== Ai Message ====
We have the Sunny Day Tee. It's a vibrant yellow t-shirt perfect for
sunny summer days. It's made from soft, breathable cotton and features
a classic crew neck and relaxed fit.
```

It's particularly noteworthy that despite the retriever tool fetching three items, the generator model correctly utilized only the first one to generate its response, as it was the only one relevant to the user's query.

This architecture offers flexibility and isn't limited to a single retrieval method. It can accommodate various retrieval types (such as one semantic and another keyword-based) or even utilize different retrievers for distinct knowledge bases. This allows the generator model to be prompted to dynamically choose the most suitable retriever based on the user's query.

RAG agents are particularly well-suited for addressing challenges involving unstructured data. In the next section, we will explore how to use agents to retrieve data from structured databases.

NL2SQL

Beyond using RAG for unstructured data retrieval, we can also use agents to analyze structured data sources. For this purpose, we can build an agent capable of querying a database and providing answers to user queries based on the results.

To work with the structured data generated previously, we'll create an SQLite database that can be used in your local environment. However, it's worth noting that any other structured data source could be used, such as Cloud SQL, by employing the `Database` interface offered within `langchain_community`. To proceed with this example, we'll need to install the `langchain_community` library:

```
pip install langchain_community
```

The following code creates a single table within the database named `ITEMS`. The columns in this table align with the structure of the data generated earlier:

```
from langchain_community.utilities import SQLDatabase

db = SQLDatabase.from_uri("sqlite:///database.sqlite")
db.run(
    """
    CREATE TABLE ITEMS (
        name TEXT,
        type TEXT,
        color TEXT,
        season TEXT,
        price FLOAT,
        description TEXT
    )
    """
)
```

Finally, we populate the database by inserting each record using individual `INSERT INTO` statements:

```
import json

with open("data.json") as input_file:
    items = json.load(input_file)

sanitize = lambda string: string.replace("'", "")  # Remove apostrophe

records = [
    ", ".join(
        f"'{sanitize(value)}'" if isinstance(value, str) else
str(value)
```

```
        for colname, value in item.items()
    )
    for item in items
]
for record in records:
    statement = f"INSERT INTO ITEMS VALUES ({record})"
    db.run(statement)
```

The cognitive architecture of a simple NLSQL agent is like that of a RAG agent, with the key difference being the tools available. In this case, the tool can execute SQL queries, as illustrated in *Figure 11.5*:

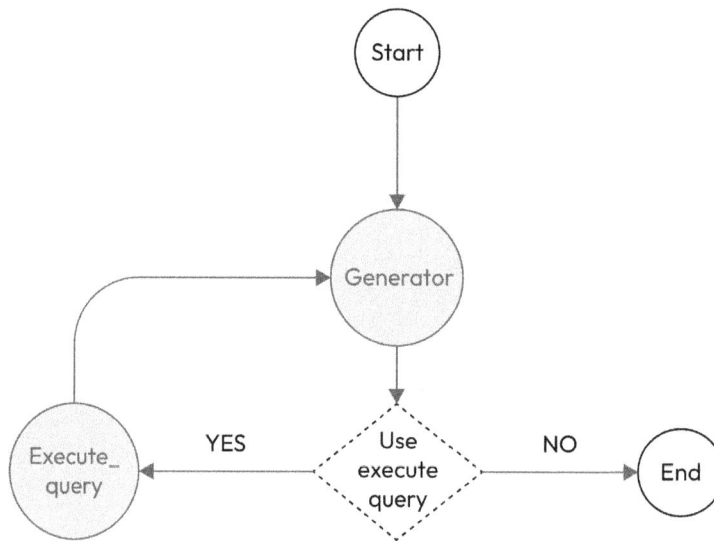

Figure 11.5 - LangGraph SQL agent cognitive architecture

Next, let's construct our tool using LangChain's `tool` decorator. Remember, it's very important to provide a clear docstring when using this decorator. The **docstring** serves as the function's description within the generator prompt. For our tool, we'll include the database schema directly in the prompt, enabling the model to generate accurate SQL statements.

For more complex scenarios, the code could be enhanced by incorporating a tool that dynamically retrieves the database schema, allowing the language model to adapt to changes in the database structure:

from langchain_core.tools import tool

```
@tool
def execute_query(query: str) -> str:
    """
    Executes a query against the clothing items database.
```

```
The schema of the database is the following:
```sql
CREATE TABLE ITEMS
(
    name TEXT, -- Name of the item
    type TEXT, -- Type of the item can be 't-shirt', 'pants' or
'coat'
    color TEXT, -- Color of the item. Can be "red", "blue",
"black" or "white"
    season TEXT, -- Can be "summer", "winter" "fall" or "spring"
    price FLOAT, -- Prize in dollars.
    description TEXT -- Description of the item
)
```
"""
return db.run_no_throw(query)
```

In the preceding code, the `run_no_throw` method executes the provided SQL query against the `clothing items` database. It returns the query result as a string if successful. If the query encounters an error, `run_no_throw` returns the error message itself. This error-handling mechanism allows the agent to identify and rectify incorrect queries and retry the query if necessary.

Let's proceed to build the LangGraph graph, similar to our approach in the prior section. However, note that, in this instance, the conditional edge is directed toward `query_tool`, and our tools list now incorporates the `execute_query` function we just defined:

```
graph = StateGraph(MessagesState)
graph.add_node("generator", invoke_generator)
graph.add_node("query_tool",
    ToolNode(tools= [execute_query]))
graph.set_entry_point("generator")

graph.add_conditional_edges("generator", use_execute_query)
graph.add_edge("query_tool", "generator")

agentic_sql = graph.compile()
```

The prompt for the generator model can be structured similarly to the one we employed for the agentic RAG but, in this scenario, we explicitly state that it can use SQL to fetch items from the database. For more complex use cases, we can also specify the SQL dialect it should use, such as MySQL or BigQuery:

```
GENERATOR_PROMPT = """
    - You are a useful assistant that help users navigate a catalog of
      clothing items.
    - You can retrieve clothing items from the catalog using a SQL
query.
```

```
        - Answer in natural language and format your output using
paragraph
        or bullet points if necessary.
    """
```

Now, we can execute the compiled application and pose a question about the database using the following code snippet:

```
messages = [
    SystemMessage(GENERATOR_PROMPT),
    HumanMessage("Can you show me the name and price of all coats?")
]

stream_generator = agentic_sql.stream(
    {"messages": messages}, stream_mode="values")

for state in stream_generator:
    state["messages"][-1].pretty_print()
state["messages"][-1].pretty_print()
```

This code initializes a conversation with the system, providing the GENERATOR_PROMPT as context. The user then asks to see the name and price of all coats. The agentic_sql.stream function processes this request, likely executing a SQL query against the database to retrieve the relevant information. The results are then streamed back and printed in a formatted manner using pretty_print:

```
=== Human Message ===
Can you show me the name and price of all coats?

=== Tool Message ====
Name: execute_query
query: SELECT name, price FROM ITEMS WHERE type = 'coat'

[('Midnight Magic Coat', 89.99), ('Autumn Hues Sweater', 49.99),
('Winter Wonderland Jacket', 79.99), ('Cozy Cabin Cardigan', 59.99),
('Fall Foliage Vest', 49.99), ('Snowy Peaks Parka', 99.99)]

=== Ai Message ===
Here are the coats and their prices:

* Midnight Magic Coat, $89.99
* Autumn Hues Sweater, $49.99
* Winter Wonderland Jacket, $79.99
```

```
* Cozy Cabin Cardigan, $59.99
* Fall Foliage Vest, $49.99
* Snowy Peaks Parka, $99.99
```

In the preceding output, we observe the agent executing a query, retrieving the results, and then generating a well-formatted response.

Granting the agent the ability to execute SQL statements enhances its capabilities, allowing it to perform calculations in addition to retrieving information. Let's consider the following question:

```
messages = [
    SystemMessage(GENERATOR_PROMPT),
    HumanMessage("What is the name and price in euros of the most
expensive coat, given that 1 euro is currently 1.1 dollars?")
]

stream_generator = agentic_sql.stream(
    {"messages": messages}, stream_mode="values")

for state in stream_generator:
    state["messages"][-1].pretty_print()
state["messages"][-1].pretty_print()
```

The agent is not only able to correctly identify Snowy Peaks Parka as the priciest coat but also accurately converts its dollar price into euros based on the provided exchange rate:

```
=== Human Message ===
What is the name and price in euros of the most expensive coat, given
that 1 euro is currently 1.1 dollars?
=== Tool Message ===
Name: execute_query
query: SELECT name, price * 1.1 FROM ITEMS WHERE type = "coat" ORDER
BY price DESC LIMIT 1

[('Snowy Peaks Parka', 109.989)]
=== Ai Message ===
The most expensive coat is the Snowy Peaks Parka and its price is
109.99 euros.
```

Using the LangGraph framework, we can easily introduce new functionalities to our existing architecture. For instance, a new node can be integrated into the system tasked with correcting the syntax of the SQL query produced by the generator when necessary. The new architecture is shown in the following figure:

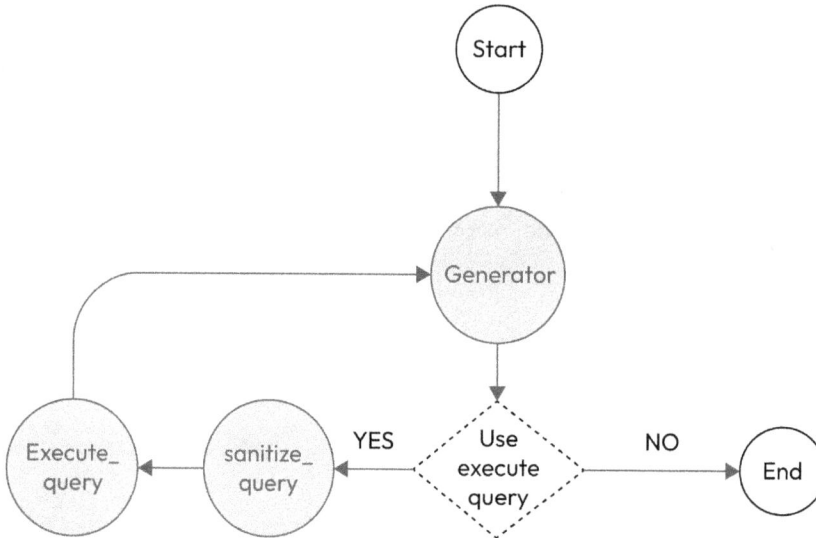

Figure 11.6 - LangGraph SQL agent with query preprocessing

This modification involves integrating a new node, sanitize_query, into the LangGraph structure. We'll adjust the conditional edge to point to this new node (thus modifying the use_execute_query function) and introduce an additional edge connecting it to the execute_query node. The new graph structure is defined as follows:

```
graph = StateGraph(MessagesState)
graph.add_node("generator", invoke_generator)
graph.add_node("query_tool",
    ToolNode(tools = [execute_query]))
graph.add_node("sanitize_query", sanitize_query)
graph.set_entry_point("generator")

graph.add_conditional_edges("generator", use_execute_query)
graph.add_edge("sanitize_query", "query_tool")
graph.add_edge("query_tool", "generator")


agentic_sql = graph.compile()
```

In scenarios where an agent might get stuck in a loop of calling the `execute_query` function, it could become necessary to introduce a mechanism to track the number of calls made. This allows the agent to break the loop once a predefined limit is reached, preventing potential infinite loops.

To achieve this, we can enhance the state representation beyond a simple list of messages. The state could include a counter variable specifically dedicated to tracking the number of `execute_query` calls. We can accomplish this using LangGraph by defining a custom state class, as shown in the following snippet:

```
class AppState(MessagesState):
    """ Extended state with a field for tracking number of queries
    """
    consecutive_queries: int = 0
```

Additionally, we'll need a node dedicated to handling errors. The conditional edge should be adjusted to redirect to this error-handling node when the call limit is reached:

```
QUERY_LIMIT = 5

def use_execute_query(
    state: AppState
) -> Literal["sanitize_query", END]:
    if not state["messages"]:  # Dummy case where no message is input
        return END

    if state["messages"][-1].tool_calls:
        has_reached_limit = state["consecutive_queries"] >= QUERY_
LIMIT
        if not has_reached_limit:
            state["consecutive_queries"] += 1
            return "sanitize_query"
        else:
            return "generate_error"

    return END
```

The resulting architecture incorporating the error-handling node and the modified conditional edge is illustrated in *Figure 11.7*:

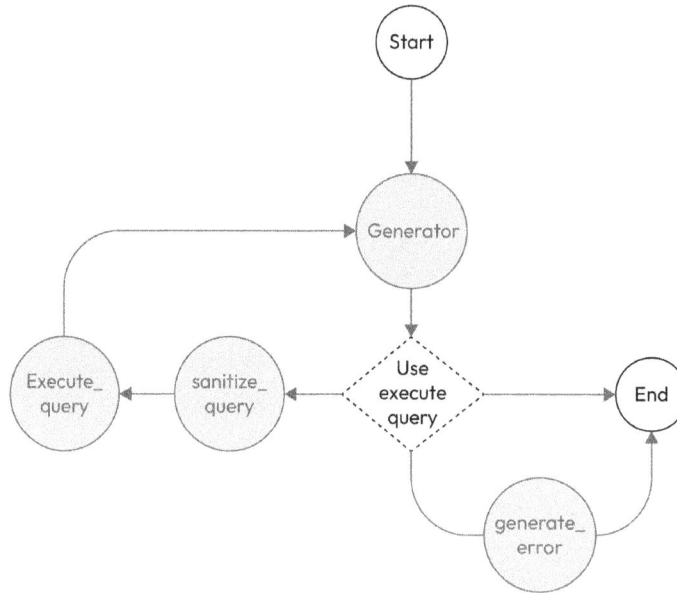

Figure 11.7 - Adding a loop break to the cognitive architecture

This approach showcases the adaptability and modularity of the LangGraph architecture. By incrementally introducing new nodes and edges, and adjusting the state representation as needed, we can progressively evolve our system to manage more intricate scenarios and fulfill evolving requirements. The key advantage lies in preserving the independence of behavior within each node, fostering a clean, maintainable, and scalable design.

Summary

In this chapter, we explored the concept of agentic RAG and its implementation using LangChain and Google Cloud's Vertex AI. We demonstrated how to create a knowledge base, build a vector store, and define a cognitive architecture using LangGraph. This architecture enables the language model to interact with the knowledge base, retrieve relevant information, and generate contextually appropriate responses.

Furthermore, we also delved into the application of agents for analyzing structured data sources. You learned how to construct an agent capable of querying a database and delivering answers based on the retrieved results. The provided examples highlighted the agent's ability to not only fetch data but also perform calculations, such as currency conversions, based on the user's query.

Part 4: Designing Generative AI Applications

We're going to talk about what additional details you should take into consideration when designing generative AI applications. Besides giving a brief overview of Google Cloud's foundations, we'll explore system design requirements for generative AI applications in enterprise settings and look into a few common architectural patterns.

If you're new to Google Cloud, we encourage you to look at *Appendix 2*, where we provide an intro to various aspects of building scalable enterprise platforms on Google Cloud.

This part has the following chapters:

- *Chapter 12, Evaluating Generative AI Applications*
- *Chapter 13, Generative AI System Design*

12

Evaluating GenAI Applications

Large Language Models (LLMs) have proved their performance on a variety of **Natural Language Processing (NLP)** tasks and even their abilities of common reasoning. When new LLMs are released, they are typically tested on various generalized datasets, and performance benchmarks and leaderboards are publicly available. Still, when building **Generative AI (GenAI)** applications, we need to evaluate their performance on the underlying task (or tasks) we're working on. We need this for two reasons – to ensure we meet product requirements and quality expectations, and to compare various architectures or prompting techniques to pick the best setup for our specific use case.

In this chapter, we're going to discuss how you can evaluate a GenAI application, briefly touch on using **LangSmith** for tracing and debugging your application's performance, and explore using **Vertex AI** evaluation capabilities with LangChain.

Here, we'll cover the following topics:

- Metrics to evaluate GenAI applications
- Methods to evaluate GenAI applications
- **Pointwise evaluation** with LangChain and Vertex Evaluation services
- **Pairwise evaluation** with LangChain and Vertex Evaluation services

Technical requirements

First, register at `https://smith.langchain.com/` and create an API key. You can use a free version for the purposes of this chapter.

To follow the examples of this chapter, in addition to specific requirements for each service mentioned, you will need an active Google Cloud project and a Python environment with the following libraries installed:

```
pip install langchain-google-vertexai langsmith
export LANGCHAIN_TRACING_V2=true
export LANGCHAIN_API_KEY=<your-api-key>
```

You can find all the code in this chapter on the GitHub repository:

`https://github.com/PacktPublishing/Generative-AI-on-Google-Cloud-with-LangChain`

Evaluating GenAI applications

Evaluating GenAI applications is still an open problem. Unfortunately, up until now, many engineering teams tend to ignore this aspect, and their preferred way of evaluating such an application remains either not doing it or manually testing on a few hard-coded examples. We believe this should be changed, and that designing an evaluation approach and an internal benchmark should be your first priority after you've demoed the capabilities of GenAI and you begin developing a production-ready application. Otherwise, after you deploy your application to production, you might see unintended consequences if you don't have a proper evaluation procedure.

A big challenge is the fact that GenAI applications are not deterministic by nature, and they provide rich answers in natural language given complex tasks. That makes evaluation of such applications difficult – for example, it's not easy to compare two different summaries of text (they shouldn't necessarily match). Let's look at another example – given the question "*What is the capital of Germany?*" and a golden answer of "*Berlin is the capital of Germany,*" we might get the following answers:

- *Berlin is the capital of Germany.*

- *The capital of Germany is Berlin.*

- *Berlin.*

- *Bern is the capital of Germany.*

- *Munich is the capital of Germany.*

- *Berlin is the capital of France.*

- *Berlin is the capital of Germany, and Paris is the capital of France.*

If we want to evaluate the factuality of our questions, it becomes difficult since most metrics measure the similarity between the expected and the received answer. In our examples, such similarities might be misleading.

A scientific approach to evaluation is the key to building scalable and reliable GenAI applications. First, such applications in general, and LLMs in particular, are non-deterministic. That means evaluating an improvement of your prompt based on a single run and a single example might not be a good idea. Second, such applications quickly become complex pipelines with multiple stages and hyperparameters, and even a small change might lead to unforeseeable outcomes. Hence, you need to build your own benchmarks and invest in collecting your domain and task-specific datasets. The good news is that you don't need large evaluation datasets. 30-50 examples is already a good starting point, and you can grow your datasets over time.

Why 30-50 examples? 5-10 examples is too small of an amount, and you might face a high risk of overfitting your prompts and your pipeline parameters. 30-50 examples are still relatively feasible to gather, and it gives you a good start. Since most metrics we discuss are proportions, your confidence range for estimating them will further narrow down as you increase the number of examples in your evaluation dataset up to 400 and over.

Let's take a look at the key approaches to evaluate GenAI applications, and then discuss each of them in detail:

- **Comparison on a benchmark**: A public or private dataset is used to evaluate a GenAI application. When running this type of evaluation, you need to choose a dataset and an appropriate metric. A metric can be computed deterministically depending on predicted input and output (e.g., a **cosine distance** between two strings), but choosing a good metric is a challenge given the complex nature of the tasks mentioned previously. Some of these metrics – such as cosine distance, edit distance, and fuzzy string match – don't require an exact match between two strings but estimate a level of "closeness" between the expected output and the predicted one.

- **Use LLMs to evaluate results**: Typically, an LLM (such as **GPT-4** or **Gemini-1.5-PRO**) is used to evaluate generative applications based on simpler models. In other words, in this case, the metric is determined by the LLM itself (maybe another LLM than the one that was used to generate the predictions). There is some evidence in the literature, however, that using LLMs as a judge should be done cautiously since they tend to prefer generated output over human output, and themselves over alternative LLMs [1], [3].

- **Human-in-the-loop evaluation**: Humans are asked to evaluate the answers produced by GenAI applications on various scales such as factuality, tone, harmlessness, and so on.

From another point of view, the evaluation pipeline can be divided into two categories:

- **Pointwise evaluation** (or **string evaluators** as LangChain names them) evaluates single input-output pairs by comparing an output generated by your GenAI application with a desired output.

- **Pairwise evaluation** (or **comparison evaluators** as LangChain names them) evaluates different foundational models (or GenAI pipelines) one versus the other. It helps to choose which combination of hyperparameters (including different versions of your prompts or fine-tuned models) to use.

In this chapter, we'll focus on the quality of your applications, but in general, you also need to evaluate the system's performance (looking into such metrics as latency, throughput, reliability, costs, etc.) and business performance. For example, if you're developing a shopping assistant for your website, measure conversion into purchase and average basket size for users being offered to use the assistant.

LangSmith

LangSmith is a commercial offering from LangChain to help developers to trace and evaluate GenAI applications. It simplifies the development and troubleshooting of such applications. With LangSmith, you can achieve the following:

- Enhance visibility with clear insights and debugging information at each stage of an LLM sequence. Identify and resolve your problems more easily.

- Natively render chat messages, functions, and retrieved documents. This, in turn, improves the overall development and debugging experience.

- Easily collect and share traces of your applications with your colleagues.

- Collect datasets from product logs and annotate them with human labelers (and manage such annotations with annotation queues).

- Organize, share, and re-use your prompts.

You can start using LangSmith with a free plan at `https://smith.langchain.com/`. You need to register and create your API key. After doing this, you can add the following configuration to your application:

```
import os
os.environ["LANGCHAIN_TRACING_V2"] = "true"
os.environ["LANGCHAIN_PROJECT"] = "Tracing example"
os.environ["LANGCHAIN_API_KEY"] = "YOUR_API_KEY"
```

LangSmith organizes traces into projects, so feel free to use your own name. Now let's take a simple example from the previous chapter, and collect traces (you can find the full code on our GitHub repository). Let's run our **Retrieval-Augmented Generation (RAG)**:

```
chain_rag = (
    {
        "context": retriever | format_docs,
        "question": RunnablePassthrough(),
    }
```

```
    | prompt
    | llm
    | StrOutputParser()
)
chain_rag.invoke("What was Alphabet's revenue in 2022?")
```

We can see all steps on LangSmith (with the latency, amount of tokens consumed, and other useful information), as shown in *Figure 12.1*.

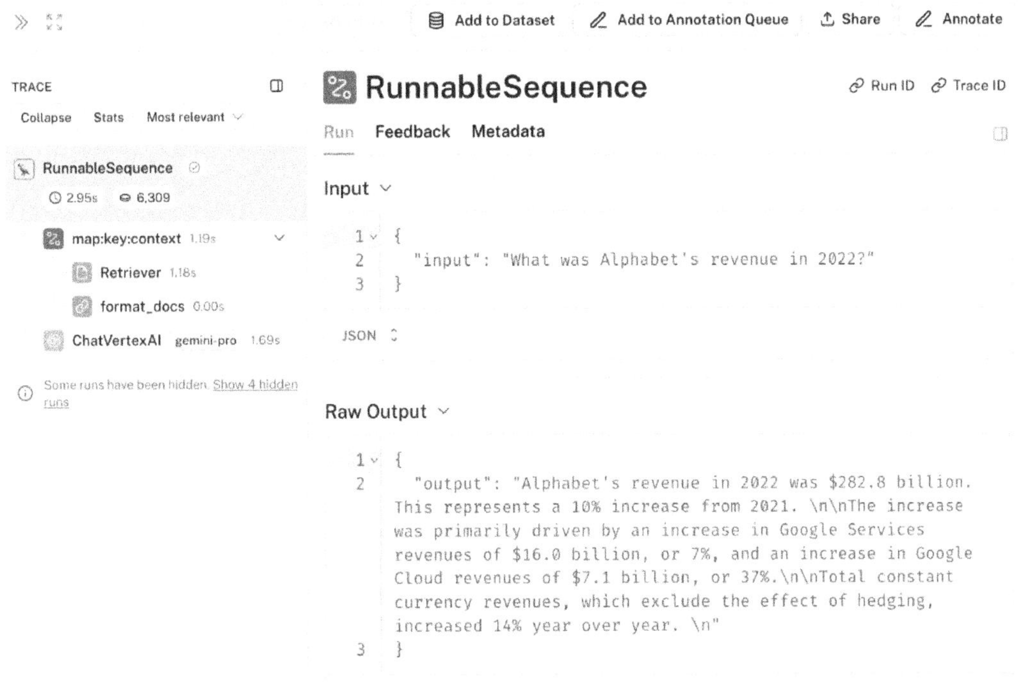

Figure 12.1 – Tracking a Runnable with LangSmith

We can explore input and outputs for each step that help debug the invocation. For example, let's explore all chunks retrieved by the chunks retriever from the vector store:

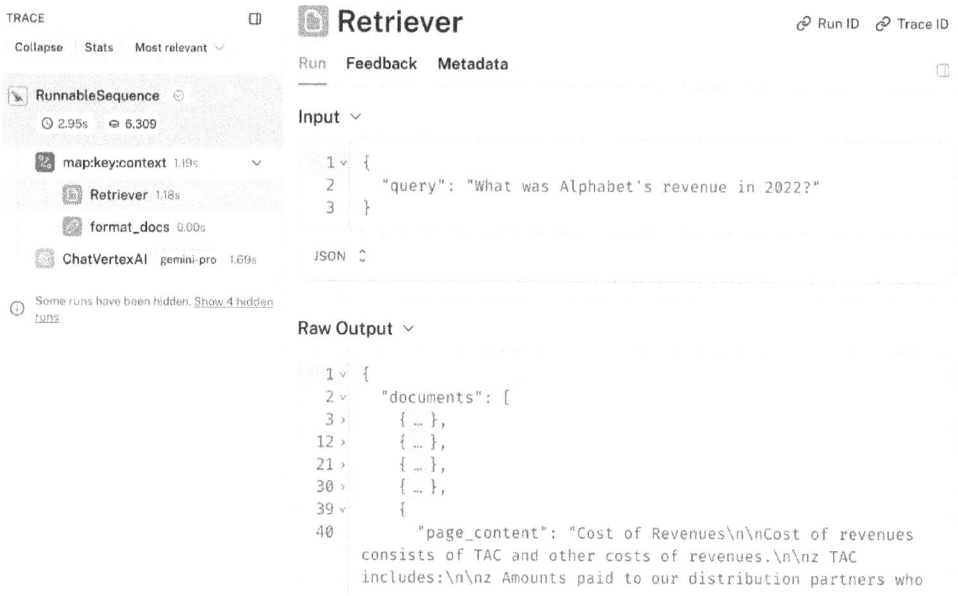

Figure 12.2 – Tracking chunks received from a retriever step

LangChain Hub for prompt management

When you're developing your GenAI applications, you typically experiment with different prompts. Your applications grow in complexity, and understanding the influence of a new prompt on the overall performance becomes more difficult. You also need a way to track your prompts and measure their performance.

LangChain offers you such capabilities with LangSmith and **LangChain Hub**. You can put your prompts on LangSmith, and then retrieve them with an API or share by link. All changes to the prompts will be saved in history, and you can traverse it back. You can also make your prompts public (or re-use somebody else's public prompts). For example, let's use a public prompt for RAG, which can be found at `https://smith.langchain.com/hub/rlm/rag-prompt`:

```
from langchain import hub
prompt_v1 = hub.pull("rlm/rag-prompt")

chain_rag_v1 = (
    {
        "context": retriever | format_docs,
        "question": RunnablePassthrough(),
    }
```

```
    | prompt_v1
    | ChatVertexAI(
        temperature=0, model_name="gemini-pro",
        max_output_tokens=1024)
    | StrOutputParser()
)
chain_rag_v1.invoke("What was Alphabet's revenue in 2022?")
>> Alphabet's revenue in 2022 was $282.8 billion. This represents a
10% increase from the previous year.
```

Datasets and benchmarks

To run your evaluations, you need to collect your own datasets. In traditional machine learning, a dataset is typically a pair of *input* and *output*. In GenAI, it might be a little bit different. First, if we use LLM-based evaluations, we don't necessarily need to provide an expected output (although it's beneficial). Hence, the dataset might consist of an input only and an optional expected output. Secondly, your dataset might have additional fields – for example, the context provided to the LLM, human evaluations, and so on.

LangChain allows you to define three types of datasets:

- A kv dataset helps you to evaluate GenAI applications (e.g., agents) that require multiple inputs or outputs. Such datasets are just a collection of arbitrary key-value pairs.

- An llm dataset contains a sequence of string input and output pairs.

- A chat dataset contains a sequence of input and output pairs where both input and output are lists of serialized chat messages.

Collecting your own dataset and building your own evaluation pipelines (or benchmarks) is extremely important to control the performance of your application and make sure your changes do impact it positively. An important note is that sometimes you can enrich your dataset with synthetic data. You can use LLMs to augment (or paraphrase) your human-gathered datasets or to create completely new examples based on a task description. You can read more in a synthetic data generation tutorial on LangChain [4].

LangChain and LangSmith allow you to construct and manage your datasets programmatically or via UI. We recommend that you store your raw datasets on **Google Cloud Storage** as CSVs and programmatically create corresponding datasets on LangSmith. You can also define your evaluation pipelines (or benchmarks), programmatically run them on specified datasets, and collect and visualize such runs in the LangSmith user interface.

We will further introduce you to LangSmith in the following sections. While discussing evaluations and providing examples, we'll collect evaluators' traces with LangSmith to better understand what's happening under the hood and how evaluations are performed.

Pointwise evaluations

Let's start our deeper discussion with pointwise evaluations. Just to recap, a pointwise evaluation is when you compare the generated output (for a given input) with the expected output. First, let's start with using existing benchmarks for evaluation.

Comparison on benchmarks

When solving enterprise problems, you typically work on already explored problem classes. Your goal is to choose the best approach from existing ones and adjust it to the specific business needs (and that's one of the distinctions between research and industry). That means that typically, it's a good idea to take a look at how this type of problem has been formulated in academic literature, what dataset has been collected, and how solutions have been evaluated.

There are dozens or hundreds of publicly available benchmarks and datasets (some of them are not intended for commercial use though, or are subject to an additional license). The industry is evolving from datasets with relatively simple **Natural Language Understanding (NLU)** tasks – such as **Language Modeling Broadened to Account for Discourse Aspects (LAMBADA)**, **General Language Understanding Evaluation (GLUE)**, **Stanford Question Answering Dataset (SQuAD)** or others – to more complex ones, such as **TriviaQA**, **Conversational Question Answering Challenge (CoQA)**, **Harder Endings, Longer contexts, and Lowshot Activities for Situations With Adversarial Generations (HellaSWAG)**, and many others [2].

The goal of our book is not to cover all existing datasets, but if you're looking for one, a good starting point is to start with **Hugging Face**, **Tensorflow Datasets**, **Kaggle Datasets**, or **Google Dataset Search**.

Take into account how a dataset is constructed (i.e., what are labels and what are examples), what its size is, and how test-train-evaluation split is performed.

Evaluation metrics

There are many different metrics used to evaluate LLMs and GenAI applications in general. We will give you a few examples since going deep into a discussion on which metric to choose is beyond the scope of this book. Depending on your application, you might want to choose a different metric. How do you choose a good one? Look at which metrics are quoted in research papers in a similar domain or on a problem like the one you're working on.

Some metrics that can be evaluated by comparing input and output pairs are as follows:

- **Distance between vectors (embedded string) or raw strings** can help measure the similarity between input and output. There are multiple ways to define such a distance (we'll briefly touch on these varieties later in this chapter) – for example, cosine distance between embeddings or editorial distance between raw strings.

- **Recall-Oriented Understudy for Gisting Evaluation** (**Rouge**) is a set of metrics commonly used to evaluate the quality of generated text, particularly in tasks such as text summarization and machine translation. Rouge measures the overlap of **n-grams** (contiguous sequences of *n* words) between the generated text and a reference text. The higher the overlap, the better the score, indicating higher similarity between the two. Examples of Rouge metrics are **RougeL** (considers the longest common subsequence, focusing on sentence-level structure rather than just individual words) or **Rouge2** (measures the overlap of word bigrams, i.e., n=2).

- **Bilingual Evaluation Understudy** (**Bleu**) **score** is another metric typically used for summarization or translation tasks. It originates from machine translation research, and it measures the similarity between the machine translation to one or more reference translations provided by humans. It's similar to Rouge since it operates on word n-gram overlaps. It's important to mention that both Rouge and Bleu scores don't have either a notion of synonyms or an understanding of syntax order. Hence, these metrics might be misleading for question-answering or free text generation tasks (and we typically favor LLM evaluators for such tasks).

Additional metrics might require the involvement of a human to label outputs:

- **Accuracy** measures how well the model generates correct responses. For example, in a question-answering use case, accuracy can be measured as the percentage of questions answered correctly.

- **Groundness** measures the extent to which your application's responses are based on and supported by the input data or context.

- **Toxicity** or fairness measures the extent to which your application generates toxic outputs, or outputs that contain perpetuating stereotypes, discrimination against certain groups, or harmful content.

LangChain interfaces

LangChain exposes a `langchain.evaluation.StringEvaluator` interface that exposes an abstract `_evaluate_strings` (and its asynchronous version, `_aevaluate_strings`). It takes the following parameters:

- `prediction`: This is a predicted string.

- `reference`: This is a label to compare a predicted string against. For some evaluators, `reference` might be optional, so these evaluators are not exactly pointwise but they just evaluate an input on a certain scale.

- `input`: This is additional input that should be provided for evaluation (if needed).

Like with any LangChain runnable, you can pass any additional arguments that your evaluator needs as `kwargs`.

For pairwise evaluations, LangChain exposes a `langchain.evaluation.Pairwise StringEvaluator` interface with a similar list of arguments, but it also expects a `prediction_b` argument – it's a prediction from the candidate application's configuration.

We will discuss out-of-the-box evaluators available on LangChain, but if you need a custom one for your application, you can build such an evaluator and use it with your applications.

LangChain pointwise evaluators

Most LangChain out-of-the-box evaluators are LLM-based.

We'll start with the **question-answering evaluators**: qa, cot_qa, and context_qa evaluate a Q&A task with an LLM by rating a prediction as correct or incorrect. You can run these evaluators directly by providing a list:

```
from langchain.evaluation import load_evaluator
from langchain_google_vertexai import ChatVertexAI

llm = ChatVertexAI(model_name="gemini-1.5-pro-001")
evaluator_qa = load_evaluator("qa", llm=llm)
example = {
    "query": "What is the capital of Germany?",
    "answer": "Berlin is the capital of Germany."}
prediction = {"result": "Berlin."}
results = evaluator_qa.evaluate(
    examples=[example],
    predictions=[prediction]

)
print(results[0])
>> {'results': 'GRADE: CORRECT \n'}
```

If we explore it on LangSmith, we can use that the evaluation made a single call to the underlying LLM with the following prompt:

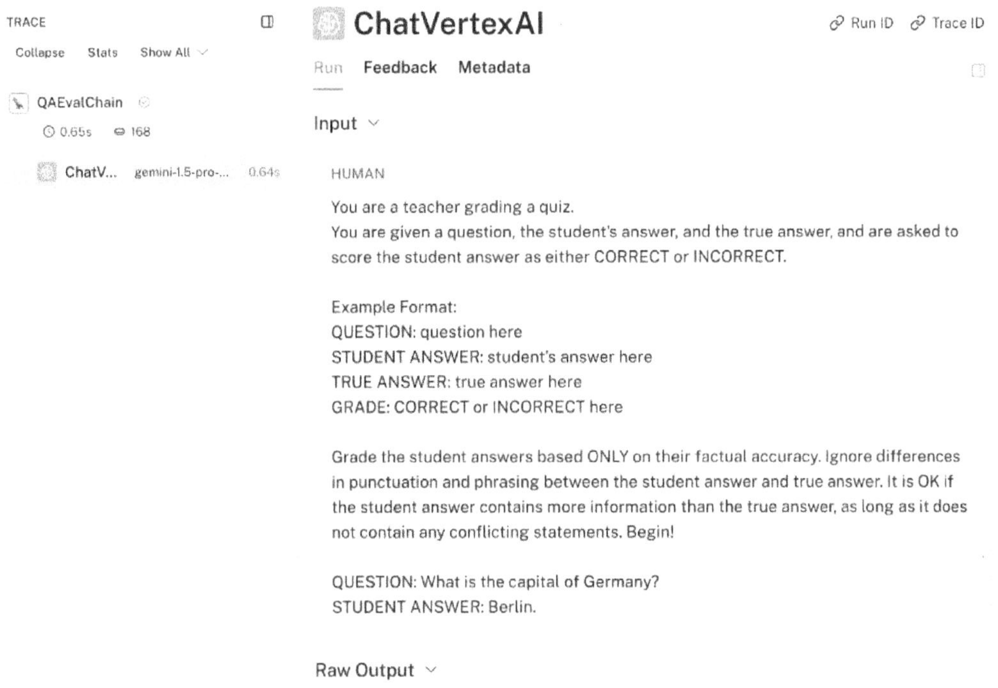

TRACE   ⊡   ⬤ **ChatVertexAI**   🔗 Run ID   🔗 Trace ID

Collapse   Stats   Show All ∨   Run   **Feedback**   Metadata   ▯

⬚ QAEvalChain ◉   **Input** ∨
   ○ 0.65s   ⊖ 168
                                                   HUMAN
      ⬚ ChatV... gemini-1.5-pro-... 0.64s
                                                   You are a teacher grading a quiz.
                                                   You are given a question, the student's answer, and the true answer, and are asked to
                                                   score the student answer as either CORRECT or INCORRECT.

                                                   Example Format:
                                                   QUESTION: question here
                                                   STUDENT ANSWER: student's answer here
                                                   TRUE ANSWER: true answer here
                                                   GRADE: CORRECT or INCORRECT here

                                                   Grade the student answers based ONLY on their factual accuracy. Ignore differences
                                                   in punctuation and phrasing between the student answer and true answer. It is OK if
                                                   the student answer contains more information than the true answer, as long as it does
                                                   not contain any conflicting statements. Begin!

                                                   QUESTION: What is the capital of Germany?
                                                   STUDENT ANSWER: Berlin.

                                                   Raw Output ∨

Figure 12.3 – Evaluation traces on LangChain

You can also use an `evaluate_strings` method, which is shared across all evaluators. It will map the `input`, `reference`, and `prediction` arguments to specific arguments for each evaluator and enrich the LLM response with parsed scores and values:

```
evaluator_qa = load_evaluator("qa", llm=llm)
result = evaluator_qa.evaluate_strings(
    input="What is the capital of Germany?",
    reference="Berlin is the capital of Germany.",
    prediction="Berlin"
)
print(result)
>> {'reasoning': 'GRADE: CORRECT', 'value': 'CORRECT', 'score': 1}
```

The `cot_qa` evaluator uses a **chain-of-thought prompting technique** (discussed in *Chapter 9*). `context_qa` doesn't require an answer but a context:

```
evaluator_contextqa = load_evaluator("context_qa", llm=llm)
example = {
    "query": "What is the capital?",
    "context": "The question is about Germany."}
prediction = {"result": "Berlin."}
results = evaluator_contextqa.evaluate(
    examples=[example],
    predictions=[prediction]
)
print(results[0])
>> {'text': 'GRADE: CORRECT \n'}
```

Since each evaluator inherits from an LLMChain class, you can inspect its default prompts by looking at the `evaluator_qa.prompt` (and you can also redefine the prompt during initialization).

Next, we have **scoring evaluators**: the `score_string` and `labeled_score_string` evaluators score an output's quality from 0 to 10 based on the question (the `input` argument) and an optional golden answer (the `reference` argument), and the second one uses the golden answer as an additional input for evaluation. All criteria are combined in a single prompt, and the LLM is asked to predict a score based on these criteria:

```
evaluator_scorestr = load_evaluator("score_string", llm=llm)
result = evaluator_scorestr.evaluate_strings(
    input="What is the capital of Germany?",
    prediction="Berlin."
)
print(result["score"])
>> 10
```

As usual, you can explore a full prompt with LangSmith:

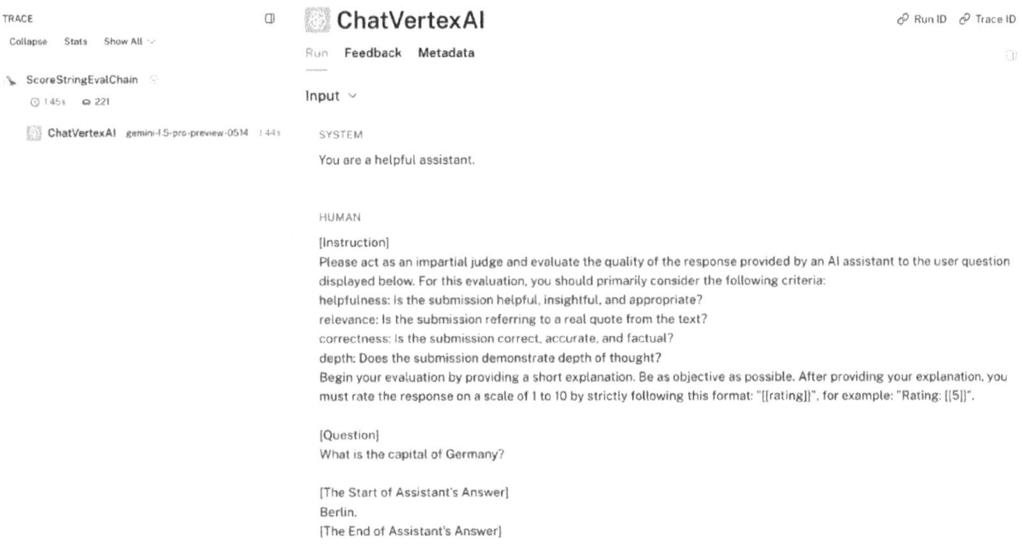

Figure 12.4 – Prompt sent to LLM using a score_string evaluator

You can also provide your custom prompt and/or change criteria during initialization.

Let's discuss how LangChain constructs criteria and adds them to the evaluating prompt. LangChain criteria are a map of scales to a text hint that is added to the prompt. You can see hints added to the evaluation prompt on the preceding trace from LangSmith.

You can take a look at the use-case for one of the pre-defined criteria:

```
from langchain.evaluation import Criteria
for c in Criteria:
    print(c.value)
```

You can also create your own.

Criteria are resolved to text hints (and these text hints are merged together into one string when substituting a prompt for evaluation):

```
from langchain.evaluation.scoring.eval_chain import resolve_criteria
print(resolve_criteria("creativity"))
>> {'creativity': 'Does the submission demonstrate novelty or unique
ideas?'}
```

You can also take a look at the default values used by evaluators:

```
print(resolve_criteria(None))
>> {'helpfulness': 'Is the submission helpful, insightful, and
appropriate?', 'relevance': 'Is the submission referring to a real
quote from the text?', 'correctness': 'Is the submission correct,
accurate, and factual?', 'depth': 'Does the submission demonstrate
depth of thought?'}
```

We also have **criteria evaluators**: the `criteria` and `labeled_criteria` evaluators are similar to the `score_string` discussed earlier, but they evaluate the output only on a 1/0 (or Y/N) scale.

There are also a bunch of **deterministic evaluators** that don't require an LLM:

- `string_distance` computes the distance between two strings (typically, distance is measured as the amount of edits needed to convert one string into another). The default distance is a **Jaro-Winkler** one, but a few other options (such as **Levenstein distance**, etc.) are available and you can pass a string `metric` argument during the evaluator's initialization that will define a type of distance measure to use.

- `embedding_distance` is similar to the `string_distance`, but it uses an embedding model to transform a text into a vector and computes the distance between two vectors.

- `regex_match` uses regular expressions to determine the quality of the output.

- `exact_match` speaks for itself.

- `json_validity`, `json_equality`, and a few others are various evaluators that are used to evaluate the quality of JSON outputs.

Vertex evaluators on LangChain

Vertex AI offers a managed GenAI evaluation service that allows you to evaluate the performance of your GenAI applications on various use case-specific metrics. GenAI evaluation offers pointwise and pairwise evaluators. Let's start with pointwise ones.

You can always check the recent list of metrics on the documentation's page (`https://cloud.google.com/vertex-ai/generative-ai/docs/models/metrics-templates#overview`), but at the moment of writing this book, the following metrics were available:

- `bleu`, `rouge1`, `rouge2`, `rougeLsum`, `rougeL`, and `exact_match` are standard NLU metrics (briefly discussed earlier) to evaluate how close a generated text is to the ground truth. They expect prediction (generated response) and reference (a ground truth) as required arguments. These metrics are evaluated algorithmically as an opposite to all other metrics that will shortly be mentioned (that are evaluated with an LLM). You can find a full list of supported computation-based metrics at `https://cloud.google.com/vertex-ai/generative-ai/docs/models/determine-eval#computation-based-metrics`.

- `coherence` evaluates the coherence of the applications' response (how well organized and cohesive it is, and whether it follows the logical flow). It expects `prediction` (generated response) as an input.

- `fluency` evaluates whether the applications' response uses natural language correctly (whether it chooses appropriate words and positions them correctly in the text, as well as whether the grammar is correct and sentences are smooth). It expects `prediction` (generated response) as an input.

- `safety` evaluates the level of safety of the application's response (there should be no hate speech, no harassing, and no dangerous or sexually explicit content). It expects `prediction` (generated response) as an input.

- `groundedness` evaluates whether the application's response references only the information provided in the context. It expects `prediction` (generated response) and `context` (background information provided to the LLM) as required arguments.

- `fulfillment` evaluates whether the application's response follows the instructions. It expects `prediction` (generated response) and `instruction` (a prompt provided to the LLM) as required arguments.

- `question_answering_quality` evaluates the quality of the application's response given the context (on four scales – groundness, comprehensiveness, relevance, and how well it follows the instruction). It expects `prediction` (generated answer), `instruction` (a Q&A prompt), and `context` (text to be used as a context to answer the question) as required arguments, and `reference` (a ground truth) as an optional one.

- `question_answering_relevance` evaluates the ability of the application to respond with clarity and only with relevant information given the context. It expects `prediction` (generated answer) and `instruction` (a Q&A prompt) as required arguments, and `context` (text to be used as a context to answer the question) and `reference` (a ground truth) as optional ones.

- `question_answering_correctness` evaluates the ability of the application to respond correctly (giving all relevant claims and not including additional claims). It expects `prediction` (generated answer) and `instruction` (a Q&A prompt) as required arguments, and `context` (text to be used as a context to answer the question) and `reference` (a ground truth) as optional ones.

- `question_answering_helpfulness` evaluates the ability of the application to respond correctly (giving all relevant claims and not including additional claims). It expects `prediction` (generated answer) and `instruction` (a Q&A prompt) as required arguments, and `context` (text to be used as a context to answer the question) and `reference` (a ground truth) as optional ones.

- `summarization_quality` evaluates the quality of the application's response (on four scales – groundness, comprehensiveness, briefness, and how well it follows the instruction). It expects `prediction` (generated summary), `instruction` (summarization prompt), and `context` (text to be summarized) as required arguments, and `reference` (a ground truth) as an optional one.

- `summarization_helpfullness` evaluates the comprehensiveness of the application's response (whether it has captured all the important details). It expects `prediction` (generated summary) and `context` (text to be summarized) as required arguments, and `reference` (a ground truth) and `instruction` (summarization prompt) as optional ones.

- `summarization_verbosity` evaluates whether the application's response was too brief. It expects `prediction` (generated summary) and `context` (text to be summarized) as required arguments, and `reference` (a ground truth) and `instruction` (summarization prompt) as optional ones.

To use Vertex evaluations, we should provide the desired metric during initialization of the `VertexStringEvaluator` instance:

```
from langchain_google_vertexai import VertexStringEvaluator

evaluator = VertexStringEvaluator(
    metric="bleu", project_id=PROJECT_ID)
result = evaluator.evaluate(
    examples=[
        {"reference": "Berlin is the capital of Germany."},
        {"reference": "London is the capital of Britain."},
        {"reference": "London is the capital of Britain."},
    ],
    predictions=[
        {"prediction": "The capital of Germany is Berlin."},
        {"prediction": "London is the capital of Britain."},
        {"prediction": "London is a capital of Britain."},
    ],
)
print(result)
>>> [{'score': 0.29071537}, {'score': 1.0}, {'score': 0.488923}]
```

Please note that the signatures of LangChain and Vertex AI APIs are slightly different. Hence, an `input` argument to LangChain evaluators is mapped to the `context` one for Vertex. The Bleu score is one of the evaluations that you can run in batches, but many others can only be evaluated one by one:

```
evaluator_qa = VertexStringEvaluator(
        metric="question_answering_relevance", project_id=PROJECT_ID
    )
```

```
result = evaluator_qa.evaluate_strings(
    instruction="Which processor does Pixel 8 has?",
    prediction="Qualcomm Snapdragon 765G ",
    contex="Google Tensor G3 works with the Titan M2 security chip
to protect personal information and make your Pixel more resilient
to sophisticated attacks. And now, Face Unlock on Pixel 8 meets the
highest Android biometric class, allowing you to access compatible
banking and payment apps like Google Wallet.",
)
print(result)
>>> {'score': 5.0, 'explanation': 'The response directly answers the
question by providing the specific processor model used in the Pixel
8, which is the Qualcomm Snapdragon 765G.', 'confidence': 1.0}
```

As we can see, relevance is high even if an answer is incorrect, but we can catch this if we use a different evaluation metric:

```
evaluator_c = VertexStringEvaluator(
        metric="question_answering_correctness", project_id=PROJECT_ID
    )
result = evaluator_c.evaluate_strings(
    instruction="Which processor does Pixel 8 has?",
    prediction="Qualcomm Snapdragon 765G ",
    contex="Google Tensor G3 works with the Titan M2 security chip
to protect personal information and make your Pixel more resilient
to sophisticated attacks. And now, Face Unlock on Pixel 8 meets the
highest Android biometric class, allowing you to access compatible
banking and payment apps like Google Wallet.",
)
print(result)
>>> {'score': 0.0, 'explanation': 'The response contains the claim
"Qualcomm Snapdragon 765G" which is not present in the reference.',
'confidence': 0.5}
```

Of course, you can use the `evaluate` method to evaluate a batch of examples, but keep in mind that the process will be sequential and might take some time in this case.

Pairwise evaluations

As we've already mentioned, pairwise evaluators use LLM to compare two different outputs from two versions of your application configured differently. A configuration change might be anything – a different prompt, a different foundational model, a new ingestion or chunking mechanism, or just a change in the `temperature` argument. You don't get a score on a specific scale, but you get preferences, and you can compute a share of cases when output from version *A* is a preferred one over output from version *B*.

LangChain offers you a few out-of-the-box evaluators:

- The `pairwise_string` and `labeled_pairwise_string` evaluators predict the preferred prediction between the two models, but the second uses the golden answer as an additional input. As usual, an evaluator with an expected output provided would most probably perform more reliably and get preferences with a higher correlation to human ones:

```
from langchain.evaluation import load_evaluator

evaluator_ps = load_evaluator(
    "pairwise_string", llm=llm)

result = evaluator_ps.evaluate_string_pairs(
    prediction="Berlin.",
    prediction_b="Berlin is a capital of Germany.",
    input="What is the capital of Germany?",
)
print(result["value"])
>> A
```

If we explore the trace on LangSmith, we can see that the evaluator made a single call to the underlying LLM with a system message and the following prompt:

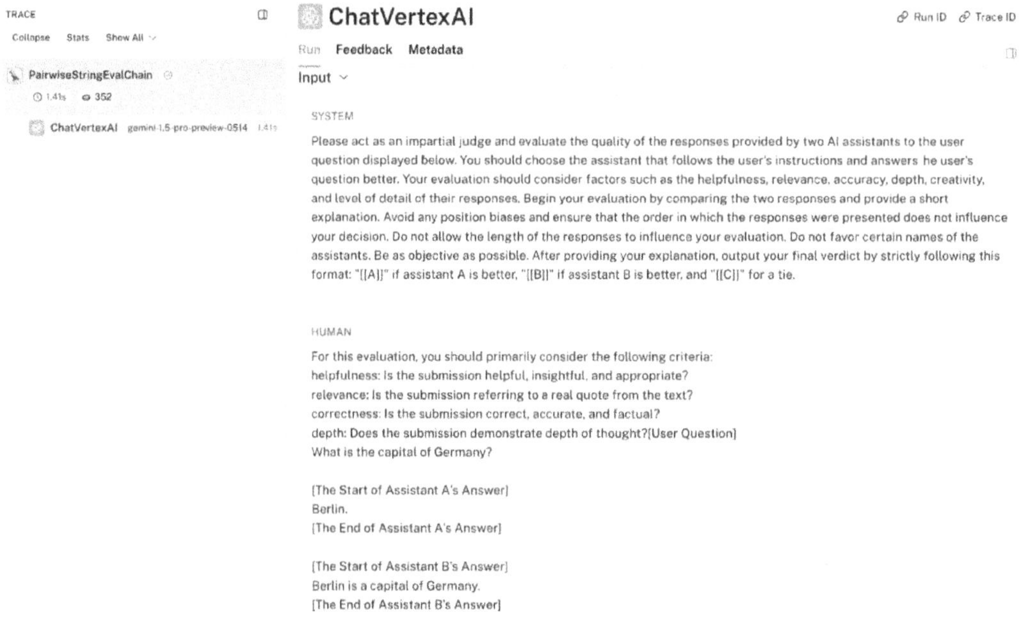

Figure 12.5 – Evaluation traces on LangSmith

- `pairwise_string_distance` and `pairwise_embedding_distance` are essentially the same as the `string_distance` and `embedding_distance` evaluators. They just evaluate how close two different candidates are instead of returning the preferences.

As mentioned earlier, you can build your own evaluators if you need custom metrics for pairwise evaluations.

Vertex pairwise evaluators

As of the time of writing, Vertex GenAI Evaluation service provided two metrics for pairwise evaluations:

- `pairwise_question_answering_quality` compares two different applications' responses given the context on four scales – groundness, comprehensiveness, relevance, and how well each of them follows the instruction. It expects `prediction` (a generated answer) and `prediction_b` (an alternatively generated answer), `instruction` (q&a prompt,) and `context` (text to be used as a context to answer the question) as required arguments, and `reference` (a ground truth) as an optional one.

- `pairwise_summarization_quality` compares two different applications' responses on four scales – groundness, comprehensiveness, briefness, and how well it follows the instruction – and picks the better one (or returns UNDECIDED). It expects `prediction` (a generated summary) and `prediction_b` (an alternatively generated summary), `instruction` (summarization prompt), as well as `context` (text to be summarized), as required arguments, and `reference` (a ground truth) as an optional one.

Let's take a look at an example:

```
from langchain_google_vertexai import VertexPairWiseStringEvaluator

evaluator_pw = VertexPairWiseStringEvaluator(
    metric="pairwise_question_answering_quality",
    project_id=PROJECT_ID
    )
result = evaluator_pw.evaluate_string_pairs(
    prediction="London",
    prediction_b="Berlin",
    input="What is the capital of Great Britain?",
    instruction="Be concise",
    )
print(result)
>>> {'pairwise_choice': 'BASELINE', 'explanation': 'BASELINE response
is concise and provides the correct answer. CANDIDATE response is not
concise and provides an incorrect answer.', 'confidence': 1.0}
```

As we can see, the evaluator has chosen a baseline answer versus an alternative one and provided an explanation together with a confidence score.

Summary

In this chapter, we discussed the importance of evaluating GenAI applications and learned the difference between pairwise and pointwise evaluators. We also learned how to use native LangChain evaluators, utilize LangSmith for debugging our applications' performance, and use Vertex AI evaluation capabilities with LangChain.

As we've highlighted, from our perspective, one of the most important (and often underappreciated) things to take care of before moving to production is creating a robust evaluation pipeline.

In the next chapter, we'll look at the further aspects of preparing your GenAI application for production deployment and putting it in front of actual users.

References

1. *G-Eval: NLG Evaluation using GPT-4 with Better Human Alignment*, Y. Liu et. al, 2023

    `https://arxiv.org/abs/2303.16634`

2. *Post Turing: Mapping the landscape of LLM Evaluation*, A. Tikhonov, I. Yamshchikov, 2023

    `https://arxiv.org/abs/2311.02049`

3. *LLM Evaluators Recognize and Favor Their Own Generations*, Panickssery et. al., 2024

    `https://arxiv.org/abs/2404.13076`

4. Synthetic data generation on LangChain:

    `https://python.langchain.com/v0.2/docs/tutorials/data_generation/`

5. LangSmith documentation:

    `https://docs.smith.langchain.com/`

6. Vertex GenAI Evaluation service:

    `https://cloud.google.com/vertex-ai/generative-ai/docs/models/evaluation-overview`

Generative AI System Design

As we've seen, generative AI is a rapidly evolving field full of opportunities for practitioners and organizations. However, due to the non-deterministic nature of LLMs and the rapid evolution of the technology, designing and building generative AI systems comes with many challenges. In this chapter, we'll guide you through the process of building generative AI systems while steering clear of these challenges, from conceptualization to implementation.

In this chapter, we'll cover the following topics:

- Architecting for generative AI systems
- Reference generative AI system blueprints
- Technical design approach
- Considerations for enterprise readiness and compliance
- How are generative AI systems different?

System design in software engineering is difficult as we need to achieve complex functional and non-functional requirements with limited resources. Almost every system is a tradeoff between performance, cost, and complexity. We aren't designing the best system – we're designing a system that will be good enough to meet our users' needs. In other words, when we design software, we typically want to build systems that are scalable, reliable, easy to maintain, and cost-effective. And we want to build them fast!

Because of these challenges, there are countless great talks, courses, and books on system design, and this book doesn't intend to replace them. Instead, we want to give you practical guidance to help you build generative AI systems.

From our perspective, there are a few important areas where generative AI systems require a different design approach to traditional applications:

- **Non-deterministic outcomes**: Outputs of generative AI applications have a certain randomness by design, meaning their outcomes aren't deterministic and might differ between executions. Dealing with this randomness requires additional guardrails and controls both on the application side and on the **user experience (UX)** side.

- **Model selection and scalability**: You'll face design choices around model choice and training data selection, its domain adaptation, and further scalability. What techniques will you use to adapt a **large language model (LLM)** to your specific tasks (fine-tuning, **retrieval-augmented generation (RAG)**, agents, or prompt engineering)? What model will you choose – foundational or open source? How will you migrate between different generations of the model and different model providers? Many more questions can be asked here!

- **Specific components**: There are a lot of well-known design patterns around messaging queues, databases, storage, and more. Generative AI applications bring additional components such as vector databases, PDF parsers, and more, all of which were typically not widely used and studied by software engineers previously.

- **Complex data flows**: Typically, generative AI applications process unstructured data, which raises additional questions on how to build ingestion pipelines, how to keep indices fresh, how to adjust existing data governance practices, how to track access controls for various data pieces and avoid data loss, and more.

- **Ethics and responsible AI (RAI)**: LLMs can inherit biases from training data or generate harmful outputs. You need to think about the RAI aspects of your applications.

Architecture design framework

As with all architecture work involving multiple parties that need to align on common goals and synchronize complex work, you should adopt an architecture framework to guide you. It doesn't matter if you go with Zachman, TOGAF, BIZBOK, or any of the other many acronyms out there. What's important is that you and your collaborators agree on one framework and stick to it. If your organization already has a different framework in place, we strongly suggest adopting that framework. Don't reinvent the wheel here! For this book, we propose a simplified architecture framework that starts with business process-aligned capabilities that map to technical designs:

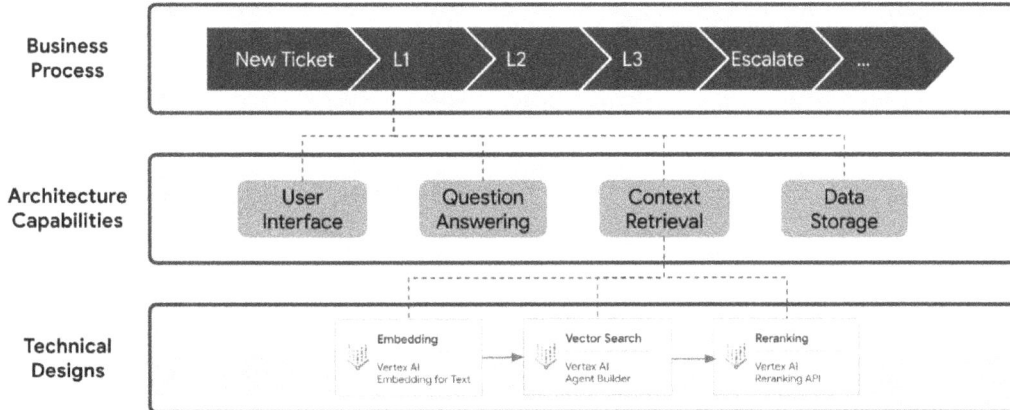

Figure 13.1: Generative AI architecture design framework

We also recommend that you create a central repository for storing the documentation associated with your generative AI system. Don't go overboard here: a simple doc or wiki is more than enough to get started unless your organization already has something different in place.

Finally, if you're part of a large team or one of multiple teams, you'll want to agree on architecture principles that guide the development of generative AI applications across teams – for example, "*We implement system evaluation based on a user query set, user feedback mechanisms, and a golden context and a golden answer to increase the performance and quality of the solution.*" Once you've agreed on a framework, a repository, and architecture principles, it's time for you to design your generative AI system!

The business process, or defining your use case

Before starting the technical implementation, you need to clearly define your use case. What problem are you trying to solve? For example, your marketing experts might struggle with writing great marketing copy, or you might spend too much money on product photography. You have many different frameworks for defining your business process. The Google favorite is **critical user journeys**. [1] In this framework, which was popularized by the YouTube product management team, we try not to identify every step our users might take but focus on the critical path that lies between our users and their business goals.

We begin by defining the goals of our users. For example, our user might want to create compelling marketing copy to impress their customers. The best goals are clearly defined and measurable. So, we don't just want to create compelling marketing copy – we want to do it instantly, and with a tangible impact on click-through-rate. Once we've identified the goal, we can define the critical user journey in the form of tasks, from the user's perspective. For marketing copy, this might be "*provide input for the marketing copy,*" "*review the output marketing copy,*" "*revise the input for the marketing copy,*" "*publish the marketing copy to a website,*" or "*review metrics for the newly published marketing copy.*" You can refer to *Appendix 1* for a use case taxonomy.

Architecture capabilities

Once the business process has been clearly defined, we can start mapping each task to architecture capabilities. This is not a one-to-one mapping. Many architecture capabilities support multiple tasks, and many tasks require multiple architecture capabilities to succeed.

An **architecture capability** is a technology-agnostic description of a feature that's needed by users to complete a task. In our example of marketing content generation, this feature could be *text generation* based on a user prompt. It would also include other capabilities, such as **data ingestion**, **prompt security**, and **frontend presentation**.

Over time, you'll build a repository of these capabilities that can be standardized, repurposed, and reconfigured to meet the needs of your users. See *Figure 13.2* for an example of some generative AI architecture capabilities that will meet the needs of most generative AI use cases:

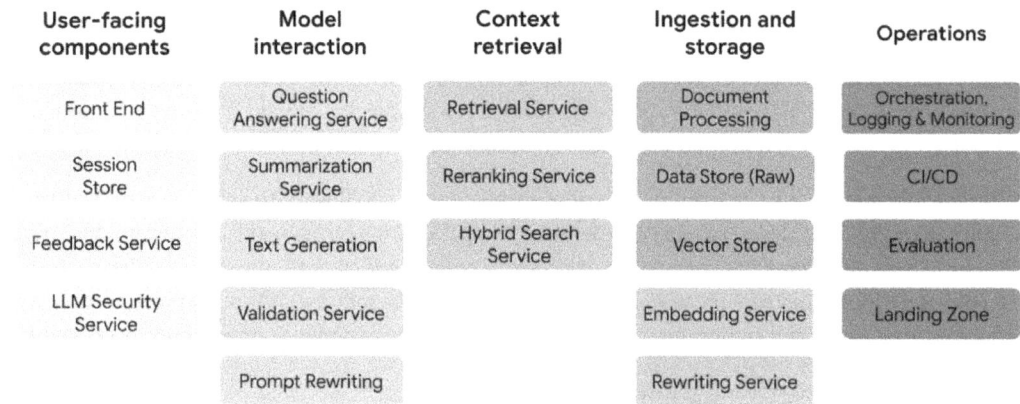

User-facing components	Model interaction	Context retrieval	Ingestion and storage	Operations
Front End	Question Answering Service	Retrieval Service	Document Processing	Orchestration, Logging & Monitoring
Session Store	Summarization Service	Reranking Service	Data Store (Raw)	CI/CD
Feedback Service	Text Generation	Hybrid Search Service	Vector Store	Evaluation
LLM Security Service	Validation Service		Embedding Service	Landing Zone
	Prompt Rewriting		Rewriting Service	

Figure 13.2: Generative AI architecture capabilities

xFor each capability, you should write a short description that will help create the corresponding technical design. For example, for document processing, you might write that the capability includes "*data preparation (for example, separating PDFs in images and text), ingesting data from a source, extracting metadata, labeling documents with metadata, and chunking documents.*" Be precise in your descriptions to ensure that the technical design meets the needs of the use case.

Technical design

After identifying the required capabilities, the technical work begins. For each capability, you must define a technical design that translates the capability description into technical components within the limits of your architecture principles. In this book, we believe in practical applications over theory, so we've prepared a bunch of technical designs for common capabilities that will help you get started with the right technical architecture.

Document ingestion and storage

Google Cloud comes with many components that will help you create an architecture for data ingestion and storage. Most (unstructured) data starts from Google's Cloud Storage, while most structured data lives within BigQuery. You can also scrape data directly from websites after domain authentication. Vertex AI Agent Builder is a managed data store for vector data and metadata that can use LLMs to answer user questions and serve as a tool for LangChain agents. Vertex AI Agent Builder comes with robust document processing capabilities and sports multiple processors for ingesting unstructured data from documents, as well as an embedding service. See *Chapter 3* for more details on document ingestion and the various options available in Vertex AI Agent Builder:

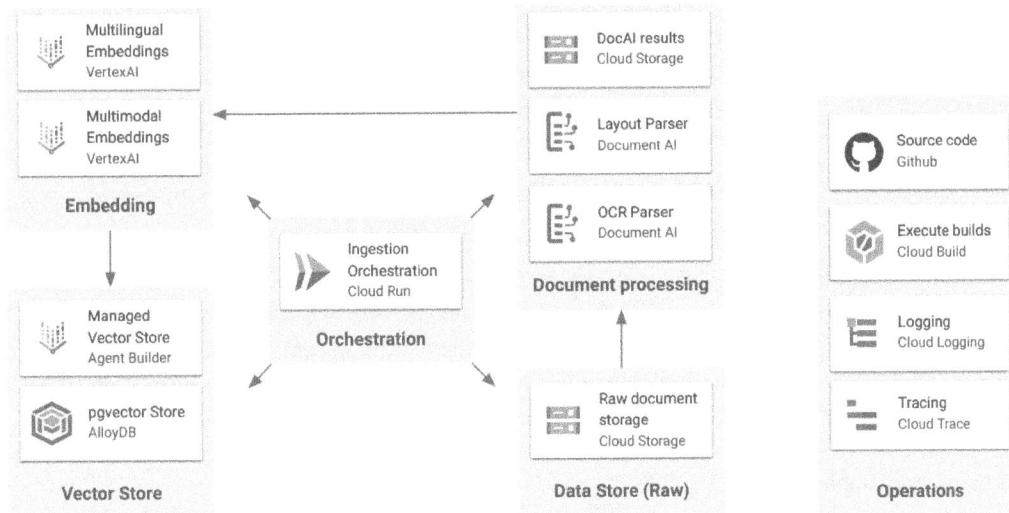

Figure 13.3: Document ingestion and storage technical design

Please note that these designs are good practice and not the only way to achieve your goals! As you learn more about Google Cloud's capabilities and implement more and more use cases, you'll refine and improve on these designs. When designing your ingestion pipeline, there are a few choices to keep in mind:

- How do you update your indices? Do you allow new documents to be added to the vector database or existing ones to be updated?

- How do you keep your unstructured data sources (for example, your PDFs or wiki pages, which may change constantly) aligned with the indexed data that you use for RAG (or other) applications? What kind of delay would you allow for changes on a confluence page to be propagated to a vector database?

- How do you track the metadata and organize it in your vector database? What kind of metadata do you have, and what kind of filters do you need during the retrieval operations?

We recommend having an indexing strategy to manage differences and changes in documents in your index. Google Cloud allows you to create a new index completely from scratch (such as a new Cloud SQL table or Vertex Vector Store instance), and then switch your applications' load. We also recommend separating transaction data (such as conversation history, user feedback, or any other operational data you persist in your application) from your vector database. For example, if you're using Postgres with pgvector on Cloud SQL, you should have two Cloud SQL instances – one containing a vector database and another for everything else (but that's another design choice to make!).

To start, you'll need operations capabilities. We recommend leveraging **Infrastructure as Code (IaC)** as much as possible. We also recommend having two repositories (use GitHub, GitLab, or any other code version control tool) with CI/CD pipelines enabled for your applications. The first repository should contain the Terraform configuration of your cloud environment as staging and production environments should only be modified through Terraform and applied from the main branch. The other repository should contain your application code. You can use CI/CD pipelines that include GitHub Actions to run checks and tests, build your artifacts (such as Docker images), and push them to Google Artifact Registry.

Another Google Cloud tool to keep in mind is **Google Cloud Secrets**. It's a very easy-to-use managed service for keeping and extracting your secrets, such as API keys. [2]

We recommend **Cloud Build** as a managed building service. [3] We also recommend leveraging **Google Cloud Logging** and **Cloud Tracing** so that you can observe what's happening in your application. Both integrate nicely with Python [4] and other common programming languages. Just keep in mind that your applications might contain users' **personally identifiable information (PII)**, so make sure that you store those logs safely and securely, such as in BigQuery. You should also take a look at **LangSmith Distributed Tracing** as a convenient way to integrate tracing capabilities with your LangChain application. [5]

We use these components to manage our resources. To land the raw documents that will power your RAG application, we recommend Google Cloud Storage. Using Google Cloud Storage, Document AI will be able to easily process your documents. Please refer to *Chapter 5* for details on using Document AI and its various parsers. Results from Document AI can then be stored in Google Cloud Storage or passed through to the Embedding Service. For embeddings, we recommend choosing the embedding type that matches your use case. *Chapters 5* and *6* cover the benefits of various embeddings.

Finally, the embedded documents land in a vector store. Here, you have many different choices, First, you need to choose between a purpose-built vector store such as Vertex AI Vector Store and running pgvector on a Postgres database. The former offers easy configuration and quick setup, while the latter offers flexibility, as well as the ability to use SQL-like language to query your data. If you decide to use pgvector, you have many options for compliant databases, ranging from managed services such as AlloyDB, BigQuery, and Spanner to self-managed options such as CloudSQL:

Vector Store	Archetype	Operations	Data Model	Size	Latency	Consistency
CloudSQL	Database	Managed	Relational	Millions	10 ms	Strong
AlloyDB	Database	Managed	Relational	Billions	< 10 ms	Strong
Memorystore	Vector store	Managed	Key-value	Millions	< 3ms	Eventual
Spanner	Database	Managed	Relational	Billions	10-100 ms	Strong
BigQuery	Warehouse	Managed	Relational	1 billion	1 s	Strong
Vertex AI Vector Store	Vector	Managed	Vector	Billions	< 10 ms	Eventual

Table 13.1: Vector store options

The preceding table provides a convenient overview of different vector store options in **Google Cloud Platform (GCP)**.

Context retrieval

Context retrieval is the next important component and is at the heart of many generative AI systems. By retrieving chunks of context using similarity search, generative AI systems can easily be customized to any business context. However, similarity search can be limited in its capabilities, which is why many practitioners couple it with filtering by metadata via an approach called **hybrid search**. Once data has been retrieved, reranking services, such as the **Vertex AI Reranking API**, [7] can help ensure that the most relevant results are considered first:

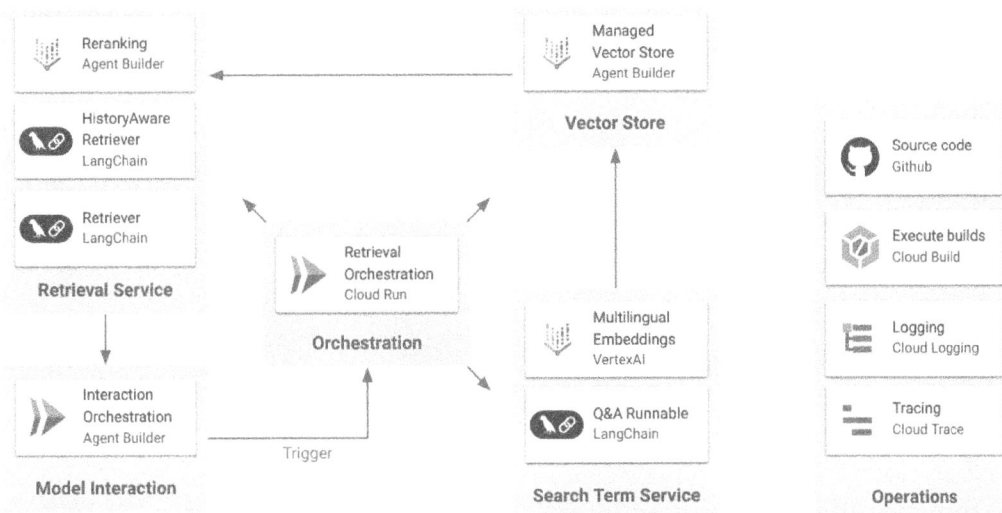

Figure 13.4: Context retrieval – technical design

Again, we recommend leveraging your orchestration service in **Cloud Run**. It will receive a prompt from the **model interaction service** that it will then pass to the **search term service**. As we saw in *Chapter 6*, rewriting the search prompt to facilitate better retrieval with similarity search (for example, by stripping out irrelevant words) can improve your retrieval performance. Next, we send the prompt to our retriever, which could be either a regular retriever or a special version such as **HistoryAwareRetriever**. After retrieving the relevant chunks, we recommend leveraging the **Reranking API** included in **Vertex AI Agent Builder** as a quick and efficient way to improve the quality of retrieved results. Alternatively, you could leverage other reranking services at this point. With our retrieval chain complete, we return the retrieved chunks to the **interaction orchestration service** so that we can include them in the generation prompt.

Model interaction

The components under model interaction control how the generative AI models that will receive your prompts interact. Commonly, you'll see services for three use cases: question-answering, text summarization, and text generation. After reading this book, you should be intimately familiar with each of these use cases. This component governs how you interact with the underlying models.

Additionally, many practitioners see success in introducing a prompt rewriting component as part of this capability. Prompt rewriting for LLMs introduces an interim step that processes user prompts to make sure they can be understood clearly by the LLM. This is done by introducing a prompt rewriting step as part of your chain. Its goal is to make your instructions more precise and effective so that the LLM gives better answers. Prompt rewriting also has a downside, mainly the latency and additional processing costs that are incurred by adding an additional call to your chain. It depends on the latency and quality requirements of your application to determine whether and where you should use prompt rewriting. Finally, validation and feedback services leverage LLMs to validate that the right data has been retrieved.

The following figure illustrates what a technical design for model interaction might look like:

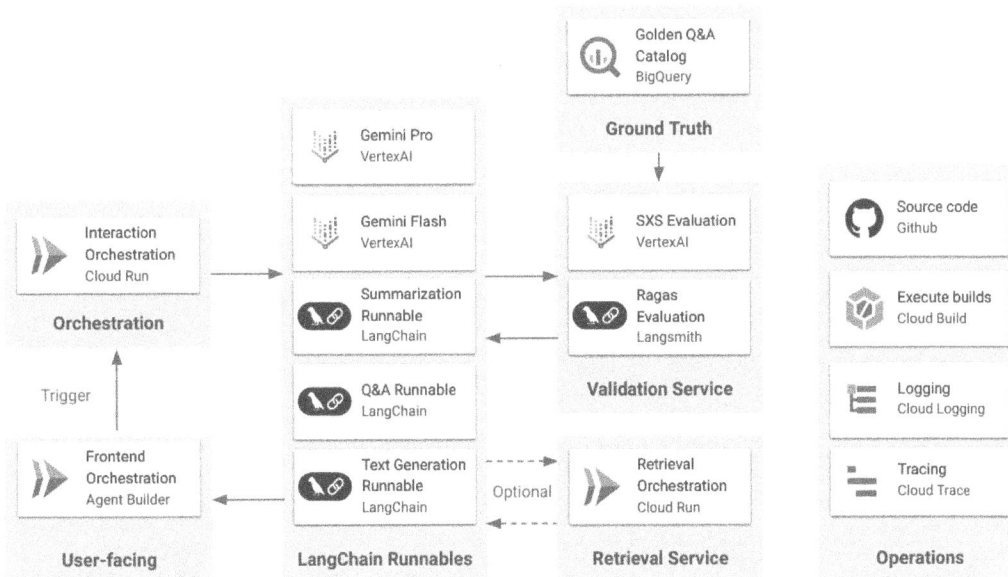

Figure 13.5: Model interaction – technical design

Just as before, **Cloud Run** serves as the core orchestration component. The **orchestration service** is triggered by the frontend with a user prompt. It then calls the relevant LangChain runnables based on its routing logic – for example, a **summarization runnable**. These runnables can invoke any available Google Cloud Vertex AI model, such as Gemini Pro or Flash, or a custom-built, self-hosted model. Additionally, the runnables might trigger the **retrieval service**. A **validation service**, such as the **Ragas Evaluation** in LangChain [8] or the **side-by-side** (**SXS**) **evaluation** offered in VertexAI, [9] should also be implemented so that you can compare the outputs of multiple models against each other (for example, when you want to benchmark different models) or compare model output against the values defined in the ground truth.

User-facing components

User-facing components act as the bridge between the inner workings of the system and the user. Imagine them as the face of your application – the part that users interact with. They encompass everything from the visual layout and design to the interactive elements that allow users to enter information and receive outputs. A well-designed frontend not only presents information clearly and intuitively but also ensures a seamless and engaging user experience. It handles user inputs, communicates those to the backend for processing, and then renders the results back to the user in a way that makes sense. For generative AI applications, the frontend also needs to deal with the latency of model responses, especially when using RAG architectures or large contexts in models. A friendly animation that occupies users while they wait for a response goes a long way.

We also recommend including the session store with user-facing components since it's closely connected to the frontend. In the session store, you would have the low-latency data store that stores your chat history, plus everything else that's relevant to the session, such as user questions and user feedback. For the session store, you have a lot of options that range from self-hosted services to fully managed, high-performance ones. See *Chapter 8* for a detailed description of the options you have for storing chat history:

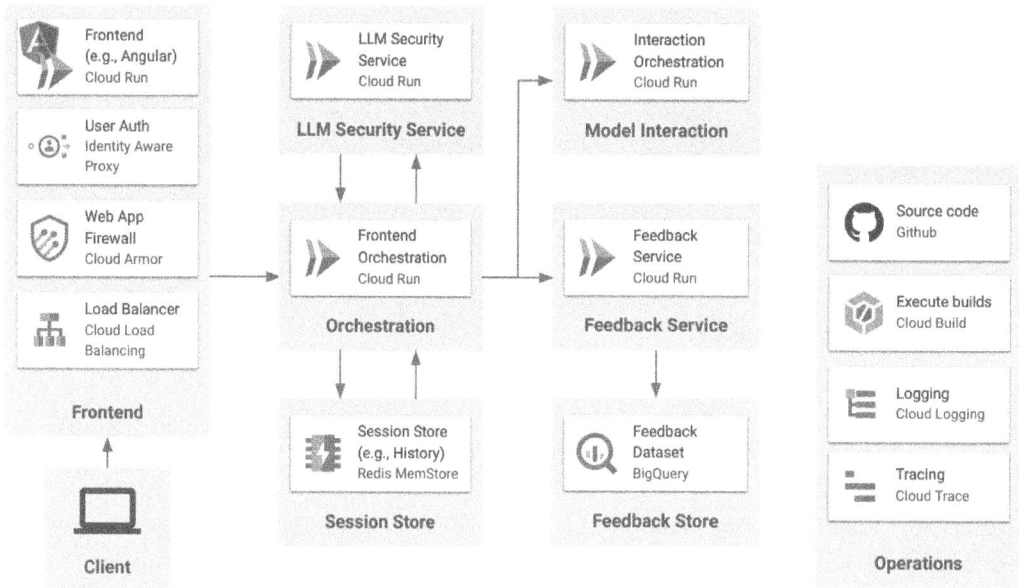

Figure 13.6: User-facing components – technical design

Figure 13.6 shows a potential technical design for user-facing components. Here, we begin with a reference frontend implementation that starts with a load balancer that uses **Cloud Load Balancing** to guide user requests. We recommend implementing a web application firewall and robust user authentication to ensure the security of your application. **Identity Aware Proxy** is a popular choice for authentication that doesn't require much management overhead. [8] Then, the frontend will connect to the **frontend orchestration service**, which will negotiate with the session store to retrieve and store messages. It will also pass the message history and the user prompt through to the **interaction orchestration service**, which will handle the communication with the backend.

Next, we recommend including a **feedback service**. What is this feedback service? Well, it's as simple as putting a "thumbs up" or "thumbs down" next to any AI message, and allowing users to give you feedback if they're not happy with a message. This will help you implement many nice features such as **Reinforcement Learning from Human Feedback** (**RLHF**) in the future. [10] We recommend storing this feedback in BigQuery since it's easy to handle and cheap, but any database will do.

Finally, you should also consider security. Since generative AI is a new and emerging discipline, we also observe new and emerging cyber security threats. To address these threats, we recommend building an **LLM security service** that reviews any prompt that's passed to it by the **frontend orchestration service** before it enters your backend application. This service should include basic filtering based on regular expressions for anything containing something that looks like code (unless you're building an application that reviews code, of course), to more advanced features such as sentiment analysis (for example, is this prompt trying to get my application to divulge its system prompt?). This can be done by processing incoming prompts using an LLM, or, much more cheaply and much more securely, by using cosine similarity to compare the embeddings of user prompts to embeddings of common prompts sent by malicious actors. You should review the Google Cloud blog for insights and recommendations regarding building secure generative AI applications. [11]

Enterprise readiness and compliance

We are neither lawyers nor auditors, just engineers. However, we want to leave you with some insights and recommendations regarding meeting compliance expectations. First and foremost, you should be aware of the requirements that prevailing regulation has for your application. For example, if you're reading this book, you likely fall under some form of data protection regulation, such as the **General Data Protection Regulation** (**GDPR**) in the European Union. You may also fall under AI-specific regulation, such as the newly published **EU AI Act**. If you work in a larger organization, you'll have access to legal and compliance departments that can inform you about the regulations that are relevant to you. If you're building something for yourself, we recommend that you get support if you intend to publish your application to users.

Regardless, you should consider establishing a **governance, risk, and compliance** (**GRC**) framework to govern your application. You should identify the risks that you're controlling (for example user data gets exfiltrated and lost), their impact (for example, your company loses user trust and goes bankrupt), and suitable controls (for example, encrypt all user data and only store user data you really need). With generative AI on Google Cloud specifically, you can leverage many built-in features to comply with regulations. [12] You can also make use of our global setup to ensure that your workloads run in the right jurisdiction and that you meet the compliance expectations of your regulators and, most importantly, users.

RAI

With an exponentially increasing number of AI applications, **RAI** is becoming more important than ever before. While there are multiple definitions for RAI, they're all related to the principles of fairness, interpretability, privacy, and safety in AI-based applications. [14]

Given the vast capabilities of generative AI models and their random, non-deterministic nature, establishing these principles challenges architects. As this is an emerging discipline, there are no established frameworks such as ISO 27001 or NIST that can guide practitioners. For this purpose of this book, we'll loosely follow the recently published EU AI Act, which will become mandatory for (generative) AI system providers in August 2026 (yes, that probably includes you!). Please keep in mind that this book doesn't provide legal guidance and that you should carefully review any system design with legal experts and your security and governance teams before you make it available to the wider public.

The EU AI Act mandates three things for providers of high-risk AI systems (basically all generative AI systems that perform tasks for users): establishing a GRC framework, ensuring that robust data is used for all model training that's free of biases, and establishing appropriate logging and monitoring of model input and output. So, let's step through those requirements:

1. A GRC framework is nothing to worry about and something that you should have in place anyway. You need to identify the risks for your application (for example, that users' personal data is breached), design appropriate controls (for example, users' personal data must always be encrypted and can only be accessed by authorized administrators), and define roles and responsibilities (for example, that an architect reviews all system designs to ensure the control is implemented appropriately). The next principle should follow automatically: one of the key risks for generative AI applications is that users will experience bias because of their race, gender, or sexual orientation, for example. You can mitigate this risk by using carefully curated training data in your model training and fine-tuning processes.

2. You must document data provenance, analyze dataset composition, and perform (sample-based) reviews, depending on the criticality of your application. Now, if you're just using a foundational model, you won't be able to review its training data. Here, the AI Act mandates special controls for general-purpose model providers that you can rely on. However, you shouldn't forget that the data in your RAG vector store and the data that's used in the prompt for in-context learning can lead to biases too!

3. Finally, as mentioned previously, you should implement robust logging and monitoring for your application. The logged data should be used by your engineers to identify, debug, and resolve errors. However, it should also be used for systematic reviews of your generative AI system. For example, you might want to implement a control for regular human reviews of model output to ensure that the system performs within acceptable parameters and doesn't hallucinate. You should also implement a reporting feature within your application that enables users to give feedback on unacceptable behavior, which is then analyzed and processed by human reviewers.

If you're using any of the Google foundational models, you'll be aware of safety settings. The model will analyze each generated response for harmful, sexually explicit, or otherwise biased content. You can determine the cut-offs within which the model can give a response. This is always a trade-off. For example, if you're working on a virtual assistant to help doctors formulate treatment recommendations for patients, the "harmful" setting will be triggered easily as the model has been configured to avoid giving medical advice out of the box. By reducing the threshold for potentially harmful answers, you enable the model to be helpful. Note that you can't fully remove the threshold for blocking responses!

Summary

In this chapter, we provided a comprehensive guide to building generative AI systems. You learned about the importance of having an architecture design framework and a central repository, as well as establishing architecture principles. We emphasized the necessity of clearly defining your use case and mapping tasks to architecture capabilities.

Then, we walked you through reference technical designs for document ingestion and storage, context retrieval, model interaction, and user-facing components. From this, you gained insights into recommended Google Cloud components and best practices for each stage. You also learned a little bit about securing your generative AI system and enterprise readiness and compliance.

With this final chapter, we conclude our journey through building and deploying generative AI applications with LangChain on Google Cloud. We started with the fundamentals of LangChain and the foundation models that are available on Google Cloud, explored techniques for grounding responses and working with vector search, and delved into advanced methods for document processing. Then, we moved on to the exciting realms of multimodality, long context windows, and chatbot development. Here, you learned how to leverage tools and function calling, design and build intelligent agents and workflows, and, finally, how to evaluate and design generative AI systems. As you move forward, remember that the landscape of generative AI is constantly evolving. Embrace continuous learning, explore new possibilities, and contribute to the responsible development of this transformative technology. The future of generative AI is bright, and with the knowledge you've gained, you're well-equipped to be a part of it.

References

1. Google Critical User Journeys, *Medium*. Available at

   `https://medium.com/initialized-capital/what-to-do-if-your-product-isnt-growing-7eb9d158fc`.

2. Google Cloud Secret Manager, *Google Cloud documentation*. Available at

   `https://cloud.google.com/security/products/secret-manager`.

3. Cloud Build, *Google Cloud documentation*. Available at

   `https://cloud.google.com/build/docs`.

4. Using Google Cloud Logging with Python, *Google Cloud documentation*. Available at

   `https://cloud.google.com/logging/docs/setup/python`.

5. LangSmith Distributed Tracing, *LangSmith documentation*. Available at

    `https://docs.smith.langchain.com/how_to_guides/tracing/distributed_tracing`.

6. Vertex AI Reranking API, *Google Cloud documentation*. Available at

    `https://cloud.google.com/generative-ai-app-builder/docs/ranking`.

7. Ragas Evaluation in LangSmith, *Ragas documentation*. Available at

    `https://docs.ragas.io/en/latest/howtos/integrations/langchain.html`.

8. SXS Evaluation in Google Cloud, *Google Cloud documentation*. Available at

    `https://cloud.google.com/vertex-ai/generative-ai/docs/models/side-by-side-eval`.

9. Identity Aware Proxy with Cloud Run, *Google Cloud documentation*. Available at

    `https://cloud.google.com/iap/docs/enabling-cloud-run`.

10. Reinforcement Learning from Human Feedback, *Hugging Face*. Available at

    `https://huggingface.co/blog/rlhf`.

11. Design considerations for secure and compliant GenAI, *Google Cloud Blog*. Available at

    `https://cloud.google.com/blog/products/ai-machine-learning/design-considerations-for-gen-ai/`.

12. Security controls for GenAI, *Google Cloud documentation*. Available at

    `https://cloud.google.com/vertex-ai/generative-ai/docs/security-controls`.

    `https://techdevguide.withgoogle.com/resources/system-design/`.

13. Responsible AI practices, *Google AI*. Available at

    `https://ai.google/responsibility/responsible-ai-practices/`.

14. *EU AI Act*:

    `https://www.europarl.europa.eu/topics/en/article/20230601STO93804/eu-ai-act-first-regulation-on-artificial-intelligence`.

Appendix

Appendix 1
Overview of Generative AI

Before we run into technical details and discuss how to build generative AI applications, let's spend some time and go back to the fundamentals. We'll try to keep this *Appendix* short and practically oriented; you'll find many links to additional materials at the end if you're interested in digging a little bit deeper.

Here, we're going to cover the following topics:

- What is generative AI?
- What are **large language models** (**LLMs**), why do they hallucinate, and why do they require alignment?
- Current trends around generative AI
- Adopting generative AI in your enterprise

Introducing generative AI

Engineers have been working on developing probabilistic natural language models for decades [1]. We need such models to solve various tasks related to understanding human language, also known as **natural language processing** (**NLP**) tasks – translation, **optical character recognition** (**OCR**), summarization, generating new text, extracting entities from text, and more.

In the last 5 years, we've observed a breakthrough in NLP related to generative AI and LLMs. Generative AI is one of the hottest topics right now – it's mentioned in over 40% of SP&500 analyst calls [2]. From this, we can observe a huge interest not only from startups and consumers but also from enterprises as they want to move fast and adopt new technology. It also drives interest across practitioners.

In this book, we discussed how to develop an enterprise-ready generative AI solution on Google Cloud with LangChain, but in this *Appendix*, we'd like to spend some time discussing the basics. We feel it's important for engineers and product owners to understand the core principles of these technologies and potential future development, so we'll try to avoid going into too much technical detail.

The current progress we see is usually associated with the groundbreaking neural network architecture called the Transformer, which was invented in 2017 due to collaboration between Google Brain, Google Research, and the University of Toronto. The authors of the original paper [3] demonstrated better performance on two machine translation tasks. What does it mean to "demonstrate better performance?" These days, there are **labeled datasets** for almost any task in NLP. In this specific case, the authors worked with a WMT 2014 English-to-German translation dataset. It contained around 4.5 million pairs of German and English pieces of text. So, the researchers took part of this dataset for evaluation purposes and demonstrated that their model had better performance based on a certain metric – in this case, the **BiLingual Evaluation Understudy** (BLEU) score, a score from zero to one that quantifies the similarity between a piece of text that's translated by a computer and its reference translation.

At almost the same time, in December 2015, OpenAI was founded as a non-profit AI research company. According to their publications, initially, they focused on research in reinforcement learning; we'll see how relevant it is for the generative AI field later. In 2018, they published GPT-1, a generative pre-trained transformer.

In 2018, Google open sourced **Bidirectional Encoder Representations from Transformers (BERT)**, the first transformer-based model that attracted a lot of attention in the industry and gained traction. BERT was one of the key enablers of transfer learning on NLP tasks, which resulted in a lot of progress in the industry and increased the adoption of NLP models to enterprise use cases. Many other models followed with evolving architectures and increasing growing sizes (T5 in 2019, LaMDa in 2020 from Google, GPT-3 from OpenAI in 2020, and more), but a real breakthrough in performance occurred in 2022. By the end of 2022, we got ChatGPT from OpenAI and Stable Diffusion from Stability.ai. The former is a text-to-text model – that is, it generates a text output based on a text input – while the latter is a text-to-image model – that is, it generates an image based on a text description.

Both garnered a lot of attention. Two months after its launch in February 2023, ChatGPT surpassed 1 billion monthly page views [4] and became the fastest-growing application in history. This result reinforced the hype and resulted in attention from investors, the community, and enterprises. In that time, a lot of great startups have been founded, many new products have been launched and are about to be launched, and many engineers and product enthusiasts are interested in this new technology.

That's how the rise of generative AI started. At this point, let's define it. Generative AI is a set of AI systems that generate new content (text, image, audio, video, or other data) using neural networks, often in response to prompts – a task description (typically, this is a piece of text, but it can also be any type of content, such as a combination of text and an image).

Another important concept we just introduced is prompts – input to the LLM that includes a description of the task in the form of natural language.

Something related to this is the emergent reasoning capabilities of LLMs, something we'll discuss shortly. If a model can generate computer programs or maintain a conversation, it's a huge step forward. There are a lot of applications that use such smart systems.

Exploring LLMs

An LLM is a model with a lot of parameters that's been trained on a huge amount of text data. When we say "a lot of parameters," we usually mean billions. For example, GPT-3 from OpenAI, which was a model used by ChatGPT, had 175 billion parameters, whereas LaMDA from Google had 137 billion parameters. These days, the boundary is shifting, which means we can use smaller LLMs – for example, Phi-2 from Microsoft consists of 2.7 billion parameters [5], and Gemini Nano-1 from Google has 1.6 billion parameters [6].

What's so special about these models? They're auto-regressive statistical models that treat a piece of text as a sequence and are trained to predict the next (or masked) word in such a sequence. Now is a good time to mention that LLMs don't exactly operate with words and that they transform a piece of text into **tokens** (a process known as **tokenization**). A token is a unit that LLMs use to operate – it's typically a subword (a character or a few characters, though sometimes it can even be longer than a word – for example, a few common words or a sentence). Different LLMs use various **tokenizers** (a small program that memorizes a mapping into tokens and can transform any piece of text into a sequence of token IDs); some of them are open source, while others are proprietary. But typically, tokens are produced according to the statistical distribution of a sequence's frequency in a large text corpus. So, a tokenizer is a program that maps text into a sequence of tokens. Different LLMs use different tokenizers (and they might have a different understanding of what a token is).

LLMs are pretrained on large datasets that represent a significant portion of all the public text that's been crawled from the internet (including Wikipedia), published books, and other sources. We're not going to discuss the nuances here, but a lot of effort is required to clean and prepare such a training dataset. However, simply put, during training, we take a random piece of a crawled text, mask a word in it, and train the LLM to predict this masked word:

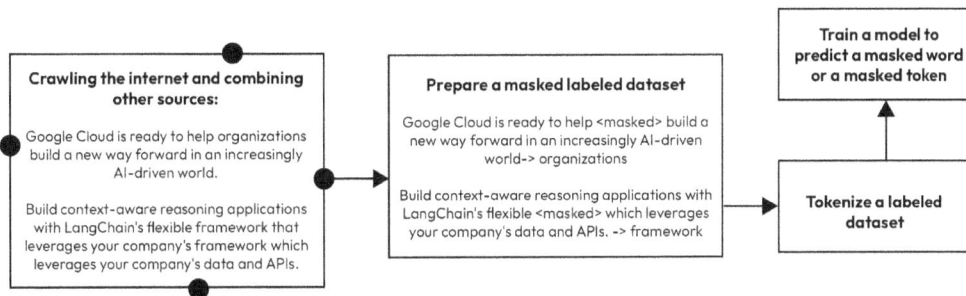

Figure A1 – A simplified view of the first step in training a LLM

While the prediction is taking place, we predict the text output auto-regressively – that is, we start with the input sequence of words, predict the next one, and then use the original sequence and the predicted word on the previous step as input to the model:

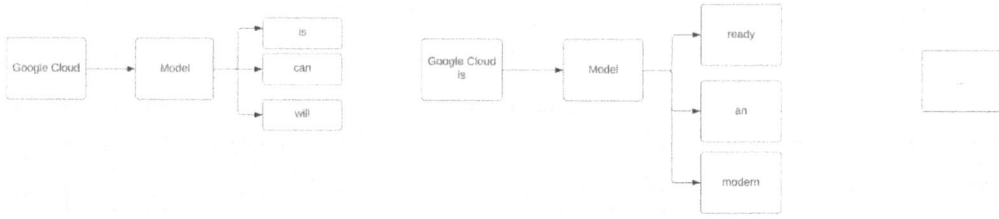

Figure A2 – A simplified prediction process. The LLM predicts the next word and uses the new text that includes this predicted word as input for the following step

One of the important outcomes of the autoregressive nature of LLMs for us, as engineers, is that the latency of LLM-based applications increases linearly with the length of expected output.

In 2020, OpenAI published a paper [7] that demonstrated that if you train an LLM with 175 billion parameters on a large corpus of text (around 300 billion tokens), it starts performing close to the **state-of-the-art** (**SOTA**) models for various NLP tasks (another reason for the high popularity of such models). Before 2020, ML engineers invented a special architecture and trained a specialized model for specific NLP tasks. We had a model for translation, another one for text summarization, and a third one that utilized closed-book question-answering. In addition, each of these models required **domain adaptation** – that is, you needed to change the behavior of your summarization model, you needed to gather a new large dataset and train a new model. This required a lot of effort and investment.

LLMs can solve tasks described as natural language

Andrej Karpathy, a well-known computer scientist and AI researcher, recently tweeted "*English is the hottest programming language.*" What did he mean by this? In this section, you'll learn that you can make a computer perform your task by formulating it properly in natural language. And it's a program, isn't it? Let's look at what this means, and how you can ask a computer to do things in plain English.

How can LLMs solve almost any task?

GPT-3 demonstrated strong performance on most language tasks (that it wasn't specifically trained for) and provided domain adaptation due to **in-context learning**. This means that you can teach a model to do what you want by describing a task in simple natural language! You don't need to undertake the costly retraining process anymore, which includes preparing a dataset and updating any weights. You can just describe what you wish and feed it as input to the model. This user input is in the form of natural language (these days, we use **multimodality**, where an input can be an image, a piece of text, or a combination of both) and describes a task for the LLM through a **prompt**.

Let's imagine we're working on a website that provides an overview of the Age of Discovery – "...*a part of the early modern period from approximately the 15th century to the 17th century, during which seafarers from several European countries explored, colonized, and conquered regions across the globe.*" [8] We need to generate short one-sentence summaries for different discoveries in this period.

First, let's start with a simple example and ask Gemini (an LLM provided by Google) a trivial question (note that this input is what we mean by a prompt):

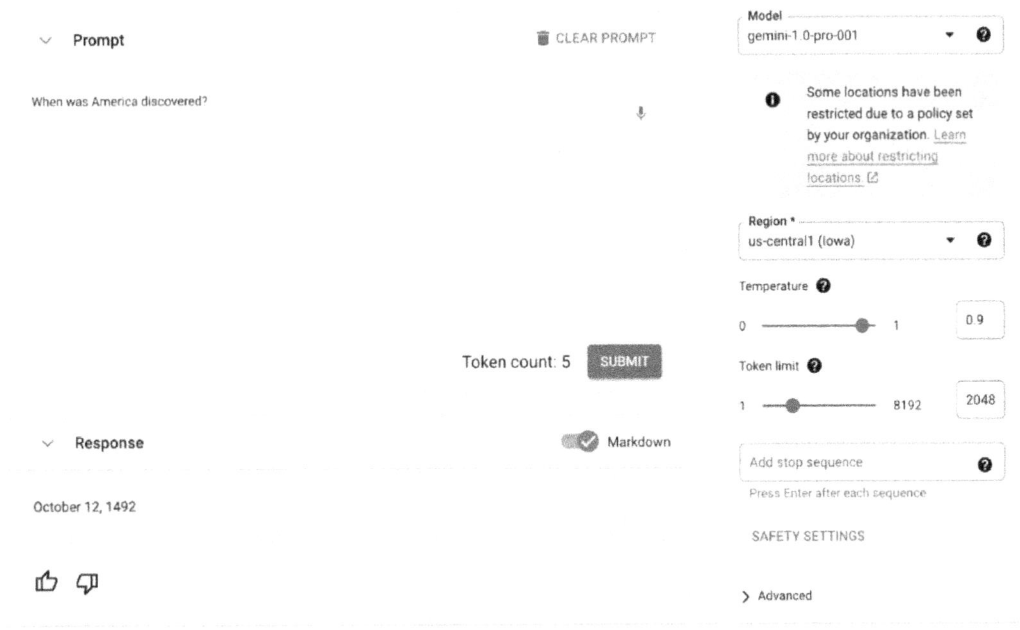

Figure A3 – Querying Gemini with a simple prompt in the Google Cloud console

From this, we can see that LLM produced a correct answer using the data it memorized during training. But our task is to generate a one-sentence summary for our website, so such a concise answer isn't exactly what we'd like to see. Let's try **zero-shot learning**, where a prompt that describes a task:

```
Answer a question about a geographical discovery by specifying a
full year, who the pioneer was, and giving a few details about the
expedition.

When was America discovered?
```

```
Response: 1492 by Christopher Columbus - He sailed across the Atlantic
Ocean from Spain and reached the Caribbean Islands.
```

As we can see, it's improved. We now have a summary instead of just a date! But let's imagine that our website editor didn't like this summary and they wanted to have a slightly different tone. Let's add an example of a desired output based on an input. This process is known as **one-shot learning**:

```
Answer a question about a geographical discovery by specifying a
full year, who the pioneer was, and giving a few details about the
expedition.

When was India discovered?

  Response: Portuguese explorer Vasco de Gama was the first European who
  reached India via the Atlantic Ocean in 1498.

When was America discovered?

  Response: Christopher Columbus, an Italian explorer in the service of
  Spain, arrived in the Bahamas in 1492 and claimed the land for Spain.
```

We don't have a special term for two or three-shot learning, but it involves performing few-shot learning multiple times. So, we can have multiple examples in a prompt. Typically, adding examples (up to a dozen) improves the performance of the LLM on a given task:

```
Answer a question about a geographical discovery by specifying a
full year, who the pioneer was, and giving a few details about the
expedition.

When was India discovered?

  Response: Portuguese explorer Vasco de Gama was the first European who
  reached India via the Atlantic Ocean in 1498.

When was Australia discovered?

  Response: Dutch East captain Willem Janszoon made the first documented
  European landing in Australia in 1606. That same year, a Spanish
  expedition led by Portuguese navigator Pedro Fernandes had landed in
  the New Hebrides and named the land "Austrialia del Espiritu Santo".

When was America discovered?

  Response: In 1492, the Genoese explorer Christopher Columbus, under
  the patronage of the King and Queen of Spain, led an expedition which
  landed in the Caribbean. Columbus had hoped to find a route to Asia,
  but mistakenly believed he had found the eastern coast of India.
```

At this point, we have an output we like, and we can potentially generate short summaries for many other discoveries for snippets on our website. As we can see from these examples, the notion of a prompt template immediately comes to mind. We can develop a prompt for our specific tasks and then insert specific context during inference. The process of tweaking the task's description in terms of natural language to improve the performance of the model is called **prompt engineering**. It's important to highlight that, unlike a classical model training process in ML, we don't change the weights of the model in this case. We can just describe what we need and give a few examples, and LLM demonstrates a huge adaptability to new types of tasks. This is called **in-context learning** – we train a model to perform well on a given task by changing only the input, not adjusting the model's weights.

Note that prompts can be even more sophisticated. There are plenty of other more sophisticated prompting techniques, such as **chain-of-thought** (**CoT**), tree-of-thoughts, and others, but they're beyond the scope of this book. You can find examples of prompts and prompt engineering techniques in the References section [9, 10] and many other great sources on the internet. This is often called **prompt design** – the process of developing prompting techniques that apply to a broad range of tasks. It's very similar to prompt engineering (and some industry experts consider there's no difference between prompt design and prompt engineering), but we might imagine that prompt engineering focuses on a specific task only, whereas prompt design results in a prompt template that can be applied in multiple use cases. In other words, prompt engineering is the process of tweaking a natural language description of a task to improve an LLM's performance on this task.

From an engineering perspective, adapting to specific tasks through prompts has another huge advantage. LLMs are large and serving them in production is expensive and requires performing a lot of tricks and optimization. In-context learning makes online inference very efficient since the same LLM that's hosted by a provider can serve multiple concurrent requests from different users or customers because the weights of the model aren't changed – only the input is adjusted to specific needs.

What is alignment, and how does it enhance LLM capabilities?

As we've discussed, LLMs have demonstrated very good performance on various NLP tasks. People quickly found that the internet (and even users' conversations) doesn't contain only high quality. For example, in 2016, Microsoft quickly turned down its Twitter chatbot, called Tay, because it became racist [11]. Researchers confirmed this by evaluating the quality of LLM's answers on various scales, such as helpfulness for the user (for example, DeepMind defined more than a dozen scales for evaluation [12]). One of the key reasons for this is that the model was trained to predict the next token in the sequence, after which we can start using it with a different set of expectations – for example, to generate truthful outputs. OpenAI researchers noted that LLMs aren't **aligned** with users, and in 2022, they demonstrated that a relatively cheap alignment procedure can significantly improve the LLMs' behavior on these scales. **AI alignment** is a process that aims to make LLMs (and other AI systems) in line with humans' goals and values (including ethical principles) [13, 14, 15].

One alignment strategy is based on the **Reinforcement Learning from a Human Feedback (RLHF)** procedure and is known as **Direct Preference Optimization (DPO)**. The idea is relatively simple, but the implementation is brilliant and it required years of hard work and research to do. To improve the LLM's behavior on a specific scale (or a few), such as truthfulness, we should collect a dataset and continue training the model. The biggest challenge is that there's a lot of randomness in the output of the model, and it is often a piece of natural text (or an image), so we need a human to evaluate each specific output on a given scale. In other words, for any given example, the LLM produced some new text, and we need to involve a human so that they can rate this text before we update the model's weights. That's a very slow and inefficient process. But with the recent advances in reinforcement learning, we can train the so-called **reward model (RM)** first to compare different outputs and rank them according to their quality. We can fine-tune an original LLM as an RM. Then, we can continue the training process by using reinforcement learning with this RM. It was demonstrated that a relatively small dataset (containing less than 100,000 prompt-output pairs) is needed to significantly improve the performance of an LLM [15]:

`https://arxiv.org/abs/2203.02155`

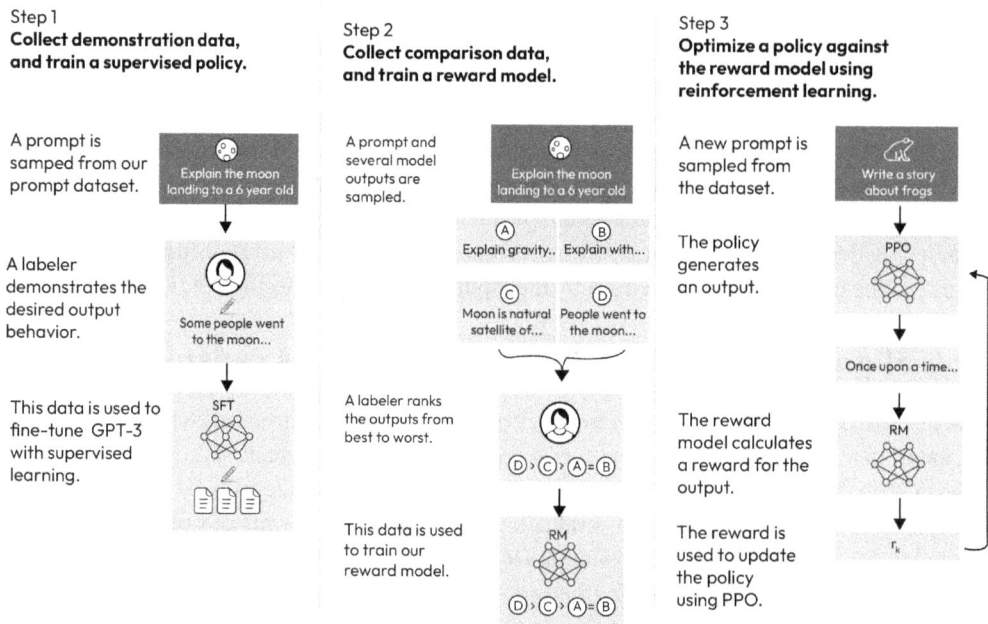

Step 1
Collect demonstration data, and train a supervised policy.

A prompt is samped from our prompt dataset.

Explain the moon landing to a 6 year old

A labeler demonstrates the desired output behavior.

Some people went to the moon...

This data is used to fine-tune GPT-3 with supervised learning.

SFT

Step 2
Collect comparison data, and train a reward model.

A prompt and several model outputs are sampled.

Explain the moon landing to a 6 year old

Ⓐ Explain gravity..   Ⓑ Explain with...
Ⓒ Moon is natural satellite of...   Ⓓ People went to the moon...

A labeler ranks the outputs from best to worst.

Ⓓ > Ⓒ > Ⓐ = Ⓑ

This data is used to train our reward model.

RM

Ⓓ > Ⓒ > Ⓐ = Ⓑ

Step 3
Optimize a policy against the reward model using reinforcement learning.

A new prompt is sampled from the dataset.

Write a story about frogs

The policy generates an output.

PPO

Once upon a time...

The reward model calculates a reward for the output.

RM

The reward is used to update the policy using PPO.

r_k

Figure A1.4 – The RLHF alignment procedure

DPO is a simpler and more direct approach, but the idea is pretty similar. Without going into too much detail, we still use the same preference data but without training a separate reward model [16]. It's a single-stage algorithm without a reinforcement learning training loop that uses direct preference data in the last training round to align the LLM with human objectives by treating it as a binary classification problem.

Tuning LLMs

Tuning is the process of adopting the LLM to the specific domain and set of tasks by training it on a relatively small labeled dataset. Technically speaking, generative AI application developers can use RLHF as one of the approaches to **fine-tuning** – a form of tuning that adjusts every weight in the LLM. The key disadvantage of fine-tuning is that it's an expensive process that requires a lot of effort to collect a large dataset and to adjust the model's weights themselves afterward.

Another disadvantage of fine-tuning is that you get a large LLM that you can use only for this task. Additionally, hosting LLMs requires expensive hardware and specialized infrastructure – for example, serving an LLM that consists of 175 billion parameters requires at least 350 GB of GPU memory (that maps to 5 H100 GPUs) [17]. LLM inference is relatively cheap because an LLM provider hosts a single model (with a lot of inference optimizations) that batches together multiple independent requests – that's how the economy of scales is achieved.

Distillation is another practical technique that's used for developing specialized models. The process involves using an LLM to train a small one by generating synthetic data [18]. It still requires unlabeled data, but labels can be generated with the help of an LLM, and the goal is to get a small model that loses its universal capabilities but can perform a specific domain task at the same level [17].

The process of fine-tuning and distillation is complex and requires a lot of effort (including data collection). **Parameter-efficient fine-tuning** (**PEFT**) is a method that's used to adjust LLMs to the specific domain task without changing the main model. It doesn't create a new model and instead introduces a set of special layers that are added to the model during inference, changing its behavior. In other words, we don't change all the weights of the model, only a small amount of them so that inference remains effective and fast and we can reuse the existing instance of the foundational model.

There are many approaches to PEFT – prompt tuning, LoRa, adapter layers, and more [19, 20, 21]. The key idea is to use a dataset to learn a small set of parameters (millions of them compared to billions of weights in the underlying foundational model) that are injected into the LLM during the inference process:

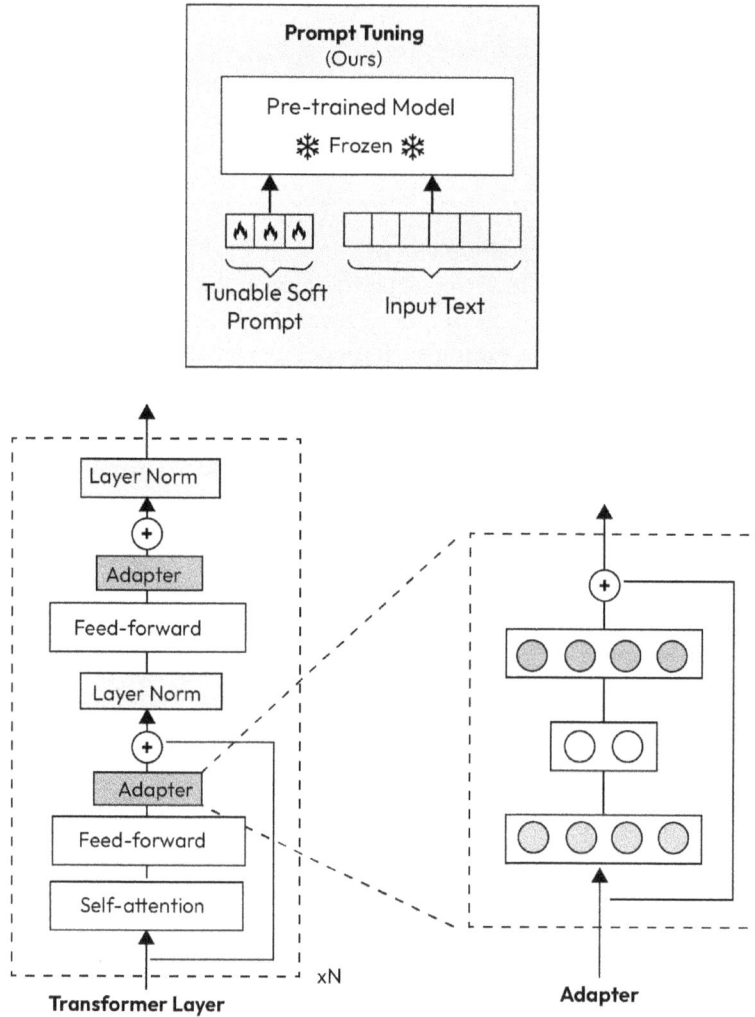

Figure A1.5 – Examples of PEFT

The key advantage is that PEFT requires a relatively small dataset (hundreds to thousands of examples) and allows the use of the same underlying frozen LLM provided by the vendor, optimized for inference. That is what makes such methods extremely useful in practice.

However, in most cases, you can start developing your generative AI application without any data by utilizing in-context learning. Here, you use prompt engineering to adapt the model to your downstream task – that is, you try to find a task description that works well. Typically, you only need a few examples to create a benchmark for your application. This is something we'll discuss in the next appendix.

Are LLMs as smart as humans?

Since LLMs are trained on a large amount of data, they incorporate knowledge about the world in many domains and often demonstrate surprising capabilities by *"demonstrating more general intelligence than previous models."* [22] Generative AI models demonstrate close to human performance on many tasks, including passing exams, even difficult ones such as law or medical exams [23, 24], or passing mock interviews on Leetcode [22]. But passing an exam doesn't mean that generative AI is ready to act as a lawyer or a doctor.

To answer this question, there have been multiple research projects on LLM reasoning capabilities. Researchers typically attack this problem head-on. One idea is to develop novel and complex prompting techniques that enhance the reasoning capabilities of such models – such as CoT, self-consistency with CoT, graph-of-thought, tree-of-thought, and others. Another is to evaluate LLM capabilities on various tasks or datasets. There are special datasets (such as CommonSenseQA and HellaSwag) that contain a set of commonsense reasoning tasks. In general, commonsense reasoning is *"a human-like ability to make presumptions about the type and essence of ordinary situations humans encounter every day."* [25] Most such datasets contain multiple-choice questions [25], as shown here:

Where would I not want a fox?

1. Hen house: A place where chickens are kept

2. England: A country in Europe

3. Mountains: A natural landform, often high and steep

4. English hunt: A hunting event, often involving foxes

5. California: A state in the United States

Why do people read gossip magazines?

1. To be entertained

2. To get information

3. To learn

4. To improve their knowledge

5. Their lawyer told them to

Evaluated on such a dataset, LLMs demonstrate accuracy in a range of 70-90%, a statistically significant improvement when using advanced prompt techniques such as CoT, yet still a significant lack of performance in specific areas such as reasoning about social interactions [26]. When used on logical reasoning datasets such as LogiQA2.0, LLMs demonstrate even worse performance, still lower than an average human's [27].

In their famous report on GPT-4 capabilities, Microsoft Research suggested that datasets might have leaked in the training data, so they focused on generating *"novel and difficult tasks and questions that convincingly demonstrate that GPT-4 goes far beyond memorization and that it has a deep and flexible understanding of concepts, skills, and domains."* [22] By demonstrating expressive examples of LLM's performance, the authors discovered significant limitations regarding the current LLM architectures, including a lack of planning for complex tasks.

To summarize, improving and evaluating the reasoning capabilities of LLMs is still ongoing. As we'll discuss in the next section, as engineers developing generative AI applications and applying them to real-world situations, we should probably focus on enhancing existing workflows with generative AI and using it to assist humans with their daily tasks.

Is it just hype or something big?

Predicting future trends is a pretty risky occupation, and that's not what this book is about. But we, as engineering leaders and product owners, who are responsible for building new products and adopting new technology, should build an intuition around it. So, let's spend some time looking at popular opinions from industry leaders and some studies.

First, there's growing confidence among industry experts that it's not just hype. Generative AI is a large technological shift, and what's even more important is that time is decreasing. McKinsey predicts that generative AI is to bring a large boost in productivity and *"add trillions of dollars in value to the global economy"* [28] in the next few years.

It's also important to note that they predict that the bigger share of generative AI impact won't be from new use cases but from the increased productivity of workers and augmenting existing routines. This is in line with our intuition and against what we sometimes observe in innovation labs across enterprises. The rule of thumb, if you're thinking about how to apply generative AI in your company, is not to start inventing new use cases but to look at the way you're currently working and think how generative AI could help increase productivity and the rate of automation.

Marc Andreessen is a veteran of Silicon Valley and a prominent techno-optimist. In his essay *Why AI Will Save the World*, he makes a point that AI would augment human intelligence. We believe it's important to keep this idea in mind when designing generative-AI-based products. At least at this current stage of development, we don't think that product owners should aim to design generative AI applications or routines that would fully automate humans' tasks [29]. From our point of view, the more realistic way to think about it is that generative AI would provide users with a lot of cheap and *relatively smart* assistants to perform a preliminary job, prepare some drafts, and let the user focus on the essentials [30]. The business value can be measured as a decreased cost per support interaction, or a decreased median response time [31].

Some evidence regarding how productivity can be improved was provided by Harvard Business School, which performed a study with Boston Consulting Group. The study tested performance on real-world tasks between consultants who were split into control and treatment groups randomly. It demonstrated that *"consultants using AI were significantly more productive (they completed 12.2% more tasks on average, and completed task 25.1% more quickly), and produced significantly higher quality results (more than 40% higher quality compared to a control group)."* [32] In other words, there was clear evidence of increased productivity by augmenting humans with generative AI.

When designing generative AI applications, we should always remember their stochastic nature, and the need to overcome problems such as **hallucinations** and **attribution**. Generative AI models tend to hallucinate – that is, they provide statistically expected but factually incorrect responses to the input (that is, the prompt) [33]. These responses might include some pieces of training data. Sometimes, this is desired since these are facts about the world that we want the model to learn. But to understand how reliable the model's response is, we should provide the end user with the correct attribution to the parts of training data that were used to generate this response. It's also important to respect the copyright for legal purposes.

As we've just seen, the tremendous progress in generative AI creates new opportunities to improve our lives. At the same time, it raises a lot of AI safety and fairness concerns [34]. There are also a lot of legal concerns around topics such as copyright. These topics are outside the scope of this book, but we recommend that you pay attention to the following aspects during the design phase:

- Generate safe content

- Avoid showing harmful content to users (check for hate speech, dangerous or harassing content, and so on)

- Respect privacy and data protection when selecting data for your fine-tuning and evaluation datasets

- Invest in the adversarial testing of your model to evaluate risks of failure (depending on the product, evaluate whether generative AI should give any medical, legal, or financial advice, or promote some goods or services)

A good first place to start might be looking at Google's AI principles [35] and how Google or Meta AI are thinking about fairness when designing AI products [35, 36]. Another aspect to keep in mind is regulations (such as the EU AI Act and the White House AI Bill of Rights).

Secrets of successful adoption

As we discussed in *Chapter 1*, LLMs can adapt to different domains. This means you can adapt an LLM to your specific task by providing instruction in the form of natural language. Therefore, sometimes, people tend to think that generative AI is different from "classical ML" and that you don't need to meet any specific data requirements to start building your application. We don't believe this is entirely true, especially not in an enterprise context.

However, you do need a high-quality dataset to build a successful generative AI application, although it could be smaller than the one required by "classical" ML approaches. And that's probably the most common misconception that leads to unsuccessful POCs in this area. So, what kind of data do we need?

First and foremost, we strongly recommend that you begin by drafting a few examples of the desired input and output for the generative AI solution you're thinking about:

	Input-Output	**Context**
Chatbot	A few dialogs between a human and a system	
Q&A system	Question-answer pairs	Examples of raw documents and pieces containing a relevant answer
Summary generator	Document-summary pairs	
Support automation	A few dialogs between a user and support agent with the desired resolution (for example, a payload sent to internal APIs)	The state of the user needed for the agent and a desired resolution

This exercise will help you narrow down your product requirements for the MVP. By doing so, you might realize that your organization doesn't have as much clean data as you thought it would. For example, you might find that you don't possess documents answering the questions your users would like to ask (or the quality of these documents is very low), or the state of the e-commerce order wasn't as good as it was at the moment a support case was handled. From this, you would realize the path to collecting more data and increasing your dataset. Why do you need more data? First, you need to build a good benchmark for evaluating your system automatically (you can read more about this in *Chapter 12*), and you might use some of these examples for few-shot learning. Second, if you can get from a few hundred to a few thousand good examples, you can consider fine-tuning as one of the ways to improve your applications.

Besides that, as industry practitioners, we should focus on business value and ROI. Sometimes, teams become over-excited with their recent progress and aim for exciting things that are far away from their practical usage. As an example, let's consider two ideas for the PoC.

First, a large international online marketplace allows sellers to place listings of cars and car accessories.

- **Use case 1 (UC1):** 20% of sellers don't fill a summary part of the listing. Such listings don't have anything to show when they're displayed in search results on the marketplace. On the other hand, listings with a concise summary tend to get X% more clicks. The idea is to auto-generate missing summaries based on the description and suggest them to the seller as a draft. The potential impact has been estimated at $7 million per year.

- **Use case 2 (UC2)**: Develop a custom natural language to SQL (NL2SQL) solution and empower every senior employee of the company to be able to interact with the corporate data and make better data-driven decisions. The potential impact has been estimated at $16 million per year.

From our perspective, use case 1 is the clear winner, despite its apparent simplicity and smaller impact. Why?

UC1 has a narrow scope and clear measurable success criteria.

UC1 uses existing frameworks and approaches, and it's based on the already-solved problem of summary generation, while the NL2SQL problem is still being attacked by researchers, deep tech startups, and database vendors.

Generating content related to car listing seems to be within the core competencies of a large online marketplace while developing a full-fledged NL2SQL solution might not be. It's a famous "buy versus build" dilemma [37] that states that in many cases, it's worth buying a third-party solution, especially when it's not a key differentiator for your business.

The company already has good data for UC1 (an existing listing with both a summary and description) and almost no data for UC2 (since it's unclear how senior managers would formulate their data-related questions and there are probably not enough examples of SQL queries that should be used to answer to such questions).

When you're not being blindsided by the larger impact of UC2, when you adjust for the unknown, as well as delivery costs and risks, UC1 becomes a clear winner in terms of ROI. On the other hand, it's important to find the right balance and not be blindsided by quick wins. Expansive 10x thinking is what's driving the true innovation culture within the company [38, 39]. It's sometimes difficult to find the right tradeoff but from our observations, teams become over-excited about new technology and try to focus on long-term gains instead of delivering business value as fast as possible.

To summarize, your POC will be successful if you manage the expectations of your key stakeholders while focusing on defining a clear scope and measurable success criteria.

Summary

In this appendix, we discussed some fundamentals that engineers and product owners might need to understand if they're involved in adopting generative AI across their products.

First, we discussed the surprising behavior of an LLM being trained to predict the missing word in a piece of text so that it can perform well on many NLP tasks. Domain adaptation can occur via in-context learning, which involves describing your task in natural language and maybe providing a few examples. This description is called a prompt, and prompt engineers try to use various techniques to increase the performance of the LLM on specific tasks by improving this prompt (for example, a task description).

Then, we touched on the problem of alignment – the process of making LLMs more performant on specific scales, such as being helpful or harmless. LLMs aren't trained for these goals, so it's not surprising they don't behave very well on these scales. However, researchers have developed a special and relatively efficient process that involves uptraining an LLM so that it performs better on these aspects by implementing reinforcement learning. In this case, we need a specially labeled dataset of preferences.

Any process that's similar to uptraining an LLM on a domain or task-specific dataset (of inputs and desired outputs) is called fine-tuning. In practice, it's not always efficient to fine-tune LLMs for your specific task since it requires a large amount of labeled data (also, keep in mind that if you're going through a complex fine-tuning process, you might end up serving your LLM and lose the economy of scale that comes from the providers of foundational LLMs).

To conclude, we briefly touched on some evidence of how good LLMs are when it comes to reasoning, and how to think about generative AI from a product development perspective. The industry is developing extremely fast and we hope to see a lot of discoveries in the future. As an analogy, we can think of generative AI as being a cheap and scalable assistant for humans that can help them perform their jobs faster and more productively. We shouldn't always blindly rely on the output of generative AI, but it's typically a good enough draft to begin with.

And like any software development project, we should start other POCs by defining and narrowing down the user journey and what exactly we're going to build. Just like any ML-related project, we should begin by evaluating the quality of our data and collecting our first labeled dataset.

In the next few chapters, we're going to discuss how to start developing a POC, how to define success criteria, and what data to collect. After, we'll put our hands on our keyboards and start having fun with some coding.

References

1. Prediction and Entropy of Printed English, by C.E. Shannon, 1950. Available at

    `https://www.princeton.edu/~wbialek/rome/refs/shannon_51.pdf`.

2. Companies double down on AI in June-quarter analyst calls, by Noel Randewich. Available at

    `https://www.reuters.com/technology/companies-double-down-ai-june-quarter-analyst-calls-2023-07-31/`.

3. Attention Is All You Need, by Ashish Vaswani and Noam Shazeer et. al., 2017. Available at

    `https://arxiv.org/abs/1706.03762`.

4. ChatGPT Passes 1 Billion Page Views, by Ben Wodecki. Available at

    `https://aibusiness.com/nlp/chatgpt-passes-1b-page-views`.

5. *Phi-2: The surprising power of small language models*, by Mojan Javaheripi and Sébastien Bubeck at

    `https://www.microsoft.com/en-us/research/blog/phi-2-the-surprising-power-of-small-language-models/`.

6. The racist hijacking of Microsoft's chatbot shows how the internet teems with hate, by Paul Mason. Available at

    `https://www.theguardian.com/world/2016/mar/29/microsoft-tay-tweets-antisemitic-racism`.

7. Language Models are Few-Shot Learners, by Tom B. Brown and Benjamin Mann et. al., 2020. Available at

    `https://arxiv.org/abs/2005.14165`.

8. Age of discovery. Wikipedia. Available at

    `https://en.wikipedia.org/wiki/Age_of_Discovery`.

9. Introduction to prompt design. Google Cloud. Available at

    `https://cloud.google.com/vertex-ai/docs/generative-ai/learn/introduction-prompt-design`.

10. Prompt Engineering Guide:

    `https://www.promptingguide.ai/`.

11. The racist hijacking of Microsoft's chatbot shows how the internet teems with hate, by Paul Mason. Available at

    `https://www.theguardian.com/world/2016/mar/29/microsoft-tay-tweets-antisemitic-racism`.

12. Improving alignment of dialogue agents via targeted human judgements, by Amelia Glaese and Nat McAleese et.al., 2022. Available at

    `https://arxiv.org/abs/2209.14375`.

13. Training language models to follow instructions with human feedback, by Long Ouyang and Jeff Wu et. al., 2022. Available at

    `https://arxiv.org/abs/2203.02155`.

14. Improving alignment of dialogue agents via targeted human judgements, by Amelia Glaese and Nat McAleese et.al., 2022. Available at

    `https://arxiv.org/abs/2209.14375`.

15. AI Alignment: A Comprehensive Survey, by J. Ji et. al., 2023. Available at

    `https://arxiv.org/abs/2310.19852`.

16. Direct Preference Optimization: Your Language Model is Secretly a Reward Model, by Rafailov et. al., 2023. Available at

    `https://arxiv.org/abs/2305.18290`.

17. Distilling step-by-step: Outperforming larger language models with less training data and smaller model sizes, by Cheng-Yu Hsieh and Chen-Yu Lee, 2023. Available at

    `https://blog.research.google/2023/09/distilling-step-by-step-outperforming.html`.

18. Distilling the Knowledge in a Neural Network, by Geoffrey Hinton, Oriol Vinyals, and Jeff Dean, 2015. Available at

    `https://arxiv.org/abs/1503.02531`.

19. The Power of Scale for Parameter-Efficient Prompt Tuning, by Brian Lester, Rami Al-Rfou, and Noah Constant, 2021. Available at

    `https://arxiv.org/abs/2104.08691`.

20. On the Effectiveness of Adapter-based Tuning for Pretrained Language Model Adaptation, by Ruidan He and Linlin Liu et.al, 2021. Available at

    `https://arxiv.org/abs/2106.03164`.

21. LoRA: Low-Rank Adaptation of Large Language Models, by Edward J. Hu and Yelong Shen et. al., 2021. Available at

    `https://arxiv.org/abs/2106.09685`.

22. Sparks of Artificial General Intelligence: Early experiments with GPT-4, by Sébastien Bubeck and Varun Chandrasekaran et. al., 2023. Available at

    `https://arxiv.org/abs/2303.12712`.

23. Generative AI, Having Already Passed the Bar Exam, Now Passes the Legal Ethics Exam Generative AI, by Bob Ambrogi. Available at

    `https://www.lawnext.com/2023/11/generative-ai-having-already-passed-the-bar-exam-now-passes-the-legal-ethics-exam.html`.

24. Capabilities of GPT-4 on Medical Challenge Problems, by Harsha Nori and Nicholas King, 2023. Available at

    `https://arxiv.org/abs/2303.13375`.

25. CommoSenseQA dataset:

    `https://www.tau-nlp.sites.tau.ac.il/commonsenseqa`.

26. Gemini in Reasoning: Unveiling Commonsense in Multimodal Large Language Models, by Yuqing Wang and Yun Zhao. Available at

    `https://arxiv.org/abs/2312.17661`.

27. Evaluating the Logical Reasoning Ability of ChatGPT and GPT-4, by Hanmeng Liu and Ruoxi Ning, 2023. Available at

    `https://arxiv.org/abs/2304.03439`.

28. The economic potential of generative AI: The next productivity frontier, by McKinsey, 2023. Available at

    `https://www.mckinsey.com/capabilities/mckinsey-digital/our-insights/the-economic-potential-of-generative-AI-the-next-productivity-frontier`.

29. Why AI Will Save the World, by Marc Andreessen, 2023. Available at

    `https://a16z.com/ai-will-save-the-world/`.

30. Unbundling AI, by Ben Evans. Available at

    `https://www.ben-evans.com/benedictevans/2023/10/5/unbundling-ai`.

31. AI: The Coming Revolution, by Sri Viswanath, Vibhor Khanna, and Yijia Liang, 2023. Available at

    `https://www.coatue.com/blog/perspective/ai-the-coming-revolution-2023`.

32. Navigating the Jagged Technological Frontier: Field Experimental Evidence of the Effects of AI on Knowledge Worker Productivity and Quality, by Fabrizio Dell'Acqua and Edward McFowland et. al. Available at

    `https://papers.ssrn.com/sol3/papers.cfm?abstract_id=4573321`.

33. On the Origin of Hallucinations in Conversational Models: Is it the Datasets or the Models? by N. Dziri et. al, 2022. Available at

    `https://arxiv.org/abs/2204.07931`.

34. To Be a Responsible AI Leader, Focus on Being Responsible, by M. Renieris, D. Kiron, and S. Mills, 2022. Available at

    `https://sloanreview.mit.edu/projects/to-be-a-responsible-ai-leader-focus-on-being-responsible/`.

35. Google AI Principles:

    `https://ai.google/responsibility/principles/`.

36. Meta AI: Responsible AI:

    `https://ai.meta.com/blog/meta-llama-3-meta-ai-responsibility/`.

37. Build vs. buy. Thoughtworks, 2022. Available at

    `https://www.thoughtworks.com/content/dam/thoughtworks/documents/e-book/tw_ebook_build_vs_buy_2022.pdf`.

38. Everyone wants a culture of innovation. So what does it look like? Google Cloud. Available at

    `https://cloud.google.com/executive-insights/everyone-wants-a-culture-of-innovation-report-what-does-it-look-like-report`.

39. Design thinking in 3 steps: How to build a culture of innovation, by Pferdt, 2019. Available at

    `https://www.thinkwithgoogle.com/future-of-marketing/creativity/design-thinking-principles/`.

Appendix 2
Google Cloud Foundations

Ready to harness the power of **generative AI (GenAI)** with LangChain? Google Cloud provides a robust platform to develop and deploy your innovative applications. In this chapter, we'll guide you through essential steps to set up your Google Cloud environment and get started with LangChain.

If you're an experienced Google Cloud engineer, you can skip this appendix. But for engineers who are new to Google Cloud and would like to use other Google Cloud tools combined with Gemini, we prepared a short intro to the cloud setup. Think of this chapter as your trusty compass, navigating you through the Google Cloud setup. By the end, you'll have a solid foundation to embark on your GenAI adventures. The Google Cloud documentation offers a handy setup checklist [1], which we roughly follow in this chapter, with some additions.

So, let's dive in and build the foundation for unlocking the full potential of LangChain with Google Cloud! We'll cover everything from creating your organization and managing users to configuring your network infrastructure, setting up your development environment, and deploying your LangChain applications. In particular, we'll cover the following topics:

- Setting up your organization
- Adding users and groups
- Managing administrative users
- Setting up billing in Google Cloud
- Centralizing logging in Google Cloud
- Securing your Google Cloud environment
- Setting up your Google Cloud network infrastructure
- Enabling your Google Cloud environment for AI/Machine Learning experiments
- Deploying LangChain applications with Google Cloud Run

Setting up your organization

The foundation of your **Google Cloud Platform** (**GCP**) environment is the organization resource. This represents your company within GCP and serves as the root of your resource hierarchy. Just like filing cabinets have folders to organize documents, your GCP organization will contain folders and projects to categorize and manage your cloud resources. But before you can start deploying applications and databases, you need to set up this essential foundation.

A **Google Cloud project** is a fundamental unit that organizes your Google Cloud resources. You can grant access on a project level, and some resources (such as network) can be shared across projects, but think about a project as a finite unit that you can organize in folders.

There are two main paths to establishing your organization, depending on your existing Google Cloud setup:

- **New customer**: If you're new to Google Cloud, you'll need to set up Cloud Identity from scratch. This involves creating a managed user account for your super administrator, who will have the highest level of permissions within your organization. You'll then link Cloud Identity to your company domain and verify ownership to complete the setup process.

- **Existing Google Workspace customer**: If your company already uses Google Workspace for email and productivity tools, you can leverage it as your **identity provider** (**IdP**) for GCP as well. This simplifies the setup process, but if you plan to have users who only access GCP resources (and not Workspace products), you'll still need to enable Cloud Identity.

- **Existing Cloud Identity customer**: If you've already set up Cloud Identity, you'll just need to verify your domain ownership (if not already done) and confirm that Cloud Identity is enabled.

Remember –establishing your organization is the first step in building a secure and scalable foundation for your GCP environment. It paves the way for creating user accounts, assigning permissions, and organizing your cloud resources effectively. So, take some time to set it up correctly – it will make managing your GCP resources much easier in the long run. If you have any questions on the best practices for setting up GCP organizations, take a look at the *Best practices for planning accounts and organizations* section of the Google Cloud documentation [2].

One important thing to mention is that despite being able to do all the setup manually in the Google Cloud console, the recommended way for a matured organization is to use Terraform to define all the configuration of the Google Cloud project (including enabling corresponding APIs and creating resources you need, such as databases or Cloud storage buckets).

Adding users and groups

Now that you've established your Google Cloud organization and created a first project, it's time to populate it with the people who will bring your cloud initiatives to life. This involves creating users and groups and following security best practices to ensure controlled access to your resources.

Understanding two key principles is crucial for effective user management:

- **Principle of least privilege (PoLP)**: A fundamental security best practice is to grant users only the minimum permissions they need to perform their jobs. This is known as PoLP. By adhering to this principle, you reduce the risk of unauthorized access and potential data breaches. For example, if a user only needs to manage billing, there's no need to grant them permissions to create and manage **virtual machines** (**VMs**). Limiting their access to billing-related tasks helps prevent accidental or malicious actions [3].

- **Role-based access control (RBAC)**: Assign permissions based on job roles, using groups to efficiently manage access for multiple users. Avoid granting permissions directly to individual accounts whenever possible [4].

Next steps

Think of groups as containers for users with similar job functions. Each group has a unique email address and inherits the IAM roles you assign to it. You can create base groups for network, security, or monitoring management and separate groups for specific services or access to certain data.

To create a group, sign in to the Google Cloud console with your super administrator credentials and navigate to the **Users & Groups** section within the Google Cloud Setup.

Now that you have your groups in place, it's time to populate them with users. Start by adding users who will be responsible for completing initial setup tasks such as organization management, networking, and billing. You can add more users later on.

You can add users either by *migrating existing accounts* or *creating new users*. If your team already uses Google accounts, you can migrate them to managed user accounts controlled by Cloud Identity. This provides centralized management and simplifies access control. For new team members, you can add them directly using the Google Admin console. You can either add users individually or upload a CSV file for bulk additions. Once you've added the necessary users, return to the **Users & Groups** section within the Google Cloud Setup.

Assigning users to groups

The final step is to assign the users you created to the appropriate administrative groups based on their roles. In the Google Cloud Setup, you'll see a list of groups with an **Add Members** option for each. Click on this option and enter the user's email address. You'll also need to select a group role, which determines the level of permission the user inherits within that group. Keep PoLP in mind as you assign users to administrative groups! Remember – *each member inherits all IAM roles granted to the group*, regardless of the specific group role you select. This reinforces the importance of assigning roles carefully at the group level.

By following these steps, you'll establish a secure and well-organized foundation for user management within your Google Cloud organization. This ensures that your team members have the necessary access to perform their jobs while minimizing security risks.

Managing administrative users

Once you've created your administrative groups and assigned users, the next crucial step is to carefully manage their access to Google Cloud resources. This involves granting appropriate permissions, or roles, to these groups.

Understanding IAM roles

In Google Cloud, IAM is the system that controls who can access your resources and what they can do with them. Roles are predefined collections of permissions that grant users specific capabilities within your organization. For example, the `roles/resourcemanager.organizationAdmin` role grants a user the ability to manage all organization resources. You should familiarize yourself with Google Cloud IAM by reading up on the documentation [5].

Granting roles to groups

The recommended approach is to grant roles to groups rather than individual users. This simplifies management and ensures consistent access control. When you assign a role to a group, all members of that group inherit the permissions associated with that role.

Reviewing and customizing default roles

When you create administrative groups, they are typically assigned default roles. It's essential to review these roles and customize them to align with your organization's specific needs. You can add or remove roles as necessary to ensure that each group has the appropriate permissions.

The importance of regular review

As your organization evolves and new requirements arise, it's crucial to periodically review the roles assigned to your administrative groups. Ensure that permissions remain aligned with current job functions and that no unnecessary access is granted.

Additional tips

Here are some additional tips to bear in mind:

- **Use service accounts**: For automated tasks, we strongly recommend using service accounts instead of individual user accounts. A service account is a special non-human account that provides a way to grant specific permissions to applications and services without requiring human interaction.

- **Leverage organization policies**: Organization policies can be used to enforce consistent security settings across your entire organization. For example, you can use policies to restrict the creation of certain resource types or enforce data encryption.

By carefully managing administrator accounts and adhering to PoLP, you can significantly enhance the security of your Google Cloud environment. This helps protect your sensitive data and prevents unauthorized access to your resources.

Setting up billing in Google Cloud

Once you've established your organization and created user accounts, the next step is to set up billing. This ensures that you can use and pay for Google Cloud resources.

Billing account types

You have two primary options for billing: **self-serve accounts** are the most common option, especially for small businesses and individuals. You sign up online using a credit or debit card, and your account is automatically set up as self-serve. You'll pay for resources as you use them. If your organization meets certain eligibility requirements, you may be able to apply for an **invoiced billing account**. This option allows you to receive a monthly invoice for your usage.

Associating a billing account

To associate a billing account with your organization, you need to sign in to the Google Cloud console as a user with billing permissions (typically a member of the `gcp-billing-admins@YOUR_DOMAIN` group). Navigate to the **Billing** section within the Google Cloud Setup and select the billing account option that suits your needs. Then, you just need to follow the onscreen instructions to complete the setup process. This may involve providing payment information, verifying your identity, or waiting for approval if you're applying for an invoiced account. Review the billing documentation [6] or the setup checklist for a great step-by-step guide if you get stuck.

Don't forget to set up billing alerts to monitor your usage and costs. By setting up billing correctly, you'll ensure that your team can effectively use Google Cloud resources while maintaining control over your organization's expenses.

Centralizing logging in Google Cloud

Logging is an essential component of any well-managed cloud environment. It provides valuable insights into your application's behavior, helps you troubleshoot issues, and is crucial for security and compliance purposes. In Google Cloud, **Cloud Logging** offers a centralized platform for collecting, storing, and analyzing logs from your various resources. By consolidating logs from different projects and resources into a single location, you can easily search, filter, and analyze log data. This offers improved security by helping you identify security threats, track unauthorized access attempts, and monitor anomalies in your system behavior. Centralizing logs also simplifies compliance efforts.

Setting up centralized logging

First, you must ensure that Cloud Logging is enabled for your organization and individual projects. This can be done through the Google Cloud console or by using the `gcloud` command-line tool. Next, you should create a **central log bucket**. A log bucket is a container for your log data. Create a central log bucket to store logs from all your projects. Next, configure your projects to route their logs to the central log bucket. This ensures that all log data is collected in a single location. Don't forget to determine the retention period for your logs. Cloud Logging offers a free monthly allotment, but you might incur costs for longer retention periods. Consider your organization's specific needs and compliance requirements when setting the retention period. Finally, if you need to export logs to external systems for further analysis or compliance purposes, you can use **Pub/Sub** to stream logs to other applications or third-party tools.

We recommend activating two kinds of logs:

- **Cloud audit logs**: These logs capture administrative activity, system events, data access, and policy denials. They are essential for security and compliance purposes.

- **Access Transparency**: These logs record actions taken by Google personnel when accessing your customer content.

By centralizing logging in Google Cloud, you'll gain valuable insights into your applications, improve security, and simplify compliance efforts. This is a fundamental step in building a robust and well-managed cloud environment. For an in-depth discussion of all things logging, visit the Google Cloud documentation [8].

Securing your Google Cloud environment

Once you've established the foundational elements of your Google Cloud environment, it's crucial to focus on security. This involves implementing measures to protect your resources, data, and applications from unauthorized access, threats, and vulnerabilities. Google Cloud offers **Security Command Center** as a centralized platform for managing security across your entire Google Cloud environment. It helps you detect vulnerabilities, identify threats, and respond to incidents. The Google Cloud setup process will automatically recommend that you enable Security Command Center. The Standard tier is free, but Premium tiers incur a cost. You can read more about it in the documentation [9].

Enabling APIs and setting up quotas

Each Google Cloud service (such as BigQuery or Gemini on Vertex AI) is an API exposed by Google Cloud. By default, most of the APIs are disabled on a project level to prevent accidental usage of such a service. If you want to start using a specific Google Cloud product, you first need to enable the corresponding API. There are two ways of doing it – manually (by going to **APIs & Services** in the Google Cloud console, searching for the API you need, and clicking the **Enable** button) or through your Terraform configuration.

After you have enabled the service, the default quotas still might be low (it's another mechanism to prevent accidental usage and waste of your money). You can always ask to increase the quota through the Google Cloud console (on the **Quotas** page).

Applying organization policies

Security in Google Cloud is mainly driven by organization policies. Organization policies are a powerful tool for enforcing consistent security settings across your entire organization. These policies apply at the organization level and are inherited by folders and projects. By applying organization policies, you can restrict access to the types of resources that can be created or modified within your organization. You can enforce security practices such as data encryption for sensitive data at rest and in transit, setting standards for password complexity, IAM roles, and other security measures. You can read more about how these constraints work in the documentation [10].

The Google Cloud setup process provides a list of recommended organization policies. Review these policies carefully and customize them to align with your organization's specific security requirements. You can add, remove, or modify policies at any time using the **Organization Policy Service**.

By taking these steps, you can significantly enhance the security of your Google Cloud environment and protect your valuable data and applications. Remember – security is an ongoing process that requires continuous attention and adaptation to evolving threats.

Setting up your Google Cloud network infrastructure

Networking is the backbone of any cloud environment, providing connectivity between your resources and the internet. In Google Cloud, **virtual private cloud** (**VPC**) networks serve as the foundation for your network infrastructure. A VPC network is a virtual, private network within Google Cloud. It provides a secure and isolated environment for your resources. VPC networks are global resources, meaning they can span multiple regions. However, they are composed of regional **subnets**, which are smaller network segments within specific regions. This allows you to optimize network performance and latency based on your resource locations. Finally, VPC networks provide connectivity for your Google Cloud resources, such as VMs, Kubernetes clusters, and App Engine applications.

Shared VPC is a powerful feature that allows you to connect multiple projects to a common VPC network. It enables you to manage network resources such as subnets, firewalls, and **virtual private network (VPN)** connections centrally from a single host project.

Creating your initial network configuration

To create your network configuration, start by *creating host projects* to represent different environments or teams within your organization. For example, you might have separate host projects for production and non-production environments. Next, *create Shared VPC networks* in each host project. This will serve as the central network for the projects attached to that host. Within each Shared VPC network, *create subnets*. Subnets are regional resources with specific IP address ranges. You can create public subnets for internet-facing resources and private subnets for internal-facing resources.

Additional tips

Here are some additional tips to bear in mind:

- **Use multiple subnets**: Create at least two subnets in each Shared VPC network to provide redundancy and flexibility
- **Consider regional distribution**: If your application requires low-latency access to resources in different regions, create subnets in those regions
- **Manage firewall rules**: Carefully configure firewall rules to control inbound and outbound traffic to your resources
- **Monitor network performance**: Use tools such as Cloud Monitoring to monitor network usage and identify potential bottlenecks

By following these steps and considering the best practices, you'll establish a solid network foundation for your Google Cloud environment. You can then proceed to deploy and connect your resources to this network infrastructure.

Enabling your Google Cloud environment for AI/machine learning experiments

Reading this book, you will see that most chapters are built around interactive notebooks that enable you to apply what you learn to practice immediately. Having a well-configured environment is essential for efficient experimentation and development with LangChain. Google Cloud offers several powerful tools to cater to different needs and preferences. Here, we'll explore three tools, each with its own advantages and trade-offs:

- **Colab Enterprise** is a fully managed Jupyter notebook environment that provides a collaborative platform for data analysis, **machine learning (ML)**, and education. It can be accessed directly from your web browser, making it easy to get started without complex setups. It facilitates real-time collaboration among team members, making it ideal for projects involving multiple contributors. It also seamlessly integrates with other Google Cloud services, such as BigQuery for data analysis and Compute Engine for running custom training jobs. However, Colab Enterprise does have limitations: while it offers a decent amount of computational resources, it may not be suitable for large-scale training jobs or extremely demanding workloads. Luckily, we don't need those with LangChain! It also only provides a preconfigured environment, which might not fully align with your specific requirements.

- **Vertex AI Workbench instances** are custom JupyterLab environments that you can create and configure according to your specific needs. This provides greater flexibility and control compared to Colab Enterprise. With Vertex AI Workbench instances, you can choose the machine type, operating system, and software packages to create a tailored environment. Instances can be scaled up or down to accommodate varying workloads. Instances seamlessly integrate with other Vertex AI services, such as AutoML and Model Registry. Vertex AI Workbench instances require more setup and management compared to Colab Enterprise.

- **Cloud Workstations**, finally, offers a fully managed desktop environment that can be accessed remotely. This provides a more traditional desktop-like experience for developers who prefer working with a graphical interface. It provides a familiar interface for developers who are accustomed to traditional workstations. Cloud Workstations is designed for demanding workloads and can provide powerful computational resources. We are also big fans of integrating Cloud Workstations with our local **integrated development environment** (**IDE**) such as VS Code, which enables us to work on a familiar device that is seamlessly connected to the cloud [11]. Unfortunately, Cloud Workstations might be overkill for simpler tasks and can be more expensive than other options.

Deploying LangChain applications with Google Cloud Run

After you have experimented with and developed your LangChain application, you need to deploy it to a production service.

Google Cloud Run is one of the options to use. It's a serverless platform that allows you to run stateless containers that are invocable via HTTP requests. Google Cloud Run takes care of load balancing your traffic and scaling your application up and down (and you can control the scaling configuration yourself). As you only pay for the resources your application consumes, it is cost-effective for many use cases. Finally, Cloud Run integrates seamlessly with other Google Cloud services, such as Cloud Storage and BigQuery, making it easy to build complex data pipelines. You can read more in the documentation: `https://cloud.google.com/run/docs/overview/what-is-cloud-run`.

To deploy a LangChain application on Cloud Run, you have two options. The first is to wrap it with an HTTP API (using Flask, FastAPI, or any other framework) and create a Dockerfile (as described in `https://cloud.google.com/run/docs/deploying`). The other option is to use the LangServe library to deploy your runnable or your chain directly to Cloud Run (`https://python.langchain.com/docs/langserve/#deploy-to-gcp`).

Summary

In this chapter, we explored essential steps to set up your Google Cloud environment for AI/ML experiments. We covered the importance of establishing your organization, creating user accounts and groups, managing permissions, and configuring billing. We also discussed the different options available for AI/ML development environments: Colab Enterprise, Vertex AI Workbench instances, and Cloud Workstations, which are the best way to get started on developing LangChain applications.

By following the guidance in this chapter, you'll be well equipped to embark on building exciting LangChain applications in Google Cloud. Remember – the choice of environment depends on your specific needs and preferences, so carefully evaluate the options to find the best fit for your workflow.

References

1. Setup checklist – Google Cloud documentation

    `https://cloud.google.com/docs/enterprise/setup-checklist`

2. Organization and identity best practices – Google Cloud documentation

    `https://cloud.google.com/architecture/identity/best-practices-for-planning`

3. PoLP – *Wikipedia*

    `https://en.wikipedia.org/wiki/Principle_of_least_privilege`

4. RBAC – *Wikipedia*

    `https://en.wikipedia.org/wiki/Role-based_access_control`

5. IAM – Google Cloud documentation

    `https://cloud.google.com/iam/docs/overview`

6. Billing – Google Cloud documentation.

    `https://cloud.google.com/billing/docs`

7. Deciding a resource hierarchy – Google Cloud documentation

    `https://cloud.google.com/architecture/landing-zones/decide-resource-hierarchy`

8. Google Cloud Observability – Google Cloud documentation

   `https://cloud.google.com/products/operations`

9. Security Command Center – Google Cloud documentation

   `https://cloud.google.com/security-command-center/docs/concepts-security-command-center-overview`

10. Organization policy constraints – Google Cloud documentation

    `https://cloud.google.com/resource-manager/docs/organization-policy/org-policy-constraints`

11. Develop code locally using VS Code with Cloud Workstations – Google Cloud documentation

    `https://cloud.google.com/workstations/docs/develop-code-using-local-vscode-editor`

Get This Book's PDF Version and Exclusive Extras

UNLOCK NOW

Scan the QR code (or go to `packtpub.com/unlock`). Search for this book by name, confirm the edition, and then follow the steps on the page.

Note: Keep your invoice handy. Purchases made directly from Packt don't require one.

Index

C

‹packt›

packtpub.com

Subscribe to our online digital library for full access to over 7,000 books and videos, as well as industry leading tools to help you plan your personal development and advance your career. For more information, please visit our website.

Why subscribe?

- Spend less time learning and more time coding with practical eBooks and Videos from over 4,000 industry professionals

- Improve your learning with Skill Plans built especially for you

- Get a free eBook or video every month

- Fully searchable for easy access to vital information

- Copy and paste, print, and bookmark content

Did you know that Packt offers eBook versions of every book published, with PDF and ePub files available? You can upgrade to the eBook version at packtpub.com and as a print book customer, you are entitled to a discount on the eBook copy. Get in touch with us at customercare@packtpub.com for more details.

At www.packtpub.com, you can also read a collection of free technical articles, sign up for a range of free newsletters, and receive exclusive discounts and offers on Packt books and eBooks.

Other Books You May Enjoy

If you enjoyed this book, you may be interested in these other books by Packt:

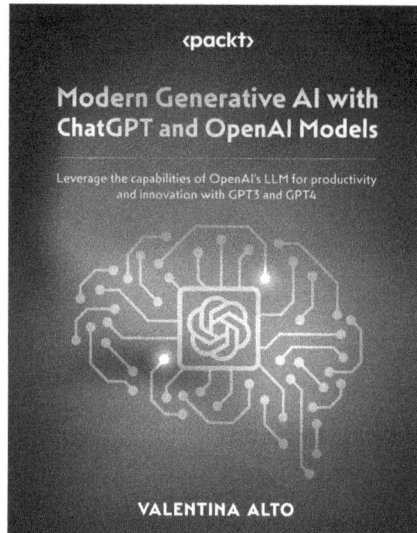

Modern Generative AI with ChatGPT and OpenAI Models

Valentina Alto

ISBN: 978-1-80512-333-0

- Understand generative AI concepts from basic to intermediate level
- Focus on the GPT architecture for generative AI models
- Maximize ChatGPT's value with an effective prompt design
- Explore applications and use cases of ChatGPT
- Use OpenAI models and features via API calls
- Build and deploy generative AI systems with Python
- Leverage Azure infrastructure for enterprise-level use cases
- Ensure responsible AI and ethics in generative AI systems

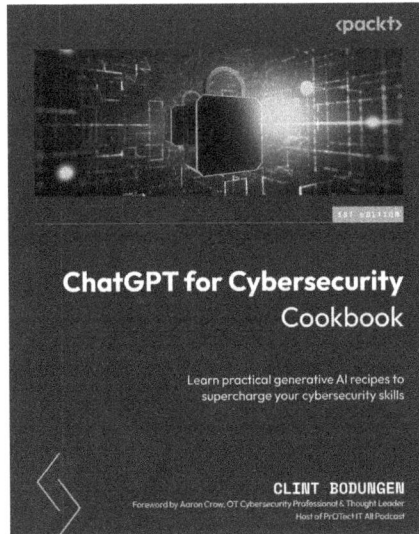

ChatGPT for Cybersecurity Cookbook

Clint Bodungen

ISBN: 978-1-80512-404-7

- Master ChatGPT prompt engineering for complex cybersecurity tasks
- Use the OpenAI API to enhance and automate penetration testing
- Implement artificial intelligence-driven vulnerability assessments and risk analyses
- Automate threat detection with the OpenAI API
- Develop custom AI-enhanced cybersecurity tools and scripts
- Perform AI-powered cybersecurity training and exercises
- Optimize cybersecurity workflows using generative AI-powered techniques

Packt is searching for authors like you

If you're interested in becoming an author for Packt, please visit `authors.packtpub.com` and apply today. We have worked with thousands of developers and tech professionals, just like you, to help them share their insight with the global tech community. You can make a general application, apply for a specific hot topic that we are recruiting an author for, or submit your own idea.

Share Your Thoughts

Now you've finished *Generative AI on Google Cloud with LangChain*, we'd love to hear your thoughts! Scan the QR code below to go straight to the Amazon review page for this book and share your feedback or leave a review on the site that you purchased it from.

`https://packt.link/r/1-835-88933-6`

Your review is important to us and the tech community and will help us make sure we're delivering excellent quality content.

www.ingramcontent.com/pod-product-compliance
Lightning Source LLC
Chambersburg PA
CBHW081054220326
41598CB00038B/7088